Extending Applied Linguistics for Social Impact

Also available from Bloomsbury

Applying Linguistics in Illness and Healthcare Contexts, edited by Zsófia Demjén
Contemporary Second Language Assessment, edited by
Jayanti Veronique Banerjee and Dina Tsagari
Identity in Applied Linguistics Research, by Lisa McEntee-Atalianis
Investigating Adolescent Health Communication, by Kevin Harvey
On Writtenness, by Joan Turner

Extending Applied Linguistics for Social Impact

Cross-Disciplinary Collaborations in Diverse Spaces of Public Inquiry

Edited by Doris S. Warriner and Elizabeth R. Miller

BLOOMSBURY ACADEMIC
LONDON • NEW YORK • OXFORD • NEW DELHI • SYDNEY

BLOOMSBURY ACADEMIC
Bloomsbury Publishing Plc
50 Bedford Square, London, WC1B 3DP, UK
1385 Broadway, New York, NY 10018, USA
29 Earlsfort Terrace, Dublin 2, Ireland

BLOOMSBURY, BLOOMSBURY ACADEMIC and the Diana logo are trademarks of Bloomsbury Publishing Plc

First published in Great Britain 2021
Paperback edition published in 2023

Copyright © Doris S. Warriner, Elizabeth R. Miller and Contributors, 2021

Doris S. Warriner and Elizabeth R. Miller have asserted their right under the Copyright, Designs and Patents Act, 1988, to be identified as Editors of this work.

Cover design by Rebecca Heselton
Cover image: © Giulia May / Unsplash

All rights reserved. No part of this publication may be reproduced or transmitted in or any information storage or retrieval system, without prior permission in writing from the publishers.

Bloomsbury Publishing Plc does not have any control over, or responsibility for, any third-party websites referred to or in this book. All internet addresses given in this book were correct at the time of going to press. The author and publisher regret any inconvenience caused if addresses have changed or sites have ceased to exist, but can accept no responsibility for any such changes.

A catalogue record for this book is available from the British Library.

A catalog record for this book is available from the Library of Congress.

ISBN: HB: 978-1-3501-3638-0
PB: 978-1-3502-4954-7
ePDF: 978-1-3501-3639-7
eBook: 978-1-3501-3640-3

Typeset by RefineCatch Limited, Bungay, Suffolk

To find out more about our authors and books visit www.bloomsbury.com and sign up for our newsletters.

Contents

List of Figures	vii
List of Tables	viii
Notes on Contributors	ix
Introduction *Doris S. Warriner and Elizabeth R. Miller*	1
1 Engaging the Public in Sociolinguistics for Social Justice: Advocating for Pidgin Speakers in Hawai'i *Christina Higgins*	13
2 Building Partnerships and Expanding Repertoires of Practice: Working with and in Museums To Improve Informal Science Education for Linguistically Diverse Young Children *Leslie C. Moore*	35
3 An Applied Linguist at Work: Tracing Language Choices in a Social Sustainability Network *Elizabeth R. Miller*	59
4 Finding Answers within the Story: The Transformative Potential of Translanguaging Praxis *Obed Arango and Holly Link*	81
5 Being, Seeing, and Hearing White: When Theater Arts Interrogate and Make Visible the Power of the Elephant in the Room *Ellen Skilton*	103
6 Language as a Social Determinant of Health: Partnerships for Health Equity *Emily M. Feuerherm, Rachel E. Showstack, Maricel G. Santos, Glenn A. Martínez, and Holly E. Jacobson*	125
7 "It Depends Case by Case": Understanding How the Practices of Cultural Health Navigators Impact Healthcare Access and Delivery for Refugee-Background Families *Katherine E. Morelli and Doris S. Warriner*	149

8 Applied Linguistic Anthropology: Balancing Social Science with
   Social Change   *Netta Avineri, Eric J. Johnson, Bernard C. Perley,
   Jonathan Rosa, and Ana Celia Zentella*   171

Afterword: Crossing Borders, Rethinking Expertise, and
   Becoming *Collaborative* Linguists   *Betsy Rymes*   195

Index   211

Figures

1.1	Museum exhibit wall for *Pidgin: How was . . . How Stay!*	23
1.2	Museum exhibit panel on Pidgin in the 1920s featuring Better English Week	24
1.3	Touchscreen computer featuring oral and visual Pidgin at the exhibit	26
1.4	Pidgin T-shirts on display	26
4.1	Story co-construction based on continual reflection and action	87
6.1	Intersections of language and health across domains	128

Tables

3.1	Top five most frequently occurring content words	68
3.2	Raw frequency of words relating to contexts for sustainability	69
3.3	Raw frequency of words relating to sustainability subtopics	70
3.4	Most frequent content-word collocations with *sustainability*	71
5.1	Snapshot of dimensions of visual/aural/gestural analysis of marked subject-as-seen/subject-as-heard at start of "Fighting" scene (adapted from Blackledge and Creese 2017)	121

Contributors

Obed Arango is a Mexican immigrant, anthropologist, and journalist living in the US since 2000. He and his two daughters are from Mexico City. Together they have learned to resist the anti-immigrant environment in the US and have explored the principles of Paulo Freire and Martin Luther King, Jr. Following this path and with the spirit of other members of the immigrant community, he founded Revolución Arte as a center for social transformation. He is RevArte's Director and is also an instructor at the University of Pennsylvania in the School for Social Policy and Practice.

Netta Avineri is Language Teacher Education Associate Professor, Intercultural Competence Committee Chair, and Collaborative in Conflict Transformation Graduate Pillar Lead at the Middlebury Institute of International Studies at Monterey. She is the author of *Research Methods for Language Teaching: Inquiry, Process, and Synthesis* (2017, Palgrave Macmillan) and co-editor of *Language and Social Justice in Practice* (2019, Routledge). Her research focuses on interculturality, critical service-learning, and heritage language socialization. She is the American Association for Applied Linguistics Public Affairs and Engagement Chair, Series Editor for Critical Approaches in Applied Linguistics (De Gruyter), and former Chair of the American Anthropological Association Task Force on Language and Social Justice.

Emily M. Feuerherm is Associate Professor of Linguistics in the Department of English at the University of Michigan – Flint. Her research explores community-based ESL program development for health with a focus on partnerships, needs analysis, curriculum, and assessment. Recent publications include "Conducting a Community-Wide ESOL Programme Needs Analysis" co-authored with Toko Oshio in the *English Language Teaching Journal* (2020), and "A Researcher's Coming-of-Age Through Participatory Action Research" in Bigelow and Warriner (eds.), *Critical Reflections on Research Methods: Power and Equity in Complex Multilingual Contexts* (2019, De Gruyter).

Christina Higgins is Professor at the University of Hawaiʻi at Mānoa in the Department of Second Language Studies, where she is also co-director of the Charlene Junko Sato Center for Pidgin, Creole, and Dialect Studies. Her research examines the sociolinguistics of multilingualism, with attention to language ideologies and interactional practices in postcolonial contexts. Her work examines language, discourse, and semiotics in the domains of tourism, family life, the media, popular culture, and the workplace.

Holly E. Jacobson is Associate Professor in the University of New Mexico Department of Linguistics. Communities impacted by health disparities constitute the driving force of her work. She has geared her research agenda to advancing our understanding of language as a social determinant of health, focusing on the contexts of mediated interaction and health literacy. Her research is informed by interactional frameworks. Recent publications include "Advancing health equity and eliminating health disparities," co-authored with Francisco Soto Mas, Diane D. Allensworth, and Camara Phyllis Jones, in Fertman and Allensworth (eds.), *Health Promotion Programs: From Theory to Practice* (2017, Jossey-Bass) and "Predictors of English health literacy among U.S. Hispanic immigrants: the importance of language, bilingualism and sociolinguistic environment" in *Literacy and Numeracy Studies* (2016).

Eric J. Johnson is Professor of Multilingual Education at Washington State University. He received his PhD in Sociocultural Anthropology from Arizona State University. His research focuses on ethnographic approaches to immigrant education programs and language policies in public schools. His publications span topics involving bilingual education, immigration, and family engagement. He has served as a member of the Executive Committee for the Council on Anthropology and Education, the Chair of the American Anthropological Association's Committee for Human Rights, and as a member of the Bilingual Education Advisory Committee for Washington State's Office of Superintendent of Public Instruction.

Holly Link directs Educational Programming and Research at Revolución Arte. A former bilingual teacher, she is also an educational consultant in the fields of English as a Second Language and Dual-Language Education. Holly teaches at RevArte, Temple University, and the University of Pennsylvania. At RevArte, she is working with teachers and community leaders on participatory research for young people and adults through which they can promote social transformation and inform public policy. Her research on Latinx students and schooling has been published in the *Harvard Educational Review*, the *American Educational Research Journal*, and the *Journal of Latinos and Education*.

Glenn A. Martínez is Dean of the College of Liberal and Fine Arts at the University of Texas at San Antonio. Dr. Martínez's research focuses on the impact of language diversity on health systems and population health. In this vein, Dr. Martínez focuses on language policies in the healthcare arena and language pedagogy for healthcare professionals. His recent publications include *Tension and Contention in Language Education for Latinx Students in the United States* (with Robert Train; 2019, Routledge) and *Spanish in Health Care: Policy, Practice and Pedagogy in Latino Health* (2020, Routledge).

Elizabeth R. Miller is Professor in the Department of English at the University of North Carolina at Charlotte. Her research focuses on issues of identity, ideology, agency, and emotions as they relate to language learning and teaching. Her research has appeared in *TESOL Quarterly, System, The Modern Language Journal, Applied Linguistics*, among other journals, and her most recent book is the co-edited volume *Theorizing and Analyzing Language Teacher Agency* (2019, De Gruyter).

Leslie C. Moore is Associate Professor in the Department of Teaching and Learning and the Department of Linguistics at The Ohio State University. Her research focuses on language socialization, bi- and multilingualism, informal science education, and linguistic diversity in education. She has published on linguistics outreach, language socialization in religious and secular schooling, and science education for young emergent bilinguals. Her research, outreach, and engagement have been funded by the National Science Foundation, the Ford Foundation, Spencer Foundation, and Fulbright.

Katherine Morelli is a Part-Time Lecturer in Northeastern University's Writing Program and an Associate Lecturer in the Center for Academic Excellence/Academic Support Programs at The University of Massachusetts Boston. Her research focuses on the role of language, literacy, and rhetoric in health communication and in accessing healthcare services, particularly in multilingual healthcare settings. She has taught English as a Second Language and undergraduate courses in writing, rhetoric, literacy, and technical communication. Currently, she teaches undergraduate advanced disciplinary writing courses including writing in the technical and health professions.

Bernard C. Perley is Director of Critical Indigenous Studies at the University of British Columbia, Vancouver. He is Maliseet from Tobique First Nation, New Brunswick. His work on Indigenous language endangerment and revitalization emphasizes a multimodal and integrated approach toward language life as "emergent vitalities." His monograph *Defying Maliseet Language Death: Emergent Vitalities of Language, Culture, and Identity in Eastern Canada* (2011, University of Nebraska Press) is a critical assessment of language experts' rhetoric on language endangerment and extinction. Perley's research and advocacy is dedicated to empowering Indigenous communities to ensure possible futures for their heritage languages.

Jonathan Rosa is Associate Professor of Education, Comparative Race and Ethnic Studies, and, by courtesy, Anthropology and Linguistics, at Stanford University. He is author of *Looking like a Language, Sounding like a Race: Raciolinguistic Ideologies and the Learning of Latinidad* (2019, Oxford University Press) and co-editor of *Language and Social Justice in Practice* (2019, Routledge). His work has appeared in scholarly journals such as the *Harvard Educational Review, American Ethnologist*, the *Journal of Linguistic Anthropology*, and *Language in Society*, as well as media outlets including MSNBC, NPR, CNN, and Univision.

Betsy Rymes is Professor of Educational Linguistics in the University of Pennsylvania's Graduate School of Education. She is the author of several books, including *How We Talk About Language: Exploring Citizen Sociolinguistics* (Cambridge University Press, 2020), *Communicating Beyond Language: Everyday Encounters with Diversity* (Routledge, 2014), and *Classroom Discourse Analysis: A Tool for Critical Reflection* (second edition, Routledge, 2015). Her work has also appeared in journals including *Language in Society, Linguistics & Education*, and *Harvard Educational Review*, and she blogs regularly at citizensociolinguistics.com.

Maricel G. Santos is Professor at San Francisco State University in the Department of English, and the EdD Educational Leadership Program. Her research explores how adult ESL participation serves as a health-protective factor in transnational immigrant communities. Recent publications include "Putting the literacy back in health literacy: Interventions in U.S. Adult Literacy and English Language Programs" in the *International Handbook of Health Literacy* (2019, Policy Press), and "The Health Literacy of U.S. Immigrant Adolescents: A Neglected Research Priority in a Changing World" in the *International Journal of Environmental Research and Public Health* (2018).

Rachel E. Showstack is Associate Professor of Spanish in the Department of Modern and Classical Languages and Literatures at Wichita State University. Dr. Showstack's research addresses the experiences of Spanish speakers in the US in healthcare, Spanish language education, and the family. Recent publications include "Making Sense of the Interpreter Role in a Healthcare Service-Learning Program" in *Applied Linguistics* (2020), and "Language Ideologies, Family

Language Policy, and a Changing Societal Context in Kansas," co-authored with Drew Colcher, in *Studies in Hispanic and Lusophone Linguistics* (2019).

Ellen Skilton is Professor at Arcadia University in the Department of Education and the Faculty Director of the Center for Teaching, Learning, and Mentoring. She is an educational anthropologist, applied linguist, and teacher educator who is interested in understanding linguistic diversity in US education. Her research interests focus on immigrant and refugee education in the US (particularly for Cambodians in Philadelphia), biliterate development, (arts-based) global/local civic education and engagement, the inclusion of English Learners and students with disabilities in general education contexts, service-learning in undergraduate and graduate education, and embodied learning.

Doris S. Warriner is Professor of English in the Department of English at Arizona State University. In her scholarship and teaching, she draws on theories and approaches from applied linguistics, literacy studies, educational anthropology, and linguistic anthropology to examine the relationship between social practices and large-scale processes such as displacement, ethnic conflict, immigration, and transnationalism. Recent publications have appeared in *Anthropology and Education Quarterly*, *Curriculum Inquiry*, the *Journal of Multilingual and Multicultural Development*, and *Theory Into Practice*. With Martha Bigelow, she co-edited *Critical Reflections on Research Methods: Power and Equity in Complex Multilingual Contexts* (2019, De Gruyter).

Ana Celia Zentella is Professor Emerita at the University of California, San Diego and Hunter College, CUNY and an anthro-political linguist specializing in US Latinu languages, language socialization, "Spanglish," and "English-only" laws. She authored the award-winning ethnography, *Growing up Bilingual: Puerto Rican Children in NY* (1997, Blackwell Publishers), co-authored *Spanish in New York: Language Contact, Dialectal Leveling, and Structural Continuity* (2012, Oxford University Press) with Ricardo Otheguy, and edited the three volumes, *Building on Strength: Language and Literacy in Latino Families and Communities* (2005, Teachers College Press and the California Association for Bilingual Education), *Multilingual San Diego* (2009, University Readers), and *Multilingual Philadelphia* (2010, Swarthmore). In 2016, she received the Award for Public Outreach & Community Service from the Society for Linguistic Anthropology.

Introduction

Doris S. Warriner and Elizabeth R. Miller

In recent years, a growing number of applied linguists and sociolinguists have noted (often with regret) that researchers from other disciplines, constituents from local communities, and other non-academic audiences often fail to recognize or appreciate the contributions or "problem-solving orientation" of applied linguistics. The central paradox is that, while applied linguistics as a scholarly endeavor claims to "address a broad range of real-life language issues" and "facilitate the advancement and dissemination of knowledge and understanding regarding language-related issues in order to improve the lives of individuals and conditions in society" (the stated mission of the American Association for Applied Linguistics, see aaal.org), we have not disseminated our findings or influenced social practice as much as we might have. It is not just where we present our work, who the audience is, or the jargon we use. Applied linguists, in general, talk and write more to each other than to scholars from other disciplines or to nonspecialist audiences. While many applied linguists acknowledge the value of dissemination and impact, the field continues to struggle to reach those outside our scholarly comfort zones.

The original motivation for this volume was inspired by a colloquium that the editors (Elizabeth Miller and Doris Warriner) organized for the American Association for Applied Linguistics (AAAL) 2017 annual conference with "transdisciplinarity" as its theme. That colloquium showcased work that analyzed language ideologies in transdisciplinary, cross-institutional, multi-sited, and/or collaborative research projects. Presenters explored how an explicit focus on language practice might facilitate understanding, engagement, and impact in a number of diverse real-world settings and in collaboration with members of local communities. Since that time, examining the real-world and impactful contributions of scholarship that focuses on language has remained a priority of the scholars contributing to this volume, and our confidence in the need for their accounts has only increased.

Contributors to this volume agree that, if the primary goal of our field and our research projects is to influence change, then we must do more than report our "findings" to each other via conferences, journals, and books. The kind of engagement we recommend and demonstrate here goes beyond describing our research process, obtaining participants' informed (and ongoing) consent, or confirming our understandings, concerns, questions, and priorities with collaborators. This volume shows that to pursue and enact the stated mission of the AAAL applied linguists must devote more energy and time to clarifying, communicating, and collaboratively exploring the relevance of our scholarship to other disciplines and local communities. To accomplish this, we propose that applied linguists need to move purposefully into spaces that we might initially find unfamiliar or uncomfortable.

Writing this introduction during the fall of 2020, we (the editors of this volume) are reminded of the many daunting challenges facing communities all over the world, the potential and promise of community engagement and social activism, and the value of locally produced forms of knowledge production. We believe that academics must do more than ever before to seriously engage with and actively respond to the various challenges of the moment. This volume responds to the exigency of this moment with three overarching goals and purposes. First, this volume demonstrates how scholars of language and linguistics might call upon their deep and robust understandings of how language works and the work that language does in order to explore problems and situations that are of interest/concern in other fields, local communities, or the public sphere. Second, the volume illustrates the value of investigating multiple layers of social process, sharing the relevance of our findings and understandings with audiences less familiar with our theories and tools, and impacting public discourse and engagement through multiple modes of communication. To this end, we showcase the contributions of scholars working closely and carefully with community partners or experts from other fields, and we acknowledge that collaborative work done well and done thoughtfully can impact a wide range of social practices, relations, and interactions. Third, the reflective contributions shared here reveal how unrealistic it is to expect a seamless, smooth, and tension-free research-engagement process. All the contributors to this volume describe, examine, and reflect on the process of pursuing projects that focus on problem spaces that have been identified in collaboration with community and/or academic partners. But they all also make clear that this kind of work can often be logistically and emotionally demanding, with many twists, turns, and false starts. We hope the accounts shared here will encourage others conducting research that is intended to have social impact to expect the challenges, frustrations, and disappointments that emerge and to lean into these dimensions of the collaboration-research-communication-dissemination process. Indeed, we invite readers to also reflect on how to better manage such dynamics when pursuing cross-disciplinary and/or community-based collaborative work.

The chapters in this edited volume are written by researchers who are invested in expanding the domain of applied linguistics scholarship and increasing the impact of that work on social practices, social policies, and social life. While some of the contributors demonstrate the value and potential of drawing on theories and methods often used by applied linguists, others turn to approaches and tools not commonly used by applied linguists to investigate and address real-life language issues. All the chapters demonstrate the value of conducting research and theorizing findings in collaboration with colleagues from other disciplines, professionals from non-academic institutional locations, and/or nonspecialists from local communities.

We see this project as building on and extending the insights of colleagues with similar priorities. Friedrich (2019: *x*), for instance, has widened the scope of applied linguistics by exploring the practical applications of linguistic knowledge and demonstrating the value of transdisciplinary linguistic research. Friedrich's book *Applied Linguistics in the Real World* shows how an applied linguistics perspective might contribute critical insights to research projects relevant to language learning and teaching, disability studies, World Englishes, translation studies, corpus linguistics and computational linguistics, forensic linguistics, peace and diplomacy, speech therapy, composition, and the democratization of communication and knowledge. Friedrich (2019: 5) celebrates and encourages mixed methodologies, partnerships with experts from other fields, and "an applied linguistics that goes everywhere and forges alliance with many disciplines in its search for expansion and further meaning."

We also honor and build on the contributions of sociolinguistic scholarship that influences how linguists, sociolinguistics, and nonspecialists alike might view the social dimensions of language and its everyday use. For instance, we are inspired by work that values the scientific study of language to advance social justice (e.g., Baugh 2018); public-facing work that engages everyday citizens in research to "speak up about their own language" and promotes their active engagement with words and the world (e.g., Rymes and Leone 2014); and scholarship that moves beyond disciplinary silos to explore language in relation to society (e.g., Lawson and Sayers 2016). This volume demonstrates how analyzing the role of language in society might contribute to socially embedded, cross-institutional, multi-sited, and/or collaborative research projects—and how applied linguistics has evolved to become "a broad, evolving, interdisciplinary field of language and language-related study across diverse social contexts" (Phakiti, De Costa, Plonky, and Starfield 2018: 5). Finally, aligned with Shaw, Coupland and Snell (2015: 2), contributors to this volume seek to demystify the research process and deprioritize "sanitized accounts" of research design, data collection, and data analysis.

With such priorities in mind, chapter authors have endeavored to address the following questions:

1. How did you build collaboration with others (e.g., in other disciplines and/or in local communities) in undertaking this project?
2. Under what circumstances did language and/or literacy issues become an important focus for the research context? How did you respond?
3. What difficulties did you encounter as a language/linguistics researcher in working with non-linguists? and how did you address them?
4. What can other applied linguistics/academics exploring the role of language, literacy, and/or communication in issues, problems, dilemmas of concern to the broader public learn from your approaches (methodological, theoretical, epistemological) to inquiry?

Each chapter author aimed to make clear arguments and provide support for those arguments and to write in way that is accessible to both applied linguists and nonspecialist readers who are interested in the social dimensions of language. Authors have provided and analyzed concrete examples, highlighted and discussed the practical/applied aspects of their research, and tried to show how a language-/linguistics-oriented research methodology can lead to insights and solutions that ultimately have social impact.

Overview of chapters

This section is organized according to three overarching and related themes that are explored in this volume. Under each heading, we have elected to highlight how certain chapters from the volume engage with and explore that particular theme even though all of the chapters address these three themes. While we argue that every chapter in the volume illustrates important ways of using language-focused research to achieve social impact, the ways in which they accomplish this differ.

Collaborating and partnering with non-language specialists

All of the chapters in this volume explore collaborations between applied linguists, sociolinguists or linguistic anthropologists, and those outside their fields, including a wide range of non-language specialists. For instance, contributors reflect on collaborative work done with healthcare providers (Feuerherm et al.; Morelli and Warriner), applied theater directors with a social justice mission (Arango and Link; Skilton), museum educators and curators (Moore; Higgins), numerous community groups (Arango and Link; Feuerherm et al.; Higgins; Skilton), and diverse professional organizations (Avineri et al.; Feuerherm et al.; Miller; Morelli and Warriner; Moore). While reporting on how they drew on their expertise in language, chapter authors also frequently highlight how much they learned from their collaborators. Their accounts demonstrate how their partnerships greatly extended the social and public impact of their work, became catalysts for new projects, and promoted their interest and engagement in cross-disciplinary work. At the same time, while moving outside of familiar academic contexts and partnering with non-language specialists, the authors encountered numerous challenges. These challenges involved misunderstandings and clashing goals among collaborators, long delays due to funding setbacks, different cultures of work, and the long periods of preparation necessary to establish trust with partners, among many others.

As an example, Moore's chapter reflects on work conducted with museum-based informal educators over many years as part of her ongoing efforts to persuade partners at a science museum to focus on the learning experiences of preschool-aged children who are dual language learners (DLLs). Moore's years-long interest in bilingualism and second language learning (and her previous work in informal science institutions) enabled her to introduce a particular language focus to the museum site that ultimately benefited her collaborators' efforts to gain funding needed to develop and enhance science education programming for the museum. Moore involved preschool DLLs, their parents, and their teachers, and Moore also collaborated with two national professional organizations and six additional science centers and children's museums who were invested in doing innovative work with community partners to make museums more welcoming to and supportive of young multilingual children and their families.

Skilton describes her collaborations with a nonprofit applied theater group called *Just Act*, a group that engages community members in exploring their everyday experiences of oppression and discrimination using the principles of Theater of the Oppressed. Skilton discusses how her engagement with this organization helped her come to understand more vividly her own experiences of privilege and reflect on how race might be inflecting her interactions and professional work. Her involvement with *Just Act* included workshop trainings, joining the board, and planning/participation in events in churches, Head Start centers, neighborhood festivals, get out the vote campaigns, and meetings in community members' living rooms. In examining the educational implications of *Just Act*, Skilton subsequently introduced these applied theater principles to her university students. This new form of collaboration between a university professor and her students points to the synergies, shared learning, and unexpected insights that can come from cross-disciplinary engagements with collaborators who might initially seem quite distant from the scholarly work of applied linguistics.

Two multi-authored chapters, one by Morelli and Warriner and another by Feuerherm, Showstack, Santos, Martínez, and Jacobson, explore the complex and dynamic nature of language in contexts of healthcare delivery, especially when minoritized communities and their literacy practices are involved. Feuerherm et al's chapter introduces three projects intended to improve access to healthcare and health information for speakers of minoritized languages. They include: (1) a partnership with community organizations to provide ESL education and more medical interpreting in response to a local public health crisis (Feuerherm); (2) a collaboration with health professions faculty and community health clinics to provide opportunities for community members to talk about their experiences with type 2 diabetes and (later) to develop researcher identities and practices around healthcare language access so that they could educate and support members of their own community (Showstack and Martínez); and (3) a partnership with public health authorities and adult ESL programs to create curricula that support ESL students' efforts to translate (linguistically and culturally) health research on lead contamination in imported foods for their own communities (Santos).

The chapter by Morelli and Warriner reflects on understandings and relationships that emerged while developing a university–clinic partnership and (later) Morelli's collaborations with a group of five Cultural Health Navigators

(CHNs) who worked for a refugee pediatrics clinic. By examining how multilingual CHNs work with the refugee and immigrant communities served by the clinic, the chapter demonstrates how brokering access to the language and literacy practices of a health clinic for families from minoritized language or cultural backgrounds requires far more than language interpreting. It also requires "interpreting" or "translating" health insurance practices, the purpose of a medical clinician's "intrusive" questions in obtaining medical histories, and the Westernized notion of time in order to assure that refugee patients follow medication protocols as prescribed. This chapter illustrates how collaborating with and learning from non-language specialists (in this case healthcare professionals) helps applied linguists identify and understand locally relevant responses to language, literacy, and communication "barriers" in the healthcare setting and address local concerns and priorities. While the chapters by Feuerherm et al. and Morelli and Warriner focus on how language experts can contribute to enhancing minoritized patients' access to healthcare services in the North American context by collaborating with health authorities, they also reveal the roadblocks these scholars often faced in gaining access to these sites and communities and the many years required to establish productive partnerships.

Collaboration with non-language specialists is also central to the four case studies that are described and theorized by Avineri, Johnson, Perley, Rosa, and Zentella. Their chapter demonstrates different ways of working closely with other scholars, practitioners, and institutions to interrogate how a particular "language problem" is framed locally or publicly. In exploring the role of time, scale, audience, and modality, each case in this chapter exemplifies how an applied linguistic anthropology perspective informs the process and outcomes of their collaborative work with community-based or institutional partners.

Employing and expanding methods and methodologies in language-focused inquiry

Many of the authors in this volume use a mix of traditional ethnographic methods including interviews, surveys, observations and field notes, group conversations, and artifact collection (Arango and Link; Feuerherm et al.; Miller; Moore; Morelli and Warriner). Others reflect on their role in organizing community events (Higgins; Moore; Skilton), contributing to artistic performances or film projects (Arango and Link; Higgins; Skilton), or lobbying to change language practices in mainstream media and the Census Bureau and educating the broader public on racist ideologies (Avineri et al.).

Several chapters provide examples of how to integrate one's research methods with an attention to language. We see this kind of purposeful action-oriented approach demonstrated by Arango and Link in their partnership with a bilingual nonprofit community organization serving the local Mexican immigrant population. Analyzing field notes from weekly theater workshops directed to young people from the community, recorded conversations with these young participants, and the written scripts that these young people created for their staged performances, Arango and Link trace the development and outcomes of their workshop interventions to highlight the transformative potential of their emphasis on translanguaging praxis. By incorporating Spanish and English in their chapter text, this chapter also demonstrates the power of translanguaging praxis. Skilton's chapter—which focuses on the power and meaningful circulation of "wordless tableaus" and other embodied forms of meaning making—reminds us that applied linguistics sometimes focuses on other forms of communication beyond language, speech, and text. Indeed, an applied linguistics that "goes everywhere" (Friedrich 2019) must be able to explore extralinguistic expression and include the body itself as a meaning-making agent.

As an example of applied linguistics work that exemplifies the value of working across disciplines and moving outside one's comfort zone, Miller's chapter analyzes her participation in a university-based social sustainability network. The network organizers wanted to develop a definition for social sustainability that would have broad application and that could form the basis for social sustainability metrics or standards. To achieve this goal, they wanted to understand how the network members (a mix of researchers and practitioners) conceptualized social sustainability while talking and writing about the topic. Miller was invited to join the network because the organizers, all non-language specialists, did not know how best to devise a method for collecting that language data or how to go about making sense of it. Although Miller was asked to focus on language, she subsequently learned that sustaining members' interaction and engagement with each other was more important to the goals of the network than arriving at a clear definition of social sustainability.

Moving from collaboration to impact and public engagement

All the chapters in this volume showcase varied forms and dimensions of collaborative work with social impact and/or the potential for public engagement, and many resulted in tangible materials, events, or performances developed for public consumption. While all of the contributors to this volume drew on their expertise in language, linguistics, or sociolinguistics to pursue projects with social impact, certain efforts were explicitly public-facing.

Higgins' chapter, for example, outlines three projects that promoted the language rights of Pidgin speakers and advocate for the legitimacy of Pidgin use in public and institutional spaces in Hawai'i. Her leadership in organizing these projects, now spanning more than a decade, is motivated by a commitment to advancing social justice for Pidgin speakers, a speech community whose history is marked by economic disenfranchisement and social discrimination. Higgins draws on the tools and theories of sociolinguistics while collaborating with community members to design, collect, analyze, and represent a range of nonstandard language practices. In one project, Higgins collaborated with a language advocacy group (Da Pidgin Coup) and a high school media program to produce a documentary film that showcased students using Pidgin in everyday scenarios. It was introduced at two public screenings, one in their local community and one at a research university. Another project involved collaborating with the Hawai'i Plantation Village Museum to create an exhibit that introduced the history of Pidgin to museum visitors as well as its contemporary vibrancy. The exhibit brings critical public attention to the marginalization experienced by Pidgin speakers. The third and most recent of these projects was a day-long Summit on Pidgin and Education that brought together 200 educators and other interested community members to learn from teachers who use or teach Pidgin in their classrooms. The event was covered by local media. The social impact of these events and projects is demonstrated by the many visitors who have attended the film screenings, the museum exhibit, and the educational summit as well as in the ever-growing number of online views of the student-made documentary.

The chapter by Avineri et al. demonstrates how applied linguistic anthropologists make sense of local issues, perspectives, and contexts to accomplish cross-disciplinary work within a social justice frame. Theorizing their individual and collective efforts, Avineri, Johnson, Perley, Rosa, and Zentella's chapter exemplifies the role of professional organizations as support for broader advocacy work as well as the power of cross-disciplinary approaches. Zentella, for instance, describes her years-long efforts to change a US Census classification label ("linguistically isolated") that was assigned to families in which no one reported speaking English "very well." After six years of lobbying efforts by Zentella and colleagues that involved numerous letters, meetings, and conference calls directed to the Census Bureau and the congressional committee overseeing the bureau, a new director of the bureau agreed to change the classification labeling. Zentella points out that, even though the replacement label was still problematic, we see the impact that a few language scholars supported by several professional organizations and Latino community organizations were able to have on the practices of a governmental organization that affects all residents of the US. In another section of this chapter, Rosa collaborated with pro-immigration activists to challenge discriminatory language choices related to the representation of immigrant families in the US. To demand that mainstream media stop using the word "illegal" when referring to undocumented immigrants, he drafted a statement in support of the "Drop the I-Word Campaign" which was widely circulated among academics and media outlets. In response to the campaign, a number of powerful national news organizations agreed to stop using "illegal" when referring to a person.

Also in this chapter, Perley describes efforts to transform public awareness regarding the "naturalized racism" inherent in sports mascots based on stereotypes. Focusing on building public coalition around this concern, Perley acknowledges that there is still much work to be done, but highlights cases where Native American sports mascots have been banned, including in Maine, California, and Washington. With a focus on stigmatizing discourses, Johnson worked to inform public and scholarly discourse surrounding the "language gap"—showing that while research on the "language gap" purports to show the effects of socioeconomic inequities on the language repertoires of low-income students, this frame reaffirms ideologies regarding the superiority of academic standard English and sheds light on the influence of discriminatory ideologies on students' experiences. Johnson's op-ed articles to major news outlets, workshops for educators, public presentations, and academic publications all demonstrate the value of academically oriented public-facing work and show there are multiple ways to measure "success" and "impact" from public-facing projects that attend to how language works in specific contexts.

Final comments

The work featured in this collection draws on theories, methods, and methodologies from applied linguistics, sociolinguistics, linguistic anthropology, and communication studies to conduct research relevant to non-language specialists and increase public awareness of how language-related issues affect individuals and society. The chapters demonstrate the value of examining language-related problems and issues through the lens of social practice while expanding the scope of the applied linguistics universe in productive ways. Finally, and most importantly, the volume demonstrates how collaboratively constructed interdisciplinary understandings might help to address pressing social problems of our time.

This volume demonstrates that there are many ways to do applied-language-focused work in the service of social action and/or social change. While some chapters showcase concepts, theories, and methods often used by applied linguists, others extend the domain of the work that applied linguists can do, the conceptual frameworks that can be used to do that work, and the role of cross-institutional collaborative work. We hope that you will enjoy reading first-hand reflective accounts written by researchers doing language-/linguistics-oriented work in the service of exploration, collaboration, discovery, and impact. We also hope this volume will inspire others to apply linguistics theories/methodologies to the scholarly pursuits in other fields, community-based priorities, and social change initiatives.

References

Baugh, J. (2018), *Linguistics in Pursuit of Justice*, Cambridge: Cambridge University Press.
Friedrich, P. (2019), *Applied Linguistics in the Real World*, London and New York: Routledge.
Lawson, R., and D. Sayers (2016), *Sociolinguistic Research: Application and Impact*. London and New York: Routledge.
Phakiti, A., P. De Costa, L. Plonsky, and S. Starfield (eds.) (2018), *The Palgrave Handbook of Applied Linguistics Research Methodology*. London: Palgrave Macmillan.
Rymes, B., and A. Leone (2014), "Citizen Sociolinguistics: A New Media Methodology for Understanding Language and Social Life," *Working Papers in Educational Linguistics*, 29(2): 25–44.
Shaw S., F. Copland, and J. Snell (2015), "An Introduction to Linguistic Ethnography: Interdisciplinary Explorations," in J. Snell, S. Shaw, and F. Copland (eds.), *Linguistic Ethnography*, pp. 1–10. London: Palgrave Macmillan.

1

Engaging the Public in Sociolinguistics for Social Justice: Advocating for Pidgin Speakers in Hawai'i

Christina Higgins

Introduction

In this chapter, I discuss a decade of my work that has sought to meld social justice frameworks with greater sociolinguistic understanding among the public about Pidgin, the creole language of Hawai'i. Pidgin emerged on sugar plantations in the nineteenth century as a result of contact among laborers who spoke languages including Cantonese, Japanese, and Portuguese. They were all exposed to Hawaiian, which was still spoken widely in the Kingdom of Hawai'i, and to English, the language of most sugar plantation owners. As a result of their interactions, a pidgin, or initial contact language, emerged so that they could communicate, and it developed further into a creole when the next generations of speakers used this language as their primary means of communication. The creole, which is still called Pidgin by all who speak it, is spoken by a majority of residents in Hawai'i despite regular efforts to sanction its use in education and despite rhetoric that denounces its value vis-à-vis English (Eades et al. 2006). While there has been growing recognition of Pidgin as a legitimate language in schools and society, it is still often referred to as "broken" English, a label which reflects a general misconception about its historical and grammatical status as a language separate from English. Furthermore, people often tolerate Pidgin in informal settings but state that it is inappropriate in institutional contexts such as workplaces and schools, even though it is widely used in these same educational contexts (Saft 2019).

The public-facing projects that I describe in this chapter have been designed to invite community engagement beyond the ivory tower of academe and to encourage greater dialogue and more appreciation among the general public about the language rights of Pidgin speakers. These projects were designed with attention to three democratizing and decolonizing principles. First, they adhere to the *principle of linguistic gratuity*, a concept that Walt Wolfram (1993) developed which refers to how linguists make use of the knowledge they have gained from communities for the benefit of those communities. At a minimum, this requires scholars to share their findings with communities. More robust forms of linguistic gratuity involve projects such as those carried out by Wolfram and colleagues on language varieties of North Carolina, which include documentary films, museum exhibits, and research that documents and addresses linguistic discrimination at their own university (Wolfram 2016). Second, the projects have been designed to critically examine language discrimination and language rights with reference to inequities of race and class, in line with recent scholarship on *raciolinguistics* (Rosa and Flores 2017). This framework draws our attention to the necessity of denaturalizing the historical linkage between language and race and seeks to challenge the ways that the languages spoken by minoritized people are targeted as inappropriate, ungrammatical, and of lesser value. Third, the projects aim to promote *critical language awareness* (CLA) (Fairclough 1992; Janks 2009), a framework which connects language and discourse to larger structures of power and inequality and encourages discursive shifts that can lead to sociocultural change. The three projects I discuss that engage with these principles are: 1) the creation of a documentary film by high school students about Pidgin; 2) an exhibit about Pidgin at a plantation museum; and 3) a public conference on Pidgin and education, held at a local high school.

My goal in writing this chapter is to show how I see my responsibility as an applied linguist and sociolinguist in making my scholarly work useful to the communities that I work with. I illustrate these projects in some detail in hopes that they are useful for inspiring other projects elsewhere. I have been encouraged to do this work myself because of examples set by others, including the early contributions of scholars such as William Labov and John Gumperz, two towering figures who engaged in public-facing work as a part of their scholarly trajectories. They have brought their research on language variation and cross-cultural communication to bear on educational and workplace contexts, in the spirit of social justice. Though many scholars do research that has the potential for real-world impact, publications which demonstrate such kinds of impact are not common in applied linguistics. It is likely that the constraints of time and resources, and the valuing of publications in academic journals over and above evidence of 'real-world impact' mean that most do not pursue these activities. A stellar project of this nature is the Wellington Language in the Workplace project in New Zealand that began in 1996 and serves to study interactions at work and to collaborate with stakeholders by way of workshops, media interviews, and research (Holmes et al. 2011). In addition, the tremendous contributions of Walt Wolfram, Jeffrey Reaser, and collaborators at North Carolina State University (NCSU) have laid a strong foundation for how to do public scholarship on sociolinguistic topics through fieldwork, educational materials, films, and more (Wolfram 2016; Wolfram et al. 2008).

While there are signs that sociolinguists and applied linguists are doing more engagement with communities, too much of this work is still demoted as mere outreach or service, and therefore is often waitlisted as tasks to be accomplished only after the 'real' research has been written up and published for academic audiences to digest. There are seldom studies that were designed from the start to engage the larger public. Very recently though, scholars have written about projects that aim to contribute to social justice through sociolinguistics (Avineri et al. 2019) and to demonstrate how scholars can work with stakeholders outside of academia to address social problems (Lawson and Sayers 2016), and these are promising beginnings for a new orientation to applied linguistics scholarship.

Why sociolinguistics for social justice?

I am personally invested in sociolinguistics for social justice because I recognize my privileged position as a White American, and I feel an obligation to design my applied linguistics scholarship in ways that engage the public and with the intention that it can lead to positive change. I believe some aspects of my personal history encouraged me to take this view. I grew up in the the 1970s and 1980s on military bases in the US and Germany. In contrast with other places in the US where White flight and institutional segregation has occurred, military bases are more racially and linguistically diverse. Of course, the rank of one's military parents matters, and there were more highly ranked White officers than officers of color. My own father started off as an officer and retired as a Lieutenant Colonel, and our military housing was always noticeably bigger than the housing of the families headed by enlisted soldiers. Nonetheless, in my childhood, I had a number of classmates, neighbors, and playmates who were not White, and this seemed normal. When I started seventh grade, my family moved off-base, into "civilian life," to the affluent suburbs of Washington DC, where we suddenly entered the American reality that was much more commonplace—suburban neighborhoods and schools that were nearly all White. It was jarring for many reasons, including the sudden appearance of wealth. In the suburbs of northern Virginia, pricey brand clothing was suddenly a marker of one's status, and teenagers who attended my school were given new, expensive cars to drive. More than 90 percent of my school was White.

In college, I was lucky enough to take a course on Civil Rights with James Farmer, the founder of the Congress of Racial Equality (CORE), who shared his own personal experiences in organizing the first Freedom Ride, which eventually led to desegregation in the interstate transportation system in the US. His stories of being persecuted while fighting for equal treatment for Black Americans are unforgettable. He narrated the Civil Rights Movement to my class of 400 people without any notes, as he had been blinded from repeated exposure to tear gas.

In graduate school, I began to focus my interests on the sociolinguistics of East Africa, and particularly, the enduring legacy of English as a colonial language. Looking back, I feel that my decision to research language in Africa was motivated by my education about the civil rights history of the US and my growing understanding of the systemic and widespread impact of European colonization on the world. Race was the common factor that cast the linguistic practices of all Black speakers as inferior, as scholars in the field of Black linguistics have pointed out for a long time (Smitherman 2000; Makoni et al. 2003). In my graduate work, I learned Swahili and wrote a dissertation on the micropolitics of English and Swahili at a newspaper office that aimed to understand whether and to what degree Tanzanians had reappropriated English as their own, in spite of its colonial legacy. My theoretical frameworks were informed by postcolonial theory, and particularly the work of Ngugi wa Thiong'o, who introduced me to the concept of decolonization in language (1986). His work examines the subjugation of the African mind to Western languages, worldviews, and epistemologies, and his writing convinced me of the need to proceed with caution with regard to the idea that colonial languages and knowledge frameworks could be easily appropriated in new contexts.

I was hired as a new professor at the University of Hawai'i at Mānoa (UHM) in 2005, and my relocation to Hawai'i opened up new avenues to think about race, class, language, and social justice. In 2011, I was appointed co-director of the Charlene Sato Center for Pidgin, Creole and Dialect Studies (www.hawaii.edu/satocenter), and while this role did not come with any additional resources, it gave me the opportunity to think deeply about how I could contribute to raising the profile of Pidgin in the community. I began to design projects that would engage more with how class, race, place, and cultural capital have more primacy than language in our world, and I started to develop opportunities to engage with the public and to invite discussions on the linkages between these social categories and language.

Language and injustice in Hawaiʻi

Hawaiʻi is a rich site for addressing social injustice on many fronts, including through language. Native Hawaiians were dispossessed of their land and language in the late 1800s, after the US government illegally annexed the islands. Though the Kingdom of Hawaiʻi was highly multilingual by the late 1800s and enjoyed widespread literacy in Hawaiian, the language suffered after 1893, when a group of US businessmen deposed Queen Liliʻuokalani, the ruling monarch, at gunpoint with the help of US marines and imprisoned her. Under this illegal occupation, the newly established Republic of Hawaiʻi passed a law in 1896 to make English the only official language of public education, thereby banning Hawaiian in this realm. Subsequently, Hawaiians were pressured to adopt English in all domains of life and the islands became a US territory in 1898. By the 1950s, most families did not speak Hawaiian at home due to pressures to Americanize and to strive for educational success in English. As in other colonial contexts, if children spoke Hawaiian at school, they received corporal punishment (Wilson and Kamanā 2006). Inspiringly, and against the odds, Hawaiʻi is also the site for success stories in terms of language revitalization through immersion schooling and a growing number of Hawaiian language programs that were begun in the 1980s (Beyer 2018; Wilson 1998). The languages of those who came to work on sugar plantations in the 1800s were largely lost as well due to schooling in English and pressures to Americanize at home. Japanese families experienced language shift from the 1920s, and the language was almost entirely lost among the Japanese diaspora after World War II. Other languages that were spoken by plantation workers suffered a similar fate, including Cantonese, Ilokano, Korean, and Tagalog.

A contributing reason for language shift was that Hawaiʻi Creole, which is known more commonly as Pidgin, became the dominant language of these groups. After the Territory of Hawaiʻi was established in 1898, more White Americans relocated to Hawaiʻi in search of opportunities. Unlike the White families who resided in the islands at the time of the overthrow, these newcomers were not wealthy and could not afford the private schools that restricted admissions to the children of White wealthy landowners and descendants of

Hawaiian royalty. As more White American families arrived, they took notice that, in schools, "their children would be outnumbered by the orientals, who have little in common with them and whose language difficulties impede the progress of all" (Bureau of Education 1920: 217). The families lobbied the Bureau of Education to create public schools for their English-speaking children that would use a language test for admission. Starting in 1924, Pidgin-speaking children were segregated into separate public schools based on a language test, in spite of the fact that all public schools were English-medium, as dictated by a law passed by the new government in 1896. The last class of English Standard school students graduated in 1960. The outcome of this segregation was that Pidgin was maintained by the majority of the population. In turn, the schools attended by Pidgin-speaking children became stigmatized in the White gaze of those at the English standard schools.

In the domain of work, people who speak English with "Pidgin accents" have also been discriminated against. In 1987, the lawsuit (Kahakua et al. v. Hallgren) was filed by two local men who worked for the National Weather Service. They had sought promotions but were passed over in favor of Caucasians with mainland accents who were less qualified but who were selected because they "sounded better." At the end of the trial, the judge, who had been brought in from California, told them "to put more effort into improving their speech" (Sato 1993: 135). More recently, it has been reported that Pidgin is seen as acceptable at work, though it is still subject to critique by others and may require defensive strategies, according to survey results from Marlow and Giles (2010). In the context of the home, residents report that one or both of their parents have reprimanded them for speaking Pidgin at home, even when their parents are also Pidgin speakers (Tonouchi 2001). This same story is also part of the legacy of language shift for Hawaiian through the 1970s, and it is also currently in effect in immigrant communities among speakers of languages such as Ilokano. Still, others identify as proud speakers of Pidgin, using the language for an advantage in the realms of local politics, advertising, and identifying as local within the community (Hiramoto 2011; Saft et al. 2018).

Engaging the public

Next, I turn to three projects that I have facilitated which have sought to engage the public in critical examinations of the nexus between Pidgin and discrimination. All of these projects were the result of collaborative efforts of members of Da Pidgin Coup, a language advocacy group comprised of UHM students, faculty, and community members that was formed in 1999 in a response to negative statements about Pidgin by the chairperson of Hawai'i's Board of Education, Mitsugi Nakashima, who publicly blamed Pidgin for low test scores. Da Pidgin Coup invited the superintendant of the public schools to meet to discuss Pidgin in education, and the result was that Da Pidgin Coup agreed to offer voluntary workshops about Pidgin for educators to help dispel misconceptions about the language (Da Pidgin Coup 2008). For more than twenty years, the group has met regularly to discuss all aspects of Pidgin, including how to advocate for Pidgin speakers' language rights and to work together on projects that challenge linguistic discrimination.

Project 1: *Ha Kam Wi Tawk Pidgin Yet?* student documentary film

In 2008, members of Da Pidgin Coup discussed how to embark on a project that would engage the community while also inviting Pidgin speakers to lead the way. We contemplated ways to avoid a project that would be centered at the university. We were inspired by the work of scholars involved in the North Carolina Language and Life Project at NCSU, who had produced a number of documentary films on language varieties, including *Voices of North Carolina* (Hutcheson 2005), a film that showcased language variation from the Ocracoke "brogue" to the "mountain talk" of Appalachia. Film is of course an effective way of telling stories about language diversity that engage audiences far beyond the university crowd, and we brainstormed how we could produce a film about Pidgin in the same vein while noting our own lack of filmmaking expertise. Through our networks, we found a way to work with Searider Productions, an award-winning media program at Wai'anae High School, a school which is otherwise largely dismissed as low-achieving, and is located on the west side of O'ahu, an area that is strongly associated with Pidgin speakers and which has a relatively high percentage of Native Hawaiian residents. It was probably easier to gain access to a media classroom than a conventional language arts or social studies classroom to make a film about Pidgin due to the focus on filmmaking rather than school-based curricular content, which normally excludes Pidgin as a topic.

Our university-based team was comprised of three faculty members, including Kent Sakoda, who is from Kaua'i and speaks Pidgin, and one UHM graduate student, Gavin Furukawa, who is a Pidgin speaker from O'ahu, where UHM is located. The other university faculty members were myself and Richard Nettell, a White, British-born professor of English. Darrell Lum, a writer, editor, and scholar from Oʻahu who speaks and writes in Pidgin, also joined the project as a mentor and guide. It was crucial for local scholars to be team members, as their knowledge of Pidgin language and local culture guided the conversations with the high school student filmmakers as they made suggestions for film content and unpacked what it means to speak Pidgin. Our team members from Hawaiʻi were personally aware of the stigma that some Pidgin speakers may feel when being filmed while speaking Pidgin, and they offered advice to the student filmmakers when they expressed frustration in getting some people to agree to be on camera. We visited the high school regularly from December 2008 through May of 2009, and we researched the project as the students went about filmmaking by carrying out pre and post interviews. We were interested in tracking any changes in the their perceptions of Pidgin as they went, and we did find that they became more reflective of the value of Pidgin in Hawaiʻi (for more, see Higgins et al. 2012). Though we were knowledgable about Pidgin from a linguistic and historical point of view, we were determined to take a hands-off approach toward the film project itself, preferring to provide the student filmmakers only minimal guidance. We held back from giving our own opinions, although it was clear that our very request for a film on Pidgin indicated our stance toward the value of Pidgin to some extent. All of the approximately twenty student filmmakers had receptive abilities in Pidgin, and most of them identified as speakers of Pidgin in addition to English and languages such as Hawaiian, Samoan, and Ilokano. We were lucky to work with the director of the video production program, John Allen, who was also local and a Pidgin speaker, and who was highly skilled at encouraging the students to work creatively and autonomously.

The final version of *Ha Kam Wi Tawk Pidgin Yet?* ("Why do we still speak Pidgin?") runs for a total of 21 minutes and is available for viewing, both with and without subtitles, online (https://www.youtube.com/watch?v=8bgP2ic38gA).[1] The documentary begins with a monologue by one of the filmmakers who tells a story about "da worse day of ma life," a feature that recurs three more times as the filmmakers tell brief personal stories directly to the camera in Pidgin. In between these monologues, Pidgin is featured as a part of family life, as spoken by a grandmother to her granddaughter; as the language used by a family who is raising puppies in their yard; and as the language used by two men who are preparing a car for a new paint job. Younger students from the nearby intermediate school are also featured in snippets explaining their favorite Pidgin words, citing examples like *da kine* ("whatchamacallit"), *braddah* ("friend, pal, guy"), and *eh* (vocative particle). A segment filmed in a social studies class at the high school features the teacher explaining how Pidgin helps him communicate with his students better and shows him interacting in the classroom. The film ends with a "day in the life" segment featuring Michael, one of the filmmakers, as he goes about his usual day at school. Expressing his own raciolinguistic understanding, Michael says, "That's our Ebonics. That's our ethnic background, that's where we came from. That's how we communicate with each other and that's how others can communicate with us." He points out how local people understand each other even though the language seems opaque, giving a particularly challenging example featuring *da kine*, a term for a reference that is known by one's interlocutors. Michael says, "Kay, go home talk to my fadda and be like 'eh dad, da kine was da kine and da kine eh li'dat' he know exactly what I was talking about. He know dat I trying to say that the transmission on the truck wen broke li'dat ('broke like that')." Michael later points to the universal nature of Pidgin, claiming "It's Hawai'i's own unique way of communicating with each odda. If you ask da governa, da maya, the state representative, you ask him 'what's up cuz' you tell him 'howzit cuz' see he gon tell you 'wassup braddah.'"

When the film was finished in April 2009, we organized two screenings and invited the students and their film teacher to sit on a panel and respond to audience questions and comments after each showing. We also asked a panel of local writers, playwrights, and linguists to offer their responses to the film at the same events. The first screening was held in the community where the students live, and the second was at UHM, in Honolulu. At the university, the students were guests on the university radio show and took a brief tour of the university's filmmaking facilities. After the screening, they took questions from the audience, often from people who were newcomers to Hawai'i and were seeking advice about how to learn Pidgin, or how to learn more about local culture. The film was later posted to YouTube, and we eventually added a version with titled transcriptions in Pidgin to benefit viewers who are not Pidgin speakers.

The film continues to be viewed online, and with more than 140,000 views across all versions, it has more "reads" than all of the academic articles and books that I will ever publish. Beyond the number of views, it is a promising example of decolonizing scholarship in that the film itself was produced by members of the linguistic community for the wider community that speaks Pidgin or who interacts with Pidgin speakers in Hawai'i. To encourage educators to use the film in ways that could benefit their own students, Da Pidgin Coup later worked with high school teachers at Wai'anae High to create lessons for high school teachers of language arts and social studies that would engage with the film's content (http://www.sls.hawaii.edu/Pidgin), as well as other documentary and narrative films featuring Pidgin. Our work is a much smaller scale version of Reaser and

Wolfram's (2007) curriculum developed in reference to the documentary *Voices of North Carolina*, which they used for eighth grade social studies students. We provided interactive grammar quizzes that invite people to show off their knowledge of Pidgin and which underscore the grammatical differences between Pidgin and English. We also created standards-based lessons that allow teachers to use Pidgin as the focal point in discussions of civil rights, a key topic covered in ninth grade social studies classes. While most of the curriculum centers on issues related to the fight for equality on the US continent, featuring figures such as Martin Luther King, the materials around Pidgin invite teachers and students to consider how the rights of people in Hawai'i have also been infringed upon, and to more deeply consider the links between language discrimination and racial discrimination. While we do not have the technological resources to track the use of these materials, we have received appreciative emails from time to time from educators who have used them in their teaching.

Project 2: *Pidgin: How was . . . How Stay* museum installation

I first began to imagine creating a museum installation when I learned about the museum exhibits that the North Carolina Language and Life Project mention in their publications in reference to the principle of linguistic gratuity. For example, they designed an exhibit titled *Freedom's Voice: Celebrating the Black Experience on the Outer Banks* in 2006, which featured images, documentary footage, linguistic interviews, and artifacts to explain African Americans' contributions to Roanoke Island, a place best known for a 1585 settlement that mysteriously disappeared, known as the Lost Colony. In 2010, I reached out to the Hawai'i Plantation Village Museum to see whether they would be interested in an exhibit about Pidgin. This was the most relevant site, as it is the main museum in Hawai'i that presents visitors with an understanding of plantation life. The plantation village is located in Waipahu, in a part of O'ahu that was remade for sugar plantations in the middle of the nineteenth century. The O'ahu Sugar Company was established in 1897 in Waipahu, and it produced sugar until 1995. It is a destination for approximately 100,000 children a year who visit on a field trip as part of their studies for Hawai'i history, which is a focus in both fourth and ninth grade social studies. The museum is also on the beaten path of many tourists who are interested in learning more about the plantation chapter of Hawai'i's history, and visitors from O'ahu and the neighbor islands are also regular visitors. I consulted with the director, who amiably agreed to allow a small team of us from UHM to update the exhibit. I managed the project and was supported by Andrew Choy, a graduate student who is from Oʻahu and speaks Pidgin. By way of a small grant,[2] the team also included a Hawaiʻi historian at UHM, John Rosa, who is from Hawaiʻi, and a filmmaker, Marlene Booth, who had recently made a documentary film about Pidgin called *Pidgin: The Voice of Hawaiʻi* (2009). Our team was particularly welcomed at the museum, which was itself lacking resources. We were given two walls that provided approximately 25 feet of horizontal space to work with. The museum had an existing display about Pidgin that was limited to a list of vocabulary words and lyrics from work songs that were sung during sugarcane harvesting. On the walls of the main building of the museum, these Pidgin words decorated sepia-toned images that depicted the plantation life at the end of the nineteenth and early twentieth centuries.

Since museums often connote the past, rather than the present, we made a particular effort to design an exhibit that would present Pidgin as a language that developed in the 1800s but which would also frame the language from a contemporary lens. We settled on a timeline approach and eventually named the exhibit *Pidgin: How come ... how stay* ("Pidgin: How did it develop ... How is it now?") One way that we depicted this timeline was in the sign for the exhibit, which features the title with a visual and lexical display of the early days of Pidgin (Figure 1). On the left side, the older forms appear near an image of plantation workers and feature *hapai ko* ("carry (sugar)cane"), *habut* ("pout"), *gasa gasa* ("busy"), *tantaran* ("arrogant"), bambucha ("big"), and *kaukau* ("food"). While these words are derived from Hawaiian, Japanese, Filipino, and Portuguese, the words on the right, which reflect contemporary Pidgin, are all English-lexified. Here, we see the popular spellings of *lataz* ("bye"), *garanz* ("guaranteed, for certain"), *rajah dat* ("roger that, gotcha"), *choke* ("a lot"), *grinds* ("food"), and *shoots* ("yes, alright") surrounding a *shaka*, the ubiquitous local gesture that gets used for a range of functions, including greeting, thanking, leave-taking, confirming understanding, and more.[3] While the older terms are still in circulation, younger speakers are primarily using English-derived terms, though they have some receptive competence in the non-English forms as well.

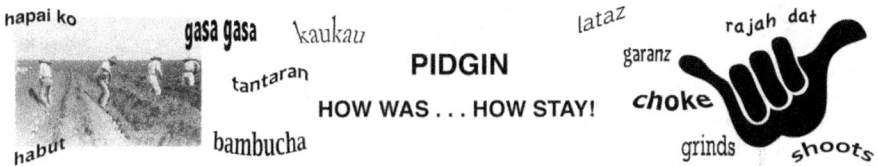

Figure 1.1 Museum exhibit wall for *Pidgin: How was ... How Stay!* (image courtesy of C. Higgins)

Most aspects of present-day Hawai'i are historically interwoven with the marginalization of Native Hawaiians and Pidgin-speaking laborers in the eighteenth and nineteenth centuries. The exhibit thus features key periods and events that examine this marginalization by using archival images and an informational sign that first summarizes the event in Pidgin, followed by more details in English, though presented in smaller font. Placing Pidgin first prioritizes the language for museum-goers and attempts to frame the presentation from a Pidgin voice.

Figure 1.2 demonstrates the enthusiasm of McKinley High School in promoting "Better English Week," in 1926 in an effort to encourage students to speak English rather than Pidgin. The student body put on a play in which they

In honor of "Better English Week," McKinley High School students conducted a wedding ceremony in which McKinley High School was married to English (top left photo). As part of the festivities, Pidgin was also killed after being found guilty of murdering good English in a trial (bottom right photo). McKinley Yearbook, 1926.

Figure 1.2 Museum exhibit panel on Pidgin in the 1920s featuring Better English Week (this image is in the public domain)

anthropomorphized Pidgin and put it on trial for killing good English. Pidgin was found guilty and sentenced to death. The bottom right image shows the students carrying a black coffin with white letters that state "Pidgin English." According to the yearbook, they buried Pidgin in the ground of the high school campus before moving on to other ceremonies, including the marriage of McKinley High to good English. All of the children in the photos are undoubtedly Pidgin speakers. It is hard to imagine how they felt about speaking their language after burying it in the ground that day.

The exhibit includes a touchscreen computer loaded with audio clips of Pidgin so that people can listen to the language as it has changed over time (Figure 1.3). In the process of finding audio clips, I learned that no known recordings of Pidgin exist in any archives prior to the 1970s, except in music recordings of songs with stylized Pidgin. This was an astonishing discovery, given that Pidgin was spoken since the turn of the century. I found recordings from oral history interviews carried out in the 1970s with elders who were born at the time when creolization was taking place, and I used excerpts from speakers such as Samuel Mock-Chew, a resident of Waipi'o who narrated the process of making kalua pork in an imu, or underground oven. The touchscreen also featured clips of two students shown in the (2009) *Ha Kam Wi Tawk Pidgin Yet?* film discussed above who represented the younger generation's Pidgin. Visitors can also use the touchscreen computer to view images of Pidgin in the linguistic landscape of Hawai'i. The presence of Pidgin in written form on signs in itself invites critical language awareness, as it raises the question of how a language that is described as having little value is used to buy, sell, and speak to local sensibilities.

The exhibit also showcases Pidgin as it is used to express local pride and local identity. A number of works in Pidgin are displayed, including novels by writers such as Lois-Ann Yamanaka and Lee Tonouchi, CD and DVD covers of local, well-loved comedians, and a copy of *Da Jesus Book*, a Pidgin-medium New Testament (Grimes and Grimes 2000). Local T-shirts with Pidgin sentiments are also on display, as these are a key way that local identity is marked in Hawai'i (Figure 1.4). In the bottom center is a T-shirt stating "Engalish Standard School Rejeck," which references the rejection of Pidgin speakers in English standard schools, discussed earlier. While the T-shirt can be interpreted as mocking those who did not get admitted to English standard schools (in the illustration, the student is even holding the book upside down), it is also often interpreted as a statement about the unfairness of English standard schools.

The museum exhibit opened in May of 2011, and we held a public program on opening day that included a talk by historian and team member John Rosa

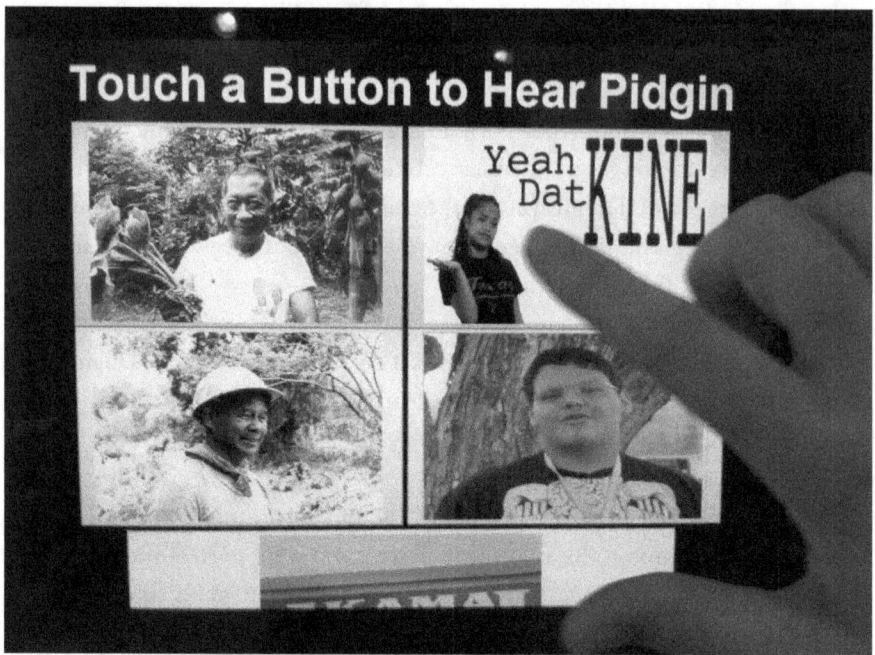

Figure 1.3 Touchscreen computer featuring oral and visual Pidgin at the exhibit (photo courtesy of C. Higgins)

Figure 1.4 Pidgin T-shirts on display (photo courtesy of C. Higgins)

about the power of Pidgin as a common language that sugar plantation laborers used to organize and demand higher wages, and as a language that expresses commonality in present-day Hawai'i. We also designed activities for people in the museum, including taking Pidgin grammar quizzes, sketching linguistic family trees to see where Pidgin entered families generationally, using Pidgin magnets to compose sentences, and watching documentary films about Pidgin, in addition to viewing the exhibit itself. As Douglas (2016) notes, it is important for museum exhibits to do more than present information to communities, and our opening day strived to engage the attendees and also learn from them about how Pidgin functioned in their own lives. We had a full house for the event and were pleased to receive nothing but positive responses from an evaluation that we gave for the opening day event. We provided handouts to the public, including pamphlets about the grammatical and lexical differences between Pidgin and English and suggestions for educators in how to talk about Pidgin in schools. Both Pidgin speakers and non-Pidgin speakers expressed interest in our materials. I particularly recall sharing a "survival Pidgin" DVD that we produced with a high school digital arts class with a man who had recently moved from the US continent and who came to the event in search of ways to learn more Pidgin. While our human and technology resources are too constrained to provide an ongoing system for collecting community members' stories and histories about Pidgin, we hope to be able to continue this work in other avenues, including podcasts or through new content on the Sato Center website, where we plan to feature brief interviews with individuals in a feature titled *Pidgin Profiles*.

Project 3: *Get Pidgin?*: Summit on Pidgin and Education

Pidgin speakers have always been stigmatized in educational contexts. It is clear that Pidgin has also long been indexical of people of color and of the lower working class in Hawai'i. Even though Hawai'i is a "minority-majority" state in the US, Pidgin has been cast as deficient to English by Americans from the US continent. The result is that there is a naturalization of Pidgin as a language of the underclass, which is made up of non-White people, just as there is a naturalization of English as the language of the upper classes, which have been historically overrepresented by White people in Hawai'i. After the US government seized Hawai'i in the 1890s, the value of English became tied explicitly to power, and while it was always ideologically linked to Whiteness by way of the *haole* ("White") businessmen and government leaders who took over Hawai'i, its associations with Whiteness increased because of the English standard school movement. To this day, speaking English is still often referred to as "speaking *haole*." Even though many White residents identify as Pidgin speakers, Whiteness is also indexical of Pidgin ineptitude. Private school education is also indexical of a lack of Pidgin ability, as it marks the higher socioeconomic class status required to pay for tuition, along with separation from public schools, where Pidgin is still ideologically located from English standard school days (Tamura 1996).

Beyond language itself, racialized perspectives that privilege Whiteness can be found in every part of the educational system in Hawai'i, as in the US as a whole. Though there has been improvement in recent decades, Native Hawaiian stories, histories, literature, art, and science are largely missing in the curriculum in spite of a state constitution mandate to teach Hawaiian language, culture, and history (Benham and Heck 1998). Public schools teach students some of this content through "Hawaiiana" classes, but these tend to be rather superficial. As in most school districts, the curriculum is shaped by the US continent's mainstream history, literature, art, science, and cultural norms for learning, with little room for local knowledge. While some teachers do incorporate local authors who write in Pidgin into their language arts classes, or introduce their students to Hawaiian ecological systems of land use, such efforts are idiosyncratic (Chappel 2018; Kawakami 1999).

To push back against discourse that positions Pidgin speakers in negative ways in schooling and to draw attention to the ways that Pidgin is a resource for teaching and learning in schools, we organized a conference in 2017 which featured educators who were all pro-Pidgin. The conference had a bilingual name: "*Get Pidgin?*: Summit on Pidgin and Education" that intended to highlight the multiple Pidgin readings of "get Pidgin," which can include "is there Pidgin?," and "do you speak Pidgin?," and from an English lens, "do you understand Pidgin?" Recordings of the conference and the conference program are available on the Sato Center website (http://www.hawaii.edu/satocenter/?p=1348). In planning the conference, my goal was to provide a platform for teachers to share their stories and their experience with other teachers and community members who wonder about the value of Pidgin. This was similar to the approach taken at a conference for the public at the University of Arizona, where graduate students organized the Language Diversity Conference in 2010 in response to a draconian state-approved educational policy that sought to remove teachers with "ungrammatical" English and who had "heavy accents" (Anya et al. 2010). *Get Pidgin?* was held at a public high school not far from the university, but also far enough to make sure that the conference would not be seen as a "UHM event" that might be off-putting to some attendees who often view the university as a site for ivory tower thinking. Of the 200 people who came, approximately seventy-five were affiliated with UHM as faculty or students. The remainder included teachers, writers, and community members. It was meaningful that a cohort of five staff from the Office of Instructional Services in the state Department of Education also accepted the invitation to attend.

To encourage interest in the conference, I invited Augie T, a locally well-known comedian who speaks Pidgin, to welcome the audience. He is an alumnus of the high school where the event was held and was able to share his own personal stories of being mistreated as a Pidgin-speaking student with his characteristic humor. The conference was divided into three parts over the course of the day (see the program at https://goo.gl/D7q4b1). First, in the segment titled "*Get Pidgin?*" we used Kahoot, a mobile app that allows for audiences to take part in quizzes, to ask people about Pidgin grammar, history, and vocabulary, and the winning team received a door prize. The second part of the day was titled "Talking Story about Pidgin" and featured a panel of local writers and educators who explained how they valued Pidgin as a vehicle for conveying characterization, place, and experience more powerfully than English. This segment featured award-winning writers Lois-Ann Yamanaka, Darrell Lum, Lee Tonouchi, and Scott Kaʻele, a doctoral student at UHM who embraced Pidgin in the composition classes he taught. After lunch, the main conference schedule began, with two tracks of breakout sessions for teacher presentations. One of the tracks featured K-12 teachers who taught ESL, language arts, and social studies, and the other track hosted the post-secondary instructors who taught community college composition, Hawaiian language at UHM, statistics in the College of Education at UHM, and a group of UHM graduate students and faculty who ran an afterschool linguistics program at a middle school, based in part on the SKILLS program at the University of California Santa Barbara (Bucholtz et al. 2014). The presenters included two high school language arts teachers who came from the island of Hawaiʻi and who had contacted the Sato Center several years before to inquire about resources for teaching Pidgin literature.

While the day provided the live audience with the chance to meet the presenters, learn about their pedagogical activities around Pidgin, and have conversations, we also posted video recordings of the presentations on the Sato Center website. We do not currently have the resources to track who views these videos or to collect information about how they might use them, but we are pleased that they are available to the general public.

In preparation for the conference, I reached out to news media to let them know about the event in hopes of getting free publicity, and this led to new forms of public engagement with Pidgin. I was interviewed on a public radio talk show prior to the event, and one local television news crew and one journalist working for a major newspaper attended the event for most of the day. The television station reported on the event on their nightly broadcast and on their website (KITV 2017), and the newspaper published a full-length feature on the summit (Lee 2017). The KITV television report's title misrepresented the intention of the conference, which was not that "Pidgin English could be used someday in the classroom," as their title stated, but rather to showcase how teachers are making use of Pidgin as an additional resource for learning and teaching. It is notable that this same misinterpretation was made in the 1997 Ebonics "controversy," when it was proposed that school teachers in Oakland CA receive information about African American English (AAE) so that they could be better informed as teachers of students who speak AAE. Despite this faulty coverage, the comment thread on the news article revealed that some people are able to challenge negative responses to Pidgin in schooling. One person's post noted the discrimination inherent in devaluing Pidgin as lazy, and then pointed out how speaking Pidgin is not a barrier to success, citing many cases of how Pidgin is important for communication and professional profit.

> Yes, Pidgin is a language. Have you considered the discrimination you're communicating when you say it's a "lazy language?" Would you say that about French? Why is Pidgin different? Have you ever learned another language? There is nothing lazy about it. Bilinguals, such as Pidgin and English speakers, benefit cognitively in many ways. My doctor, governor, favorite actor, and many highly successful people in Hawai'i are bilingual English and Pidgin speakers who can use these linguistic resources whenever needed. These bilingual skills are extremely useful for employees in many sectors in Hawai'i, such as hospitals, the court system, managers, hospitality, police and more. Pidgin speakers are laughing all the way to the bank, just ask Augie T (posted by Celebrateourbilinguals).

Future directions

As a malihini, or non-native to Hawai'i, I feel it is my responsibility to consider how my presence in Hawai'i can contribute to positive change. My scholarly contributions are embedded in a history of colonial settlerhood that has not given sufficient attention to local and indigenous people and their languages.

As a university researcher, I am in a position to address this problem. One outcome of doing more public scholarship is that I have felt more enthusiastic about academia than ever. I think this is primarily because it is for the community, including those who speak Pidgin and those who do not, and I see this work as an opportunity to engage with people who often judge Pidgin speakers negatively, whether consciously or not. As I hope to have shown through discussing these projects, sociolinguistics can play a central role in encouraging people to consider how they think about speakers of particular languages and why they have devalued languages such as Pidgin vis-à-vis languages like English. Knowing the history of this discrimination is a necessary step in (re)examining one's language ideologies. Listening to the stories of Pidgin speakers is another crucial way to disrupt discourses of deficiency and to build lines of communication, empathy, and appreciation.

In the future, I plan to invite Pidgin speakers to develop more public-facing resources by using web-based platforms that allow for a citizen sociolinguistics approach (Rymes and Leone 2014). I am in the early stages of building a website that will invite people to upload photos that they take of Pidgin in public spaces and to crowdsource a linguistic landscape database of Pidgin that the community can create, browse, enjoy, and even analyze for a sociolinguistics project of their own. Such work has the potential to democratize the process of both data collection and analysis regarding Pidgin by inviting Pidgin speakers to identify various aspects of contemporary Pidgin. Through web-based citizen science projects, Pidgin speakers could address questions that often arise, including how Pidgin has changed over the generations and whether the English-influenced Pidgin of the younger generations is a sign that Pidgin will no longer be spoken in the near future. Another topic that is often discussed is how much Pidgin varies across the islands. A citizen sociolinguistics approach could lead to more robust data in a shorter period of time than it takes for conventional academic research, and by encouraging residents of Hawai'i to engage in the research process, more conversations about Pidgin would surely take place that address language ideologies, language inequalities, and the relationship between language and identity in today's world.

Notes

[1] The student documentary project and the website that followed were funded by small grants from the Hawai'i Council for the Humanities. The website is available at http://www.sls.hawaii.edu/Pidgin/.

2 The museum installation was funded in part by a grant by the Hawai'i Council for the Humanities.
3 There are many legends about the origin of the shaka, but it is most often associated with surf culture. Native Hawaiians have long been expert surfers. The gesture is also associated with the concept of "hang loose," which is thought to have originated in Hawai'i but is now more strongly associated with California surf culture.

References

Anya, U., N. Avineri, L. Carris, and V. Valencia (2010), "Languages, Identities, and Accents: Perspectives from the 2010 Linguistic Diversity Conference," *Issues in Applied Linguistics*, 18(2): 157–69.

Avineri, N., L. R. Graham, E. J. Johnson, R. C. Riner, and J. Rosa (eds.) (2019), *Language and Social Justice in Practice*, New York: Routledge.

Benham, M. K. P. A., and R. H. Heck (1998), *Culture and Educational Policy in Hawaii: The Silencing of Native Voices*, New York: Routledge.

Beyer, C. K. (2018), "Counter-hegemony in Hawai'i: The Success of the Hawaiian Language Immersion Movement," *American Educational History Journal*, 45(1/2): 55–71.

Bucholtz, M., A. Lopez, A. Mojarro, E. Skapoulli, C. VanderStouwe, and S. Warner-Garcia (2014), "Sociolinguistic Justice in the Schools: Student Researchers as Linguistic Experts," *Language and Linguistics Compass*, 8(4): 144–57.

Bureau of Education (1920), *A Survey of Education in Hawaii*, Bulletin, No. 16. Department of the Interior, Washington DC: Government Printing Office.

Chappel, J. (2018), "Engendering Cosmopolitanism on the Ground through Place-Based and Culturally Relevant Curriculum: The Experiences of Four Teachers of World Literature in Hawai'i," *Journal of Curriculum Studies*, 50(6): 805–19.

Da Pidgin Coup (2008), "Pidgin and Education: A Position Paper," *Educational Perspectives*, 41: 31–9.

Douglas, F. (2016), "Sociolinguistics in the Museum: Enrichment, Engagement, and Education," in R. Lawson and D. Sayers (eds.), *Sociolinguistic Research: Application and Impact*, pp. 66–86, London: Routledge.

Eades, D., S. Jacobs, E. Hargrove, and T. Menacker (2006), "Pidgin, Local Identity and Schooling in Hawai'i," in S. Nero (ed.), *Dialects, Englishes, Creoles, and Education*, pp. 149–63, Mahwah, NJ: Lawrence Erlbaum.

Fairclough, N. (1992), *Discourse and Social Change*, Cambridge: Polity Press.

Grimes, J., and B. Grimes (2000), *Da Jesus Book: Hawai'i Pidgin New Testament*, Orlando: Wycliffe Bible Translators.

Higgins, C., R. Nettell, G. Furukawa, and K. Sakoda (2012), "Beyond Contrastive Analysis and Codeswitching: Student Documentary Filmmaking as a Challenge to Linguicism in Hawai'i," *Linguistics and Education*, 23(1): 49–61.

Hiramoto, M. (2011), "Consuming the Consumers: Semiotics of Hawai'i Creole in Advertisements," *Journal of Pidgin and Creole Languages*, 26(2): 247–75.
Holmes, J., M. Marra, and B. Vine (2011), *Leadership, Discourse, and Ethnicity*, Oxford: Oxford University Press.
Voices of North Carolina (2005). [Documentary film] Dir. Neil Hutcheson. USA: Language and Life Project, North Carolina State University.
Janks, H. (2009), *Literacy and Power*, London: Routledge.
Kawakami, A. J. (1999), "Sense of Place, Community, and Identity: Bridging the Gap between Home and School for Hawaiian Students," *Education and Urban Society*, 32(1): 18–40.
KITV (2017), "Pidgin English Could be Used Someday in the Classroom," *KITV News* (October 11). Available online: https://www.kitv.com/story/36576417/pidgin-english-could-be-used-someday-in-the-classroom.
Lawson, R., and D. Sayers (eds.) (2016), *Sociolinguistic Research: Application and Impact*, London: Routledge.
Lee, S. (2017), "Educators: Pidgin Belongs in Hawai'i Schools," *Civil Beat* (October 12). Available online: https://www.civilbeat.org/2017/10/pidgin-belongs-in-hawaii-schools-educators-say/.
Makoni, S., G. Smitherman, A. Spears, and A. Ball (eds.) (2003), *Black Linguistics: The Social, Linguistic and Political Problems of Languages in Africa and the Americas*, New York: Routledge.
Marlow, M. L., and H. Giles (2010), "'We Won't Get Ahead Speaking Like That!': Expressing and Managing Language Criticism in Hawai'i," *Journal of Multilingual and Multicultural Development*, 31(3): 237–51.
Ngugi wa Thiong'o (1986), *Decolonising the Mind: The Politics of Language in African Literature*, London: J. Currey.
Reaser, J., and W. Wolfram (2007), *Voices of North Carolina: Language and Life from the Atlantic to the Appalachians*, Raleigh: North Carolina Language and Life Project. Available online: http://www.ncsu.edu/linguistics/dialectcurriculum.php.
Rosa, J., and N. Flores (2017), "Unsettling Race and Language: Toward a Raciolinguistic Perspective," *Language in Society*, 46(5): 621–47.
Rymes, B., and A. R. Leone (2014), "Citizen Sociolinguistics: A New Media Methodology for Understanding Language and Social Life," *Working Papers in Educational Linguistics*, 29(2): 25–43.
Saft, S. (2019), *Exploring Multilingual Hawai'i: Language Use and Language Ideologies in a Diverse Society*, New York: Rowman & Littlefield.
Saft, S., G. Tebow, and R. Santos (2018), "Hawai'i Creole in the Public Domain," *Pragmatics*, 28(3): 417–38.
Sato, C. J. (1993), "Language Change in a Creole Continuum: Decreolization," in K. Hyltenstam and A. Viberg (eds.), *Progression and Regression in Language: Sociocultural, Neuropsychological, and Linguistic Perspectives*, pp. 122–43, Cambridge: Cambridge University Press.

Smitherman, G. (2000), *Black Talk: Words and Phrases from the Hood to the Amen Corner*, New York: Houghton Mifflin Harcourt.

Tamura, E. H. (1996), "Power, Status, and Hawai'i Creole English: An Example of linguistic Intolerance in American History," *Pacific Historical Review*, 65(3): 431–54.

Tonouchi, L. A. (2001), *Da Word*, Honolulu: Bamboo Ridge Press.

Wilson, W. H. (1998), "The Sociopolitical Context of Establishing Hawaiian-medium Education," *Language Culture and Curriculum*, 11(3): 325–38.

Wilson, W. H., and K. Kamanā (2006), "'For the Interest of the Hawaiians Themselves': Reclaiming the Benefits of Hawaiian-Medium Education," *Hūlili: Multidisciplinary Research on Hawaiian Well-Being*, 3(1): 153–81.

Wolfram, W. (1993), "Ethical Considerations in Language Awareness Programmes," *Issues in Applied Linguistics*, 4(2): 225–55.

Wolfram, W. (2017), "Public Sociolinguistic Education in the United States: A Proactive, Comprehensive Program," in R. Lawson and D. Sayers (eds.), *Sociolinguistic Research*, pp. 107–28, London: Routledge.

Wolfram, W., J. Reaser, and C. Vaughn (2008), "Operationalizing Linguistic Gratuity: From Principle to Practice," *Language and Linguistics Compass*, 2(6): 1109–34.

2

Building Partnerships and Expanding Repertoires of Practice: Working with and in Museums To Improve Informal Science Education for Linguistically Diverse Young Children

Leslie C. Moore

Introduction

Many science centers and children's museums seek to engage more effectively with preschool children who are acquiring basic language skills in their first language while at the same time acquiring English as an additional language (ASTC Dimensions 2004, 2009). Museum professionals face the challenge of doing so in the absence of research on informal science education[1] for this population (Moore and Smith 2015). This chapter describes the Expanding Repertoires of Practice project, in which a university-based applied linguist partnered with museum-based informal science educators to begin the work of systematically studying science and children's museum programs and practices for preschool dual language learners (DLLs) from diverse communities, their families, and the community organizations and early childhood educators who serve them.[2] The partnership included local early childhood education (ECE) providers; seven other museums and their community partners who were engaged in innovative work with young learners from linguistically diverse communities; and two key professional organizations, the Association of Children's Museums (ACM) and the Association of Science-Technology Centers (ASTC).

I discuss the project as an example of engaged applied linguistics research, by which I mean collaboration between applied linguistics researchers and community partners to conduct investigations in real-life contexts that are designed to expand our understanding of language-related phenomena and problems. Such projects have great promise to narrow the gap between research and direct benefit to community partners as they address critical issues, promote the sharing and development of knowledge and skills among participants, and lead to improved, evidence-based practices. Community-engaged approaches are being taken by more and more researchers in the US, and there is increasing support from universities and funding agencies for such work (National Science Foundation 2015). My intention is not to hold up the Expanding Repertoires project as an exemplary model of such research, but rather to describe my own "practical personal experiences" in order to help other researchers "open up their own path and adapt their own approach", in the words of Heller et al. (2017: 11).

Over the past fifteen years, researchers, practitioners, and policy makers in the US have paid increased attention to DLLs. This interest is motivated by growing understanding and awareness of the importance of early learning and by demographic shifts. The population of children entering school in the United States who are growing up with two or more languages has increased 40 percent since the turn of the millennium, and nearly a third of all children participating in Head Start are DLLs (Espinosa 2013; Park, Zong, and Batalova 2018). Research in this area is concerned with equity, seeking to understand and address the persistent differences between DLLs and their English-speaking monolingual peers in terms of school readiness and academic achievement (Castro, García, and Markos 2013). Thus, a focus on early learning environments and the experiences provided for DLLs are a key concern in the twenty-first century (Espinosa 2013; Gutiérrez, Zepeda, and Castro 2010). Science centers and children's museums have expanded their traditional focus on the K-12 age ranges to include preschool children and support school readiness (ASTC Dimensions 2004). More recently they have sought to engage more effectively with children and families who have a primary language other than English (ASTC Dimensions 2009). The Expanding Repertoires project focused on the intersection of these two trends in informal science education.

My path to engaged applied linguistics research[3]

The Expanding Repertoires project brought together my graduate training in applied linguistics; my postdoctoral training in informal science education; my work as an educator of educators; and my research with young Somali-American children, their families, and their teachers in Central Ohio. I became interested in bilingualism and second language acquisition while earning a BA in Language Studies at the University of California at Santa Cruz and teaching preschool in multilingual classrooms in San Jose CA. I then served as a Peace Corps Volunteer in Cameroon and Togo, working in communities where multilingualism was the norm. After Peace Corps I went to graduate school with the aim of researching additional language learning in multilingual contexts. I earned a Masters in Teaching English as a Second Language and a doctorate in Applied Linguistics, specializing in language socialization. In my MA thesis and my dissertation, I examined the social and cultural organization of children's language learning in rural and urban multilingual communities in northern Cameroon (Moore 1999, 2006).

After completing my graduate studies, I took up a postdoctoral fellowship in the Center for Informal Learning and Schools, a National Science Foundation (NSF) Center for Learning and Teaching (CILS). CILS was a multi-institution research group focused on making K-12 science education more compelling and accessible to a diverse student population, including students who come from families with little formal experiences in K-12 schools and science learning (National Research Council 2009: 189). CILS researchers studied science learning in out-of-school settings (including informal science institutions) and sought to build bridges between out-of-school and school science learning. My primary motivation for taking the postdoctoral fellowship was that it was an opportunity to work with developmental psychologist Barbara Rogoff at the University of California at Santa Cruz, but I soon discovered that informal science spaces were rich sites for studying language use and learning and that I was stimulated by collaboration with colleagues at the Exploratorium in San Francisco.

Today I am Associate Professor in the Departments of Teaching and Learning and (by courtesy) Linguistics at The Ohio State University (OSU). I teach courses on second language acquisition, language socialization, informal science education, and linguistic diversity in education. My research examines the social and cultural patterning of learning and language development in communities whose members use multiple languages and participate in multiple learning traditions. I have long had two overarching goals in studying children's educational experiences and developmental trajectories as learners and users of multiple languages across contexts: (1) to expand and deepen our understanding of diverse community practices of language use, teaching, and learning and how they vary across time and space; and (2) to contribute to the empirical and theoretical bases on which formal and informal education may be made more effective for children learning in an additional language by understanding and drawing upon the repertoires of practice they develop across multiple sites and activities.

I added a third goal when I began collaborating with the Center of Science and Industry (COSI): to participate in and contribute to the translation of research into educational practice. I front the verb "participate" because I have come to understand that my contributions are best developed and communicated in dialogue and collaboration with other stakeholders in the educational settings and processes I study. It was with this orientation that I have engaged with my colleagues at COSI.

How the partnership developed

My first connections with COSI were forged during my postdoctoral fellowship. CILS organized conferences and professional development workshops for informal science professionals in order to disseminate the center's work, and it was at these meetings that I first came to know COSI team members. Soon after moving to Columbus in 2006 for my new job at OSU, I reached out to these colleagues at COSI to meet and talk about future collaboration. I specified "future" because, as I said in that meeting, I believed that it would be strategic and wise to earn tenure before diving into the complex and risky territory of collaborative cross-institutional work.

Pre-tenure I focused my research and community outreach and engagement on the Somali community in Central Ohio and the educators who worked with them (Moore 2011, Moore and Joseph 2011, 2013). In 2012, I began outreach and engagement work at COSI as the Educational Director of the Buckeye Language Network Language Sciences Research Lab. Affectionately called the Language Pod, the lab is a permanent research space in COSI that provides the public with a research-in-real-time experience. At the Language Pod and throughout the science center, OSU faculty and students engage the public with research and interactive activities that promote excitement about and understanding of language science (Wagner et al. 2015). One of our goals is to support COSI in helping the public to better understand issues of linguistic diversity. We have developed outreach activities that highlight bi/multilingualism, additional language learning, and languages other than English; successfully recruited linguistically diverse college students for the Pod's NSF Research Experience for Undergraduates program; and recently been awarded a grant from the university to expand our Spanish-language activities.

Once my promotion and tenure were assured, I began discussions with COSI colleagues about developing a proposal to submit to the NSF's Advancing Informal STEM Learning (AISL) program. The AISL program "seeks to advance new approaches to and evidence-based understanding of the design and development of STEM learning opportunities for the public in informal environments; provide multiple pathways for broadening access to and engagement in STEM learning experiences; advance innovative research on and assessment of STEM learning in informal environments; and engage the public of all ages in learning STEM in informal environments" (National Science Foundation 2017).

I embarked on this collaboration with the idea that it would be central to what I thought of as the next chapter in my career at OSU. I was eager to partner with COSI and to become more active in the wider informal science education community. I saw the intersection of informal science education, early childhood education, and dual language learners as an exciting opportunity space, one in which we might have real impact on practice and policy. And, crucially, my institution was supportive of my collaboration with COSI. The Language Pod was and is a part of a partnership relationship negotiated between OSU's Office of Research and the leadership of COSI. The Office of Research leaders were eager see more OSU researchers conducting research at COSI, and they were hopeful that some of us would conduct research *with* COSI and thereby strengthen the university–museum relationship.

How the project took shape

The process of developing the grant proposal took almost a year, from initial negotiations about our focus to submission of the full proposal. I worked most closely with COSI's Director for Early Childhood Education Strategic Initiatives, and we met periodically with the Director of COSI's Center for Research and Evaluation and an OSU Extension specialist who worked with COSI on capacity building. My COSI colleagues wanted to focus on Kindergarten readiness. I made clear that I wanted to do work in which language and linguistic diversity were central. We came to agree that our proposal would focus on preschool-age DLLs and that we would orient to the National Association for the Education of Young Children's (NAEYC) definition of Kindergarten readiness: "readiness includes ready children, ready families, ready communities, ready early care and education, and ready schools" (National Association for the Education of Young

Children 2009: 1). We chose to use the term "dual language learner" instead of "emergent bilingual" (García, Kleifgen, and Falchi 2008), which I had used previously (Moore and Smith 2015), because the former term was used by NAEYC and Head Start and was thus most recognizable for the ECE practitioner audience we wanted to reach.

Initially, my COSI colleagues did not share my interest in focusing on DLLs, but they became more so as they learned that such a focus increased the likelihood of our proposal being funded. In a conference call, an AISL program officer emphasized that successful proposals were focused proposals, so our focus on preschool DLLs was better than studying preschoolers in general. In the NSF webinar for aspiring AISL grantees, the presenters stressed the importance of addressing issues of diversity and identified English learners as a population of particular interest. And it was not just the NSF that expressed interest in DLLs. As we engaged with local ECE providers as prospective community partners, my COSI colleagues learned that they were eager to be part of efforts to improve early learning for DLLs, who were joining their classrooms in increasing numbers.

Having agreed upon our focus, my COSI colleagues and I worked on formulating our project goals and research questions and designing a project to meet and answer them. After playing around with ideas for an intervention-based study, we decided to pursue an AISL Pathways grant, which was intended for exploratory work that could serve as a foundation on which to develop a proposal for a larger grant. The Pathways made sense because we were proposing to explore a space that was largely unexamined. Research on science education for English language learners had focused on children in third grade and older, and there was very little published research on science education for preschool DLLs (Moore and Smith, 2015). Thus, practitioners of science education for young DLLs have had to extrapolate from research on first-language early childhood science education, science education for linguistically diverse K-12 students, and English language and literacy development for children learning English as an additional language (also mostly K-12). This gap in the research left science centers and children's museums without a firm research base on which to build their programs and practices for improving informal science learning experiences and school readiness for preschool DLLs.

In the end, we articulated the overarching goal of the Expanding Repertoires project as being to advance our knowledge and awareness of needs and practices related to science education for preschool DLLs. The project had three core questions:

1. What are science centers and children's museums currently doing and/or want to do to improve informal science learning experiences and school readiness for preschool DLLs?
2. What do science centers and children's museums identify as needs with respect to reaching and serving preschool DLLs, their families, and the ECE professionals who serve them?
3. Which programs and practices hold the most promise in terms of potential to (a) improve science learning experiences and school readiness for DLLs and/or (b) be adapted for use in diverse contexts?

As Heller et al. (2017: 8) point out, the first key moment in a research project is the formulation of a question that "makes sense in the discipline." In formulating our research questions, we oriented to the interdisciplinary community of informal science education. These questions were meaningful for my COSI colleagues and me, and I was satisfied as an applied linguist because language and linguistic processes were central to all three questions.

To answer our questions, we designed a project comprised of three interconnected activities:

1. The national needs assessment: an online survey of science centers and children's museums across the country concerning their perceived needs and abilities to address linguistic diversity and to serve DLLs and bi/multilingual families, their relationships with diverse language communities, and resources museums drew on to address the needs of these communities.
2. Virtual and in-person convenings: a series of meetings that brought together teams from seven partner museums engaged in innovative work with DLLs and families, as well as the project's Committee of Visitors and Board of Advisers, to share experiences and expertise and to discuss promising practices and directions for future research.
3. The exploratory study of COSI's programs and practices related to the support of access, participation, and learning for preschool DLLs and their families: a study of the experiences and perspectives of DLLs, parents, preschool teachers, and museum professionals, in which we conducted participant observation, interviews, focus groups, and video recording of interaction on the museum floor and during museum outreach in preschool classrooms.

Each of the three activities played to the strengths and interests of a project team member. The Director of COSI's Center for Research and Evaluation would lead the national needs assessment, which would help us identify ongoing work and pressing needs at the national level. The Director of COSI's Early Childhood Education Strategic Initiatives, who had a strong national network of museum practitioners focused on early childhood, would take the lead on the convenings. The exploratory study (discussed below) was my bailiwick.

Sociocultural learning theory (Cole 1998; Lave 1988; Vygotsky 1978) was the overarching theoretical framework guiding the project. While sociocultural theory is one of the main frameworks used by informal science education researchers (National Research Council 2009), my practitioner partners were not very familiar with it, and they relied on me to explain to them and in the proposal what it meant for us to use the theory. I explained that it meant we took the perspective that informal science learning and school readiness are accomplished collaboratively and are shaped by the broader contexts in which they occur (cf., Falk and Dierking 2000; Leinhardt et al. 2002; Paris 2002; Schauble et al. 1997). That is, we saw children and their families, early childhood professionals, and informal science educators together creating opportunities for developing knowledge, strategies, and skills through apprenticeships in which designed environments and intentional guidance scaffold children's learning. We viewed these processes as entailing the use of cultural tools—including language—and occurring within activity settings and institutions that have histories and associated values and ideologies. Thus, we would examine informal science learning for preschool DLLs not only on the individual and interpersonal planes of analysis, the foci of social constructivist learning theory, which was more familiar to my COSI colleagues, but also on the institutional and community plane (cf., Rogoff 2003).

The exploratory study

The exploratory study examined COSI's programs and practices related to preschool DLLs and their families and had three main goals: (1) gain insight into the experiences and perspectives of participants and stakeholders in COSI's early childhood programs that serve preschool DLLs—the children, their families, early childhood professionals, and the COSI team; (2) identify needs, challenges, and opportunities related to reaching and serving preschool DLLs in Central Ohio; and (3) establish an empirical basis on which to develop new and/or adapted programs and practices to improve science learning experiences and school readiness for DLLs, the study of which we hoped would be funded by the NSF.

We made a case for COSI as a representative lab in which to study informal science education for preschool DLLs where that population had yet to receive much attention from science centers and children's museums. First, like many informal science institutions in the Midwest and the South, COSI served a region experiencing new and rapid growth in linguistic diversity but had yet to develop programs and practices specifically to serve diverse linguistic communities. Second, Central Ohio's linguistically diverse population is highly heterogeneous with respect to language background, ethnicity and race, cultural values and beliefs, economic resources, experiences with literacy and schooling, and (im)migration history, as is the case for the US overall. This would allow us to explore issues concerning the applicability and adaptability of programs and practices for diverse communities. And third, COSI had extensive and well-developed ECE programs that included a large exhibit area designed for children birth to Kindergarten, multiple on-site and outreach programs for families and early care and education centers, and professional development for early childhood professionals. This would allow us to study a wide range of ECE programs and practices in which DLL children, their families, and early childhood professionals participate.

The exploratory study was informed by language socialization theory and methodology (Ochs and Schieffelin 2011), meaning that we combined ethnographic methods (participant observation, interviewing, documentation of artifacts, and collection of documents) with analysis of video-recorded interactions in order to identify and illuminate patterns in participants' use of language, gesture, artifacts, and structure in the physical environment. We documented and analyzed how language use was organized in COSI contexts (on the museum floor and during outreach in preschools), how DLLs' science learning was organized, and how that organization reflected participants' values, beliefs, and circumstances. In examining interactional patterns in and participants' reflections on teaching-learning experiences at COSI and outreach sites, we sought to understand how existing practices supported or hindered DLLs and others (family members, peers, early childhood educators) in scientific meaning-making, as well as to explore potential changes to improve support.

My research team included, at different points during the life of the grant, five doctoral students and five undergraduates. Between us we spoke twelve languages, including six of the top eight languages spoken in Ohio (Spanish, Somali, Arabic, Chinese, Japanese, and French). This got us a long way but fell well short of the number of languages we encountered at COSI and outreach sites (over sixty). COSI's Manager of Early Childhood Initiatives played an important role, helping me identify and connect with outreach sites. The data set includes participant observation field notes from 110 hours on the COSI floor and 19 hours at COSI outreach sites, fifty-nine audio-recorded interviews/focus groups with DLL families (forty-three at COSI, sixteen at ECE outreach sites), eight audio-recorded interviews/focus groups with informal and early childhood educators (three at COSI, five at ECE outreach sites), and 30 hours of video-recorded naturalistic interaction (20 hours at COSI, 10 hours of COSI outreach visits).

I designed the exploratory study to answer project questions and to provide me with a data set that I could continue to mine after the project ended. I would have liked to have taken a longitudinal approach in our study of DLLs' science and/or language learning, but we were limited to a microgenetic approach because our data collection schedule was dictated by the rhythms of COSI's preschool outreach (at most two visits per classroom) and the sporadic nature of family visits to COSI. To date we have been focused on disseminating findings of interest to the informal science education community. I plan also to use the video recordings to explore issues that would be of interest to applied linguists but much less so to informal science educators (e.g., how young DLLs use languages, gesture, objects, and interactional routines to position themselves as competent participants in play with resistant monolingual English peers).

Working across fields

I enjoyed working with my COSI partners, who were passionate and thoughtful professionals deeply committed to informal science education for all. I had a great deal to learn from them about COSI as an institution and informal science education as an industry, and they were kind and patient in teaching me. There were many practical benefits for me in partnering with COSI (cf., Callanan 2012). It gave me VIP access to the museum as a research site, which meant that permissions to conduct interviews or video record interactions were swiftly granted and COSI team members helped with the identification of good times and locations for our research purposes. Being linked to their highly valued preschool outreach gave me an almost automatic "in" with early childhood educational centers that might otherwise not have been open to me as a researcher. In interviews with caregivers and teachers, our association with and framing focus on COSI seemed to engage people and put them at ease and thus may have made our questions about language, language learning, and bi/multilingualism more productive than if we had presented ourselves as applied linguistics researchers.

To be part of science center–university partnership is to work across fields, which presents challenges along with benefits. I use the word "field" both in the general academic sense of a domain of study and the community of researchers engaged therein and in the Bourdieusian sense of an arena "of production, circulation, and appropriation and exchange of goods, services, knowledge, or status, and the competitive positions held by actors in their struggle to accumulate, exchange, and monopolize different kinds of power resources (capitals)" (Swartz 2016: 1). While I was well versed in informal science education research, I knew much less about science centers as workplaces and social worlds. To work effectively with my COSI colleagues, I had to learn about how their work lives were organized, which issues mattered to them, and what kinds of activities and products were valued and prioritized by the institution.

Organizational change happened more often and more quickly at COSI than I was used to as a professor at a large public research university. The COSI colleague with whom I had worked most closely during the proposal development phase and who was to lead the convenings left COSI for a new job two months before the proposal was due. A member of COSI's senior leadership whom I had never met stepped into the role of co-Principal Investigator (PI). Shortly after we were awarded the grant, my co-PI left COSI for another job, and another member of senior leadership, the Senior Vice President of Engagement and Impact, stepped into the role. Not long after we launched the project, COSI underwent a major restructuring. The Director of the Center for Research and Evaluation experienced a major shift in her role and responsibilities that made it difficult for her to lead the national needs assessment, and the position of Director of Early Childhood Education Strategic Initiatives was redefined and remained unfilled for over a year. Midway through the project, two more key COSI members of the project team left for other jobs. During the last year of the project, my co-PI was assigned additional leadership roles and responsibilities, diminishing the time and energy she had for our project.

These changes meant that the division of responsibilities for the three project activities made during the proposal writing phase became far less clear, and the lack of clarity created tensions within the project team (for a discussion of tensions in community-based research partnerships, see Avineri 2019). So did differences between our institutions with regards to how time and effort spent on grant-related activities were tracked and valued. I used standard course release figures in our reports and never kept track of the time I spent on the project, which exceeded the time reported but which I and my employer regarded as time well spent. In contrast, my COSI colleagues were obliged to keep careful records of their project work and were not to exceed the hours covered by the grant. Whereas I had the freedom and institutional support to make the project a priority, the reality of my partners' work lives was that our project was just one of many responsibilities and most of the time not the most pressing.

Our institutions' different value systems also affected how my COSI colleagues and I thought about the dissemination of project findings. We were equally motivated to write the reports required by the NSF. My partners regularly submitted proposals to present on the project at national conferences of their professional organizations, and I presented at my usual language-focused conferences. In the spring of 2019 I worked with the Director of COSI's Center for Research and Evaluation to develop and deliver a webinar about the project for the membership of the Association of Children's Museums (Moore and Deedrick 2019), and we were both very excited about the process and the product. However, my partners were less motivated to participate in the writing of empirical research articles because they were unaccustomed to the activity, were not allocated work time for such efforts, and because scholarly publication was not of high value to them or their institution.

For us to function well as a team, we all had to recognize these differences in our work lives and adjust our expectations, timelines, and distribution of responsibilities accordingly. This occurred not just once, but several times, as circumstances shifted and new challenges arose. For example, as the end of the grant period neared, two of my COSI colleagues and I felt strained in our efforts to produce the final project report and supplementary materials for the NSF. To lessen the strain, we decided to use the remaining grant funds to hire a COSI team member who had not previously been involved in the project (and was the mother of a DLL) to compile profiles of our museum partners.[4] Working with materials produced for and during the convenings, she compiled structured overviews of each museum's programs and practices for serving DLLs. This adjustment reduced our stress and brought a fresh and valuable perspective to bear on the materials.

As I discussed above, my COSI colleagues came to embrace the project's focus on DLLs during the proposal writing phase. However, that did not mean that they developed a deep interest in and understanding of issues related to language and linguistic diversity. Like all informal science educators, they were concerned with effective communication and were aware that language was an important tool for engaging, informing, including, and inspiring a wide range of audiences.

But my COSI colleagues were accustomed to doing informal science education in English for English speakers. While they were aware that COSI served a linguistically diverse region and were eager to engage diverse communities more effectively, they did not have clear ideas about the role that multiple languages could play in doing so.

I was sometimes frustrated by the evident inadequacy of my own efforts to convince my colleagues of the importance of changing science center practices in ways that took linguistic diversity seriously into account. Recommendations I made based on the exploratory study were received with interest but rarely implemented. When I pushed for bi/multilingualism to be a priority for a new hire in early childhood, I was told that, as wonderful as it would be to increase the cultural and linguistic diversity of the team, other considerations were more important. I made several suggestions of ways to adapt outreach practices so that they would provide some support for children's home languages and/or make English-language input more comprehensible, suggestions that I believed were modest and feasible. Only a few were taken up, all of which involved making picture book read-alouds in English more engaging and understandable for DLLs (e.g., introducing core vocabulary by taking a 'picture walk' through the book before reading it aloud). These changes in practice may have been adopted because they were easy to make and because my colleagues understood that these practices supported the early literacy development of *all* children.

After a longer time than I like to admit, I realized that I needed to approach these frustrations as opportunities to learn about and address the kinds of challenges that would arise in any informal science institution where efforts to support DLLs were new. One place to start was developing a shared vocabulary for talking about language, language learning, and language use. How could I expect my colleagues to commit their energies to ideas and changes they did not understand and could not readily talk about? I began incorporating into project team meetings preplanned explanations of linguistic concepts and issues that were relevant to the activities being discussed, and I grounded these explanations in concrete examples of museum practice. The key concepts of language ideology (Irvine 2016) and language as a social practice (Heller 2007) were two that we frequently discussed and that my colleagues came to appreciate as useful tools for thinking and talking about how to improve the informal science educational experiences of DLLs and their families. These ideas helped them recognize that the way we use language reflects our understanding of the world and the places we and others occupy in it, and that our attitudes and beliefs related to language shape educational practices in ways that can either limit or expand DLLs' engagement with science content and process skills, their bi/multilingual language development, and their families' engagement with their child's learning.

Other project partners also played a key role in deepening my COSI colleagues' understanding of linguistic diversity and its significance in informal science education. These partners—the seven museums teams that were doing innovative work with DLLs, our Advisory Committee, and our Committee of Visitors (three experts who reviewed our work at regular intervals, provided us with feedback, and submitted reports to the NSF)—ranged in training and experience and included museum practitioners, university professors with long histories of collaboration with museum partners, community partners of museums who were members of and advocates for diverse languacultural communities, and leaders of two national organizations for museum and science center professionals. They could share experiences, knowledge, and insights about working with linguistically diverse audiences in concrete and museum-specific terms that were meaningful and inspiring for my COSI colleagues. Hearing from multiple, respected sources in their own professional world had more impact on my colleagues than I ever could have had as an academic.

Researching and advocating for change

The concept of repertoires of practice—the idea that individuals engage routinely in and develop fluency in multiple forms of participation over the course of their lives and different endeavors (Gutiérrez and Rogoff 2003)—was central to our project because it emphasizes the diversity and dynamism of teaching-learning practices. Practices transform as individuals and communities expand, prune, hybridize, and adapt their repertoires to changing circumstances (Rogoff et al. 2014). In our exploration of the roles that science centers and children's museums play and have the potential to play in supporting the science and language learning of DLLs, we called upon informal science institutions to reflect on their repertoires of practice, share practices that were successful, and take up the challenge of expanding their repertoires in order to engage linguistically diverse young children and their families more effectively.

Across the three project activities, six major themes emerged. First, informal science education for preschool DLLs needs to be grounded in an understanding that language and culture are profoundly intertwined. Second, the development of relationships and partnerships between informal science institutions and language minority communities is fundamental to engaging those communities in the process of creating effective informal science education for preschool DLLs and their families. Third, when informal science institutions develop relationships and partnerships with publicly funded ECE providers, they amplify their ability to engage effectively with and provide high-quality science experiences for preschool DLLs and families from underserved communities. Fourth, science learning experiences that are hands-on, multimodal, and do not depend heavily on language can be engaging and successful for preschool DLLs, their families, and their teachers. Fifth, informal science educators need nevertheless to recognize the centrality of language to science and science learning for all young children. And sixth, there is a need for research on informal science education for preschool DLLs, particularly in multilingual contexts, where bilingual education approaches may not apply. Our hope is that these themes, in which language and linguistic processes are central, may guide future research and practice.

I noted above that language ideology and language as social practice were key concepts that my COSI colleagues came to value and use. These concepts were salient for me because, as the project progressed, I became increasingly aware that language ideologies that circulated in informal science and/or early childhood educational spaces functioned together locally in ways that reinforced a monolingual habitus and an orientation to informal science education for DLLs as being in English and in service of English and English-language development. In formal and informal science in the US, English is widely regarded as the language of science, an ideology that coexists with the belief that science transcends language. The consequence is that English dominates informal science spaces and too little attention is paid to how language mediates thinking and learning (National Research Council 2009). In preschools, English-only ideologies influence the focus on English-language development as fundamental to Kindergarten readiness and support practices that create a professional hierarchy that places bi/multilingual aides below English-monolingual teachers. We heard from several early childhood educators that home languages other than English hampered children's learning and created more work for their teachers (cf., Piller 2016; Viesca and Poza 2018). In both spaces, the multilingualism in Central Ohio was frequently cited as justification for English-only practices.

In writing our grant proposal, we made the argument that science centers and children's museums are uniquely positioned to improve preschool DLLs' early science learning environments and experiences because these institutions specialize in the kinds of hands-on and multimodal science experiences that several studies with older children have shown to support English learners' participation, science learning, and their understanding and use of English (Moore and Smith 2015). Working on the project, I have learned from innovative practitioners who have adapted old practices and developed new ones to engage DLLs and their families more effectively and then gone further by sharing that knowledge with other educators and institutions. Such work is crucial, and I believe that informal science institutions can and should do even more. They can raise awareness among educators and the wider public of DLLs' strengths and needs, promote children's bi/multilingual language development, and foster critical examination of the language ideologies underlying educational practices that limit DLLs' science and language learning and their families' engagement therein.

One of my goals for the Expanding Repertoires project was to listen to and amplify the voices of linguistically diverse caregivers. Every DLL caregiver we spoke to at COSI and the outreach sites expressed a strong desire for their children to be bi/multilingual, and a large majority were interested in seeing more bi/multilingualism at COSI and in their children's preschools. Several people had specific recommendations, including more bi/multilingual staff, bi/multilingual pedagogical materials, practices that make children's home languages more present and visible, and events where linguistic and cultural diversity are central. I have shared caregivers' perspectives and input with my COSI colleagues and continue to share such feedback with the wider informal science education community through various dissemination forms.

If informal science education is to become more language-focused, asset-based, family- and community-engaged, and supportive of bi/multilingualism, applied linguists need to be involved. As Graham et al. (2018: 8) note, by "examining contexts where minoritized languages and/or dialects confront dominant norms of communication, we can identify how/why certain linguistic forms are situated to either perpetuate or limit access to information and networks of interaction." Without such understandings, informal science educators will not get far in the kinds of efforts required to engage diverse children, families, and communities. For a start, museums need to deepen their thinking about language and language practices in multilingual communities, initiate dialogue with local communities, and reflect on current practices for engaging multilingual audiences (Garibay and Yalowitz 2015).

Looking back and moving forward

The Expanding Repertoires project was envisioned as the initial DLL-focused collaboration between my COSI colleagues and me, the foundation on which we expected to build for years to come. The AISL Pathways grant ended in 2018, and we have yet to move forward on developing a next project. It is currently unclear how linguistic diversity in general and DLLs in particular fit into COSI's new strategic plan and new Inclusion, Diversity, Equity and Access initiative, and the early childhood program is very much in flux. Nonetheless, I continue to collaborate with COSI colleagues. There is much yet to do with regards to the dissemination of project findings. We have recently partnered on a professional development workshop on hands-on and inquiry-based science with English learners, which we presented at the state TESOL conference. The workshop was based in part on several I had developed and delivered with two COSI colleagues as part of the Expanding Repertoires project for the preschool teachers and aids of our local city school district. I am hopeful that we will continue to do this work and further develop our partnership.

In this chapter I present the Expanding Repertoires project as an example that other researchers might consider if they are intrigued by the potential of museum–university partnerships to be mutually beneficial and enriching for a wider public. Douglas (2016: 66) cautions that "we must think hard about how we approach these relationships, how we value the knowledge and expertise that others bring, and how we inhabit the complex interrelated roles of academic researcher, university teacher, and public ambassador for our subject." Maureen Callanan (2012), a developmental psychologist with whom I had the pleasure of working as a postdoctoral fellow, offers good counsel on how to approach such partnerships. I recommend reading the whole article, but here is how she sums up her advice: find overlapping goals, get to know the organization, recognize museum staff as professionals, recognize that your outsider status has both benefits and drawbacks, give something back, and keep an open mind. In my own experience, and as parts of my account here demonstrate, I found careful consideration of and action on these points were critical to a positive and productive partnership.

While my COSI colleagues were not initially interested in linguistic diversity, cultural diversity was of interest. Most museums are trying to increase the diversity of the audiences they reach, and many are eager to work with researchers if doing so can help the museum improve or expand their efforts (Wagner et al. 2015). Applied linguists who focus on issues of equity and access can make common cause with museums and help them to recognize the importance and complexity of language and linguistic processes in efforts to reach diverse audiences.

I embarked on my partnership with COSI already having relationships with team members, being part of an existing partnership between COSI and my university (through the Language Pod), and having training and experience in informal science education. It is not reasonable to advise other applied linguists to spend years laying the groundwork for a partnership, but I urge them to take the time to learn about the new field they want to enter, the specific institution, and the people with whom they will be working.

I went into my collaboration with COSI with informed appreciation of and interest in the knowledge, skills, experiences, and perspectives of my partners. Having informal science education training, experience, and passion helped me recognize my COSI colleagues and all they brought to the project. I continued to learn about informal science education from my partners in ways that enriched me as a researcher and an educator, and I was intentional and often explicit about this. I recommend making a practice of communicating your respect and appreciation to your partners regularly. This goes a long way to sustaining the partnership and their commitment to your work together.

As I discussed above, I had a lot to learn about how the science center functioned and the lived experiences of my colleagues within that institutional context. Consistently, frustrations I experienced with COSI colleagues could be traced to differences in the organization and values of our respective institutions. Recognizing and understanding these differences helped me work with my colleagues more thoughtfully, respectfully, and effectively. It also helped to involve other (more peripheral) partners who had the expertise and experience to act as translators between the practitioner partners and me. Recognizing and addressing differences was an iterative and recursive process.

The issue of giving back was not one I grappled with much because my research was directly connected with science center practice and my researcher skills were recognized by my COSI colleagues as essential to the project. Nonetheless, I had to learn about and take seriously what my colleagues valued in terms of project-related products and activities. The webinar for the Association of Children's Museums is one example. Webinars are not widely or highly valued by universities as a form of research dissemination, but they are an important form for practitioners. I put time and energy into the webinar because I knew how much it mattered to COSI and because they assured me that it was a high-profile and effective way to reach a key audience. I also knew that I would draw upon my work on the webinar in subsequent publications. Another way I gave back was through developing and delivering the teacher professional development workshop mentioned above. Such workshops had not been part of the grant proposal, but they were important to my colleagues, valued by our local ECE partners, and allowed me to work directly with an audience of practitioners.

In my collaboration with COSI, I went in with an open mind about what we could do together. My only nonnegotiables were that we had to (1) make language issues central; and (2) focus on children and families for whom English was an additional language and communities that had been underserved by informal science institutions. And, of course, we needed to design the project with my research knowledge and skills in mind, otherwise I would be of no use. Beyond that I was quite flexible and approached our proposal development meetings with genuine interest in the ideas and other contributions of my COSI colleagues. It can be challenging for researchers to share control over the direction and design of a project, but that is what it takes to do engaged research.

Friedrich (2016: 4–5) argues for "an applied linguistics that goes everywhere and forges alliances with many disciplines in its search for expansion and further meaning" as we apply and expand our knowledge in order to "influence the key elements of social development in our time." As an applied linguistic researcher, I plan to continue to engage with children, families, and community partners. I hope to do so in informal science and early childhood education spaces and thereby contribute to the advancement of researchers' and practitioners' understanding of early science and language learning processes, the improvement of programs and practices to better engage and support DLLs and their families, and the expansion of applied linguists' repertoire of practices for conducting and sharing research for the public good.

Notes

1 The widely-used definition of informal science education presented on informalscience.org, the website of the Center for Advancement of Informal Science Education (CAISE) is "lifelong learning in science, technology, engineering, and math (STEM) that takes place across a multitude of designed settings and experiences outside of the formal classroom."
2 This museum–university partnership was funded by a National Science Foundation Advancing Informal STEM Learning (AISL) Pathways grant (DRL #1420724).

3 For the 2017 American Association for Applied Linguistics Conference, Netta Avineri, Beth Dillard, and Johanna Ennser-Kananen organized an interactive colloquium that described, promoted, and invited conversation about how applied linguists can become engaged in community-based and mutually beneficial research for social change.
4 The partner profiles were not one of the deliverables in the original proposal. We developed, proposed, and received positive feedback on the idea during the in-person convening.

References

Association of Science-Technology Centers (2004), "Science for Early Learners: Reaching Very Young Audiences," *ASTC Dimensions*, July/August. Available online: https://www.astc.org/DimensionsPDFS/2004/JulAug.pdf.

Association of Science-Technology Centers (2009), "In Any Language: Serving Multilingual Communities," *ASTC Dimensions*, July/August. Available online: https://www.astc.org/DimensionsPDFS/2009/JulAug.pdf.

Avineri, N. (2019), "'Nested Interculturality': Dispositions and Practices for Navigating Tensions in Immersion Experiences," in D. Martin and E. Smolcic (eds.), *Redefining Teaching Competence through Immersive Programs: Practices for Culturally Sustaining Classrooms*, pp. 37–64, London: Palgrave Macmillan.

Avineri, N., L. R. Graham, E. J. Johnson, R. C. Riner, and J. Rosa (eds.) (2018), *Language and Social Justice in Practice*, New York: Routledge.

Callanan, M. A. (2012), "Conducting Cognitive Developmental Research in Museums: Theoretical Issues and Practical Considerations," *Journal of Cognition and Development*, 13(2): 137–51.

Castro, D. C., E. E. García, and A. M. Markos (2013), "Dual Language Learners: Research Informing Policy," *Chapel Hill: The University of North Carolina, Frank Porter Graham Child Development Institute, Center for Early Care and Education – Dual Language Learners*, May. Available online: https://fpg.unc.edu/node/6000.

Cole, M. (1998), *Cultural Psychology: A Once and Future Discipline*, Cambridge MA: Harvard University Press.

Douglas, F. (2016), "Sociolinguistics in the Museum: Enrichment, Engagement and Education," in R. Lawson and D. Sayers (eds.), *Sociolinguistic Research: Application and Impact*, pp. 66–86, New York: Routledge.

Espinosa, L. M. (2013), "Early Education for Dual Language Learners: Promoting School Readiness and Early School Success," *Migration Policy Institute*, November. Available online: http://www.migrationpolicy.org/research/early-education-dual-language-learners-promoting-school-readiness-and-early-school-success.

Falk, J. H., and L. D. Dierking (2000), *Learning from Museums: Visitor Experiences and the Making of Meaning*, Walnut Creek: AltaMira Press.

Friedrich, P. (2019), *Applied Linguistics in the Real World*, New York: Routledge.
García, O., J. A. Kleifgen, and L. Falchi (2008), "From English Language Learners to Emergent Bilinguals," *A Research Initiative of the Campaign for Educational Equity, Teachers College, Columbia University*, 1: 1–61.
Garibay, C., and S. Yalowitz (2015), "Redefining Multilingualism in Museums: A Case for Broadening Our Thinking," *Museums & Social Issues: A Journal of Reflective Discourse*, 10(1): 2–7.
Gutiérrez, K. D., M. Zepeda, and D. C. Castro (2010), "Advancing Early Literacy Learning for All Children: Implications of the NELP Report for Dual-Language Learners," *Educational Researcher*, 39(4): 334–9.
Gutiérrez, K. D., and B. Rogoff (2003), "Cultural Ways of Learning: Individual Traits or Repertoires of Practice," *Educational Researcher*, 32(5): 19–25.
Heller, M., S. Pietikäinen, and J. Pujolar (2017), *Critical Sociolinguistic Research Methods: Studying Language Issues that Matter*, New York: Routledge.
Heller, M. (2007), "Distributed Knowledge, Distributed Power: A Sociolinguistics of Structuration," *Text & Talk: An Interdisciplinary Journal of Language, Discourse & Communication Studies*, 27(5–6): 633–53.
Irvine, J. T. (2016), "Language Ideology," *Oxford Bibliographies* (Anthropology), New York: Oxford University Press. Available online: https://www.oxfordbibliographies.com/view/document/obo-9780199766567/obo-9780199766567-0012.xml.
Lave, J. (1988), *Cognition in Practice: Mind, Mathematics and Culture in Everyday Life*, Cambridge: Cambridge University Press.
Leinhardt, G., K. Crowley, and K. Knutson (eds.) (2002), *Learning Conversations in Museums*, Mahwah NJ: Lawrence Erlbaum.
Moore, L. C. (1999), "Language Socialization Research and French Language Education in Africa: A Cameroonian Case Study," *The Canadian Modern Language Review*, 56(2): 329–50.
Moore, L. C. (2006), "Learning by Heart in Public and Qur'anic Schools in Maroua, Cameroon," *Social Analysis: The International Journal of Cultural and Social Practice*, 50(3): 109–26.
Moore, L. C. (2011), "Moving Across Languages, Literacies, and Schooling Traditions," *Language Arts*, 89(2): 288–97.
Moore, L. C., and R. Deedrick (2019), "Museums in Service to Young Multilingual Learners: Findings from an Exploratory Project," *Webinar for the Association of Children's Museums*, April.
Moore, L. C., and L. Joseph (2011), "The OSU K12 Teacher Somali Workshop Project," *Bildhaan: An International Journal of Somali Studies*, 11(15): 135–49.
Moore, L. C., and L. Joseph (2013), *Somali History, Language, and Culture: A Workshop* [DVD set], Ohio State University Foreign Language Publications.
Moore, L. C., and Smith, M. M. (2015), "Science Education for Young Emergent Bilinguals," in K. C. Trundle and M. Sackes (eds.), *Research in Early Childhood Science Education*, pp. 325–51, New York: Springer.

National Association for the Education of Young Children (2009), "Where We Stand on School Readiness," *NAEYC*. Available online: https://www.naeyc.org/sites/default/files/globally-shared/downloads/PDFs/resources/position-statements/Readiness.pdf.

National Research Council (2009), *Learning Science in Informal Environments: People, Places, and Pursuits*, Washington DC: The National Academies Press.

National Science Foundation (2015), "Perspectives on Broader Impacts," *NSF*. Available online: https://www.nsf.gov/od/oia/publications/Broader_Impacts.pdf.

National Science Foundation (2017), "Advancing Informal STEM Learning (AISL)," *NSF*. Available online: https://www.nsf.gov/funding/pgm_summ.jsp?pims_id=504793.

Ochs, E., and B. B. Schieffelin (2011), "The Theory of Language Socialization," in A. Duranti, E. Ochs, and B. B. Schieffelin (eds.), *The Handbook of Language Socialization*, pp. 1–21, Malden: Wiley-Blackwell.

Park, M., J. Zong, and J. Batalova (2018), "Growing Superdiversity Among Young U.S. Dual Language Learners and its Implications," *Migration Policy Institute*, February. Available online: https://www.migrationpolicy.org/research/growing-superdiversity-among-young-us-dual-language-learners-and-its-implications.

Paris, S. G. (2002), *Perspectives on Object-Centered Learning in Museums*, Mahwah NJ: Lawrence Erlbaum.

Piller, I. (2016), *Linguistic Diversity and Social Justice: An Introduction to Applied Sociolinguistics*, New York: Oxford University Press.

Rogoff, B. (2003), *The Cultural Nature of Human Development,* Oxford: Oxford University Press.

Rogoff, B., L. C. Moore, M. Correa-Chávez, and A. L. Dexter (2014), "Children Develop Cultural Repertoires Through Participation in Everyday Routines and Practices," in J. E. Grusec and P. D. Hastings (eds.), *Handbook of Socialization: Theory and Research*, 2nd edn., pp. 472–98, New York: Guilford Press.

Schauble, L., G. Leinhardt, and L. Martin (1997), "A Framework for Organizing Cumulative Research Agenda in Informal Learning Contexts," *Journal of Museum Education*, 22(2&3): 3–8.

Swartz, D. L. (2016), "Bourdieu's Concept of Field," *Oxford Bibliographies* (Sociology). Available online: https://www.oxfordbibliographies.com/view/document/obo-9780199756384/obo-9780199756384-0164.xml#obo-9780199756384-0164-bibItem-0005.

U.S. Department of Health and Human Services and U.S. Department of Education (2016), "Policy Statement on Supporting the Development of Children who are Dual Language Learners in Early Childhood Programs," *An Office of the Administration for Children & Families*. Available online: https://www.acf.hhs.gov/ecd/dual-language-learners.

Viesca, K. M., and L. E. Poze (2018), "Colorado's READ Act: A Case Study in Policy Advocacy against Monolingual Normativity," in N. Avineri, L. R. Graham,

E. J. Johnson, R. C. Riner, and J. Rosa (eds.), *Language and Social Justice in Practice*, pp. 72–9, New York: Routledge.

Vygotsky, L. S. (1978), *Mind In Society: The Development of Higher Psychological Processes*, Cambridge MA: Harvard University Press.

Wagner, L., S. R. Speer, L. C. Moore, E. A. McCullough, K. Ito, C. G. Clopper, and K. Campbell-Kibler (2015), "Linguistics in a Science Museum: Integrating Research, Teaching, and Outreach at the Language Sciences Research Lab," *Language & Linguistics Compass*, 9(7), 420–31.

3

An Applied Linguist at Work: Tracing Language Choices in a Social Sustainability Network

Elizabeth R. Miller

Introduction

This chapter reports on my affiliation with a Social Sustainability Research Coordination Network (SSRCN) whose mission was to create a network of professionals from various academic disciplines and non-academic organizations who could work together to arrive at a better understanding of social sustainability, including how to promote social sustainability initiatives. Social sustainability focuses on how humans are affected by environmental and economic sustainability initiatives, and, as such, is closely tied to social impact concerns. In this chapter, I demonstrate several ways that I used corpus analysis tools to account for SSRCN members' language choices in relation to their goal of developing a definition for social sustainability. I used these analytic tools to examine the topics that emerged as network members talked about social sustainability in breakout session interactions at the SSRCN's first two annual conferences. In discussing my involvement with the network and the language analysis that I conducted on their behalf, this chapter points to small successes, useful strategies, as well as cautionary tales for other interdisciplinary collaborations that involve applied linguists or language scholars as they work with organizations which seek to have a positive social impact on the world.

Getting involved

I was invited to participate in the SSRCN as a language analyst in 2012 even though I had no prior research experience related to sustainability initiatives. My involvement in the network was facilitated by one of the original members of the

SSRCN steering committee who was a colleague from my own department, the Department of English, at the University of North Carolina at Charlotte. This colleague is a Shakespeare and Early Modern British literature expert whose work has focused on representations of the natural world in Early Modern literature. More significantly, she has helped to develop and advance the field of Ecofeminism in literary studies (see Munroe 2008; Munroe and Laroche 2011; Munroe and Geisweidt, 2016; Laroche and Munroe 2017). As such, her research profile was a good match for the SSRCN organization, given their goal of developing cross-disciplinary affiliations among individuals interested in sustainability efforts. The other founding members of the steering committee included an anthropologist, a philosopher, an architect, a bioethics specialist, and several environmental and civil engineers. My research up to that point had focused on the issues related to ideology, identity, power, and agency among adult immigrants learning and using English in the US (e.g., Miller 2010, 2012, 2013) and thus would likely never have caught the attention of the steering committee. However, my departmental colleague had become familiar with my use of discourse analysis in my published research after having served on my tenure committee in Fall 2011, and she saw the potential for me to contribute to the network through providing an analysis of how members wrote and talked about social sustainability.

When she approached me to see if I might be interested in joining the organization, I was open to trying something new given that I had recently been awarded tenure, and the notion of working with a cross-disciplinary team appealed to me. The broad goals of the organization matched my personal interests in living more sustainably (an environmental sustainability concern) as well as my professional and personal interests in ideologies and practices that promote equity and agency among marginalized populations (a social sustainability concern). I was brought on board with the charge of analyzing network members' language choices relating to the topic of defining social sustainability. I began to participate in the steering committee's bimonthly meetings and contributed a paragraph to the proposal submitted to the US-based National Science Foundation (NSF) that outlined my language analysis activities for the network—as I understood them at the time. Based on the kinds of networking activity the steering committee envisioned at this early planning stage, I indicated in the proposal that I would examine members' posts to the organization's website or to its Twitter feed, as well as meeting minutes and any white papers or other manuscripts produced by network members, with a focus on key words, metaphors, and other emergent language patterns.

Language and social sustainability

The steering committee members who wrote the proposal for the NSF grant—which was subsequently awarded late in 2012 and which funded the organization for five years—understood that language played a key role in social sustainability work. Their heightened interest in and attention to language came about because they began to organize the network during a time when a number of scholars and other professionals were working to expand the ways in which sustainability was conceptualized and defined. During the 2000s and early 2010s, many efforts were made to push beyond environmental and economic domains and to include social or human domains. Scholars argued that sustainability should incorporate concerns such as quality of life, social justice, democratic processes, education, and health and safety (Colantonio 2007; Cuthill 2010; Dempsey et al. 2011; Griessler and Littig 2005; Raworth 2012; Vallance, Perkins, and Dixon 2011). The broader concept of sustainability was thus regarded as needing to simultaneously promote and/or preserve a) natural resources in keeping with environmental sustainability concerns; b) healthy economic systems in keeping with economic sustainability; and c) strong social and cultural conditions or relationships in keeping with social sustainability. These three components have sometimes been referred to as the "three pillars" of sustainability (Boström 2012; Murphy 2012).

While there was strong support among sustainability experts for this expanded conceptualization of sustainability, a core challenge for them was arriving at a clear and comprehensive definition of its social component. This third "pillar" was characterized as "a concept in chaos" (Vallance et al. 2011), "conceptually elusive" (Murphy 2012), a "contested concept" (Boström 2012), and even a concept with no working definition at all (Griessler and Littig 2005). Such conceptual and definitional confusion for social sustainability was typically contrasted with the environmental and economic domains of sustainability, which had, years earlier, been assigned clearer definitions that allowed professionals in various fields and across national boundaries to develop standardized metrics for measuring both the need for and the (lack of) success of efforts to promote these two domains of sustainability. For example, just as the U.S. Green Building Council had developed an internationally recognized green building system, often referred to as LEED (Leadership in Energy and Environmental Design) certification, so, too, the social aspect of sustainability was viewed as needing an internationally recognized conceptualization and clear definition. As Boström (2012: 4) argued, "sustainability strategies and indicators should have both analytical depth and clarity, including clearly defined ideas about what kinds of social values to promote." Scholars who came primarily from environmental and civil engineering contended that an agreed-upon definition of social sustainability could serve as the foundation for creating standardized assessment measures that could then be incorporated into development policies in order to safeguard the priorities and address the needs of people, particularly economically marginalized communities (e.g., Bourgious 2014).

Given this scholarly discussion and the growing call for a workable definition of the social component of sustainability, the newly formed SSRCN developed the following mission statement for its research network: "to create and sustain a network of individuals from various jobs and professions who engage in dialogue in order to accelerate the rate of coming to a clear understanding of social sustainability, including how to define it and measure it and implement it" (NSF grant application). My role in the network was to attend to the following: "An important goal of the [SSRCN] is establishing clarity in understanding how network members write or talk about social sustainability differently. For this reason, we are also conducting a study of the language used during network activities" (taken from the NSF grant application and IRB consent form). Ultimately, the organizers of the SSRCN hoped that documenting network members' language choices related to social sustainability, and particularly how members defined it, would enable them to develop a clear definition for the concept that, in turn, could serve as the foundation for developing metrics for measuring implementation practices.

It is important to point out that while the organization's goal of bringing together individuals from a variety of backgrounds was important for their goal of creating a broad-based understanding of social sustainability, the impetus for its formation developed in response to the NSF's growing support for interdisciplinary research. NSF funding of Research Coordination Networks (RCNs) in particular, funding which was introduced in 2001, emphasizes research or education that crosses "disciplinary, organizational, geographic and international boundaries" (nsf.gov). The benefits of such cross-disciplinary efforts, as outlined by NSF (beyond advancing research agendas), are that they can "foster new collaborations, including international partnerships, and address interdisciplinary topics" (nsf.gov). While communications studies scholars have examined the enormous challenges that come with attempts to communicate across disciplinary boundaries (e.g., Bracken and Oughton 2006; Gilligan 2019; Stoddart 1987), particularly in the early years of an interdisciplinary project (Thompson 2009), there has been less attention to such interactional contexts among applied linguists. One of the few venues dedicated to publishing applied linguistics analyses of language use in professional contexts is the *Journal of Applied Linguistics and Professional Practice* (see Sarangi and Candlin 2010). However, research on language use among cross-disciplinary research or professional cohorts by applied linguists is still limited (though see Gotti 2016, 2019).

It is also important to note that research at the intersection of applied linguistics and social sustainability initiatives remains limited. Sustainability has garnered interest among language scholars in the field of ecolinguistics, which focuses on the language–environment connection (Chen 2016; LeVasseur 2015; Mühlhäusler 2003; Steffensen and Fill 2014; Stibbe 2015). Stibbe (2015: 1), for example, characterizes research in ecolinguistics as "critiquing forms of language that contribute to ecological destruction" but also as "aiding in the search for new forms of language that inspire people to protect the natural world." Other applied linguistic research related to sustainability has focused on the vitality of particular languages and/or cultures (Phillipson and Skutnabb-Kangas 1996; Stanford and Whaley 2010), particularly in light of the current global dominance of English (Phillipson 2008). In this way, the research has focused on language ecology (i.e., the need to sustain endangered languages). The language-related research that is perhaps best aligned with the social sustainability emphasis of the SSRCN is MacPherson's (2012: 202) "critical sustainability theory." He describes this approach as a "hybrid theory" that can "critique how social hierarchies based on dominance and oppression are rooted in deep cultural assumptions concerning the relations between humans, and human and non-human realms." However, with its focus on language policy, MacPherson's work does not draw on empirical analyses of how language is used to construct particular meanings related to social sustainability—the focus of my engagement with the SSRCN.

Building the network, adapting to change

In their first year of activity, after receiving confirmation of NSF funding, the steering committee focused on building a network of participants who shared the interests and aims of the SSRCN. They did this through reaching out to university colleagues (primarily in the US and in the UK). Because they wanted to include non-academics (often referred to as "practitioners" by committee members), they also reached out to city planners and community leaders as well as other sustainability-oriented associations and organizations. Commitment to the SSRCN from potential members developed very slowly that first year. A strong incentive for participation was the promise that members' travel expenses to the annual conferences, hosted at my university, would be covered by the NSF grant. Given that I was a newcomer to the world of sustainability research and practice and thus was of little help in making contacts that could build the network, I agreed to assist the steering committee in preparing for the first conference by handling all of these travel arrangements and funding documentation for the conference participants (approximately eighty). Although this assignment to handle travel arrangements allowed me to contribute to the overall work of the network, it turned out to be an extremely time-consuming activity over the space of several months. I agreed to this level of collaboration with the SSRCN because I thought that I would be able to manage the language analysis activity on my own time; however, it turned out that during that first year I was able to conduct almost no language analysis—both due to the substantial time required to manage the travel planning but also because there was almost no networking language to analyze.

The initial plan that I had developed for my language analysis work, as detailed in the NSF proposal and as noted earlier, was for me to conduct "discourse analysis of various participants' interactions, which might include network postings, meeting minutes and final manuscripts." However, as often happens with the best-laid plans, the steering committee's desire to nurture ongoing interactions among network members via Twitter or in response to collaboratively produced documents was not realized. Instead, during the first year of the SSRCN, nearly all of the steering committee members' energy and time was spent on building a member list, and in the subsequent two years (I participated in the SSRCN for only the first three years of the five years of the grant), the networking activity among members, other than those who were part of the steering committee, occurred almost exclusively at the annual conferences.

For this reason, instead of analyzing online interactions and written texts, I shifted my focus to recording members' interactions at the first two SSRCN annual conferences, attended by roughly seventy to eighty participants both years. Given the organization's focus on networking, these conferences emphasized group discussion in breakout sessions rather than research presentations. There was, for example, only one keynote address and several case studies that were presented to the whole group of attendees at the Year 1 conference. As noted earlier, the SSRCN mission statement states that the purpose of the network was to provide a forum which enabled members "from various jobs and professions [to] engage in dialogue." This guiding ethos of democratic dialogue developed out of the ideological discourses within the broader social sustainability scholarship, work that overtly promotes "human activity and interaction that is equitable [and] inclusive" (Dempsey et al. 2011: 290), "bottom-up participatory democracy" (Murphy 2012: 19), with an emphasis on "human dignity and participation" (Littig and Greißler 2005: 72). This commitment to having all voices be heard and a desire to hear a mix of perspectives and experiences shaped the development of the network itself along with the conference structure with its emphasis on breakout sessions.

Even with this commitment to and emphasis on the interactional processes among SSRCN members, the steering committee was hoping for "results" from the breakout sessions, too. Namely, they hoped "to accelerate the rate of coming to a clear [or at least clearer] understanding of social sustainability, including how to define it and measure it and implement it" (SSRCN mission statement). In the Year 1 conference, breakout session facilitators were explicitly instructed to elicit discussion from participants on how they understood and defined social sustainability. The steering committee's simultaneous orientation to process *and* product at the early conferences is supported by research on organizational decision-making. Priem, Harrison, and Muir (1995: 692), for example, cite a number of studies that support the view that "high quality decisions by groups facing complex, ambiguous situations often require multiple perspectives." My role as language analyst was to attempt to trace how individual network members put their understandings of social sustainability into words and then to compile such utterances into a report for closer examination by the steering committee. The nature of this report was not predefined given the bottom-up, emergent nature of the language data.

I collaborated with the conference planners in setting up software on the smart podiums located in each of the meeting rooms where the breakout sessions were held. This software allowed me to video record (with the aid of webcams) and audio record the discussions. The data that I then worked with consisted of the transcribed recordings from twenty-five of these breakout sessions from the Year 1 and Year 2 conferences. The sessions involved five to ten participants in each and lasted for roughly 50–60 minutes. All participants at both conferences consented to being recorded in the breakout sessions and the study was approved by the Institutional Review Board at my university. However, the large quantity of video and audio data that I collected posed an enormous challenge for me in terms of language analysis. It is important to add that while the NSF funding covered a broad range of *networking* activity, it did not cover *researching* activity. This is a unique feature of RCN awards. As spelled out on the NSF web page, such awards "do not support primary research" but rather "the means by which investigators can share information and ideas, coordinate ongoing or planned research activities, foster synthesis and new collaborations, develop community standards, and in other ways advance science and education through communication and sharing of ideas" (nsf.gov). Given that I could not personally commit to the extensive time required to transcribe the lengthy, multiparty, and quite messy video/audio recordings by myself, I applied for an internal university grant so that I could hire students to help me complete this first step of the language analysis process.

The student transcribers were asked to provide word-for-word written records of the breakout session talk as best they could, but they did not incorporate additional features such as pauses, intonational shifts, or turn overlaps. Because of the sometimes poor sound quality of the video recordings and the fact that the webcams often could not visually capture all of the participants in a session, I determined that it was better to work with more "barebones" transcripts. I was more concerned about creating a record of *what* was said rather than *how* it was uttered because of focusing on the content of members' *definition talk*. Furthermore, creating highly detailed transcription records from the messy video texts would have been prohibitively time-intensive and, thus, expensive, even though the transcribers were being paid student hourly wages. Here again, an issue like transcription quality points to the kinds of compromises one must sometimes make when working on a large-scale project, particularly when funding is limited and an individual researcher's priorities (e.g., excellent video or transcription quality) are not shared by all participants in a collective endeavor. Even with this assistance of student transcribers, the sheer quantity of recorded interactional data made my next steps as a language analyst quite daunting. The complete corpus of transcribed breakout sessions consists of 178,518 words and roughly 340 pages of text. I recognized that I needed to adapt my language analysis approach. Although I had anticipated using more fine-grained discourse analysis for my analytic work, in considering how best to provide an accounting of network members' talk related to social sustainability that in some way covered the complete set of transcribed interactions, I decided to learn about and implement corpus analysis. This need to adapt to unexpected developments is likely unavoidable for most cross-disciplinary, large-scale research, and it almost certainly is true for any new project (see Warriner and Bigelow 2019).

In the following section, I describe the corpus analytic approaches that I used in order to provide an accounting of the network members' languaging activity back to the membership based on the breakout session conversations at the Year 1 and Year 2 conferences. The "accounts" consisted of a presentation to the whole conference at the Year 2 conference (based on the Year 1 conference interactions), a poster presentation at the Year 3 conference (based on Year 1 and Year 2 conference interactions), and a report to the steering committee (based on Year 1 and Year 2 conference interactions).

Using corpus analysis tools

Even though I determined that corpus analysis would be the most manageable approach in my attempts to provide an overall accounting of the language data, I also wanted to incorporate some more detailed analysis of network members' interactions given my familiarity with the power of discourse analysis for illuminating meaning-making activity among individuals in interaction (e.g., Miller 2011, 2013). For this reason, I pursued a corpus-assisted discourse analysis approach (Partington, Duguid, and Taylor 2013). Corpus analysis requires the use of computerized tools to examine digitized text and usually involves numbers or counting in some form given that it is used to examine language patterns in large sets of language data or corpora (Baker 2006). For my analysis of the SSRCN breakout session transcripts, I used the free downloadable corpus software AntConc (Anthony 2019). In keeping with the analytic approaches typically adopted in corpus-*assisted* discourse analysis (Partington et al. 2013), my analysis was a bit eclectic in that the quantitative analysis of the large corpus was *assisted* by a "close, detailed analysis of particular stretches of discourse" (Partington et al. 2013: 11). The aim of using this combination of quantitative and qualitative analysis, according to Partington et al. (2013: 11), is to help researchers come to grips with "non-obvious meaning [in language data], that is, meaning which might not be readily available to naked-eye perusal" due to the large volume of language data to be accounted for, while still coming to grips with some of the particularities in the language data.

Frequency analysis

The first corpus analysis tool that I used was frequency analysis. The raw frequency of word types—literally the number of times a word or phrase appears in a given corpus—can *suggest* topical salience if a word or phrase is produced very frequently in relation to other words. As Baker (2006: 121) notes, beginning with frequency analysis is often a first step in corpus analysis because it can "giv[e] the researcher an idea about what to focus on." Though frequency by itself provides only a crude tool for determining the topical "aboutness" of a discourse, it does help analysts begin to identity how patterns in language choices relate to contexts of usage and to develop a sense of the topical foci of a corpus. For example, and as one would expect for this organization, I found the words *people, social,* and *sustainability* were among the top five most frequently occurring "content" words to emerge in the breakout session talk (see Table 3.1). (I will comment on the relevance of the high frequency of *think* and *know* in a later section.)

In reporting this simple and unsurprising frequency outcome to the SSRCN, I was able to demonstrate how corpus analysis can help a researcher identify members' particular interests, concerns, and meaning associations. Of more use to the network were my frequency tallies of words and phrases related to more refined topics connected to social sustainability concerns. For example, I was able to report that network members had focused on urban sites more frequently than rural sites and that they seemed to orient to local contexts far more frequently than those more global in scope (see Table 3.2). While the urban vs. rural orientation was not regarded as problematic in itself, in showing the membership and particularly the steering committee quantitative trends such as these, I was able to point to some of the "non-obvious" (Partington et al. 2013: 11) or unconscious preoccupations that emerged in their discussions. In this case, steering committee members commented that they suspected members' discussions around sustainability likely reflected the urban contexts where the majority of them worked and lived.

I also used frequency analysis to identify the humanistic or social qualities associated with sustainability that emerged in the breakout session talk. I found

Table 3.1 Top five most frequently occurring content words

Words	Rank of frequency	Raw frequency
think	21	1439
know	23	1284
people	39	868
social	40	868
sustainability	41	856

Table 3.2 Raw frequency of words relating to contexts for sustainability

Word	Raw frequency
City/cities	130
Urban	63
Town	15
Rural	12
Farm/Farming	9
Local/-ly	62
Global/-ly	19

that SSRCN members used words related to existential values such as *well-being, values, ethics, quality of life, resilience*, and/or *hope* as well as to structural issues such as *access, inequality, social justice, empowerment*, and *equity* (see Table 3.3). These terms align with many of the concepts associated with social sustainability that have been proposed in the scholarly literature, suggesting members' attunement with broader scholarly concerns. In showing lists such as the one displayed in Table 3.3 to SSRCN members, I was able to point them to the relative infrequent occurrence of humanistic terms (i.e., *Spiritual/Religious, Hope*) compared to terms connected to structural issues (*Access, Inequality, [Social] Justice*) in their breakout session networking. Again, these different emphases were not regarded as troubling in themselves for the steering committee. Even so, the snapshot summaries that I created of how members tended to focus their discussions when talking about social sustainability, through using the tools of corpus analysis, allowed the steering committee to gain some sense of how "network members [wrote] or talk[ed] about social sustainability differently" (SSRCN mission statement).

Perhaps more useful, I was able to show the SSRCN that despite their desire to focus on the *social* dimensions of sustainability, network members still referenced *environmental* and *economic* topics disproportionally more frequently (see bottom of Table 3.3). Given that this difference in emphasis could have been cause for concern, I undertook collocation analysis in order to explore this more frequent association of environmental and economic topics with sustainability more fully.

Collocations

Collocations are words that regularly appear next to or near another word. Corpus software such as AntConc can determine when this co-occurrence is

Table 3.3 Raw frequency of words relating to sustainability subtopics

Word	Raw frequency
Access	69
Inequality	48
Well-being	43
(Social) justice	43
Values	40
Ethics	25
Empower/-ment	22
Equity	22
Quality of life	21
Resilience	13
Spiritual/Religious	12
Hope	11
Vibrance/-y	4
Flourish/-ing	3
Subtotal	376
Environmental	262
Economic	105
Subtotal	367

statistically significant rather than occurring merely by chance. As Baker (2006: 96) explains, collocations "suggest discourse traces" of some of the "assumptions" assigned to concepts in particular textual or interactional contexts. Using the word *sustainability* as the word of interest, I examined which words appeared within a 5-word window to the left or right of it with statistically significant frequency. I found, again quite unsurprisingly, that the word *social* appeared near or next to the word *sustainability* most frequently (see Table 3.4). More useful, I found that the remaining most frequent content-word collocations with *sustainability* included the words *environmental, definition,* and *economic*.[1] These collocations corroborated the frequency analysis findings noted above in Table 3.3 which suggested that network members incorporated topics relating to environmental and economic issues relatively more frequently than social-impact topics when engaging in talk that focused on definitions of social sustainability.

Table 3.4 Most frequent content-word collocations with *sustainability*

Collocation	Raw frequency of collocation occurrences
Social	489
Think	57
Sustainability	34
Environmental	34
Definition	28
Economic	19

Selective discourse analysis

Using these more targeted findings related to participants' definition talk, gained through collocation analyses, I turned to where the collocation terms noted above clustered in the transcripts. In this way, the quantitative findings provided some guidance in terms of how to undertake selective and somewhat more detailed discourse analysis of the very large corpus. In doing so, I found that the network members' emphasis on environmental and/or economic topics often developed as they compared what was understood about sustainability in these domains to what still needed to be understood about social sustainability. This finding is illustrated in Excerpts 1–2 below in which breakout group members were participating in the assigned task of discussing how to define social sustainability at the Year 1 conference. In Excerpt 1, one network member comments on the difficulty of teaching engineering students about social sustainability and contrasts that with environmental sustainability which is "easier to define" because they "have metrics" and can "measure these things." Taking a somewhat different approach to the challenge of defining sustainability, in Excerpt 2, the network member who was part of a different breakout session comments that even economic sustainability is difficult to define, noting that these definitions will vary depending on one's "political approach" to the economy. He then comments that it will be even more difficult to define the social aspect of sustainability, adding that arriving at "one final definition of social sustainability" may not be possible and that such efforts should, in fact, be resisted. Key words related to sustainability in the definition talk excerpts are bolded.

Excerpt 1: *I think with the course I teach it's a bit difficult um to specifically **define** what a soc- what is part of **social sustainability**, right? Because obviously engineering projects should be doing something for the **common good**, right? That's the point of civil engineering, right? But to to really (.) to really **define** that aspect of why it is part of **sustainability** and whether or not the project is **socially sustainable**, we've been having a lot of trouble trying to teach the students about that, uh so that's something that is missing, because **environmental**, it's a lot more easier to **define**. [Right.] It's easier, you know we have metrics, we can measure these things, but **social** is still kind of something that's too qualitative for our students to really grasp.*

Excerpt 2: *Well yeah so on the **economic** front, and I think this is one of the (..) cases for multiple **definitions**, is that it is, this is a kind of political concept, [Right.] and even to talk about **economic sustainability**, there is vastly [Right], different theoretical approaches to the economy, and vastly different political approaches to the economy, so you know an environmental economist, or a neoliberal economist, or uh ecological economist would come up with a very different **definition** of ecology- **economic sustainability**. So I think that's where we need to (.) resist this sort of urge to uh to converge upon one final **definition** of **social sustainability**.*

In both of these cases in which network members talked *about* definitions and social sustainability, they did not, in fact, produce any potential definitions of social sustainability. It is also important to add that these two turns of talk did not elicit follow-up or clarification discussion by fellow participants in their respective breakout sessions. Although I did not engage in a detailed discourse analysis of each of the breakout session transcripts, I found that this monologic style often dominated much of the definition talk. That is, participants often took relatively long turns in presenting their individual understandings of sustainability, turns which included frequent use of epistemic markers such as "I think" and "you know" (see Table 3.1 and Table 3.4), but they tended not to build on the contributions of others in order to refine, sharpen, or critique others' understandings of social sustainability. It seems that SSRCN members actively engaged in "on-task" definition talk, often by comparing what they knew about environmental or economic sustainability, but without producing definitions of social sustainability—at least none that differed in any meaningful way from the kinds of contested definitions found in the published scholarship.

However, there were some occasions, such as is shown in Excerpt 3, in which network members did talk about how they understood social sustainability. In this excerpt, the network member utters the term *well-being* four times along with *justice, autonomy,* and *participation agency* in voicing his understanding of social sustainability. Even so, this speaker emphasizes that *well-being* by itself is insufficient for conceptualizing social sustainability given that in an unjust world, some people's "well-being comes at the cost of many other people's." He suggests that simply associating *well-being* or *justice* with a definition of social sustainability would be inadequate.

> **Excerpt 3:** *Well so the point is that we are not supposed to* **define** *what* **social sustainability** *looks like for the whole world, right? We are supposed to set some parameters within which people can decide for themselves what* **sustainability** *looks like and how to pursue it, and I do not think we are here like the master planners to determine what everyone should do. So I think our challenge is so there are things that have, like* **well-being***, right, as one of these parameters? But then probably* **well-being** *with some consideration of* **justice***, right? In our current social configuration there are some people who are* **being very well***, right, but their* **well-being** *comes at the cost of many other people's, right? So so how do we-* **well-being** *is one parameter,* **justice** *is another parameter. I would say* **autonomy** *or* **participation agency** *is another one, right? So that ability of localities and people who live in them to* **determine** *to some degree* **their own path.**

While the steering committee was quite aware that the breakout sessions had not resulted in any candidate definitions for social sustainability, I was able to provide some insight into why those "on-topic" discussions did not lead to clearer outcomes by pointing them to the kind of talk illustrated in the above excerpts. Guided by the frequency counts of terms noted in Tables 3.3 and 3.4, I came to understand that SSRCN members more often *talked about* social sustainability as it contrasted with environmental or economic sustainability, and often the complexities and difficulties involved in trying to define it, rather than *engaging in* the task of producing new definitions for social sustainability, or even in discussing their own definitions of the concept.

Even so, by the time I was able to provide the steering committee with these still-preliminary accounts of network members' talk on social sustainability, using frequency and collocation corpus analysis as well as selective content analysis (around the time of the Year 3 conference), they were already moving away from their early goal of establishing a single definition for the concept. Although I chose to terminate my involvement with the network after the Year 3 conference (discussed further below), I was granted continuing access to the DropBox folder that stored the steering committee meeting minutes for research purposes. In a meeting that took place nearly seven months after the Year 3 conference, I found that the steering committee members were expressing doubts about the viability of coming up with a single, clear definition. According to these notes, one person argued that they "may never settle on a definition." In notes from a meeting held a few weeks later that documented developing plans for the Year 4 conference, one note tersely states: "Focus on specific questions that avoid definition issues – perhaps split into small groups." This was the last time that defining social sustainability was an agenda item in the steering committee meetings. It seems that in the busyness of addressing the new challenges that emerged as they planned each year's conference, they no longer deemed this early goal of arriving at a definition of social sustainability as a priority and perhaps they simply forgot about it. In separate informal conversations with two of the steering committee members, several years after the Year 3 conference, I learned that neither one could remember how or why they had decided to abandon definition efforts. Furthermore, nearly a year after the Year 4 conference, a review article whose authors included several members of the SSRCN steering committee argued for a vision of social sustainability that rejects closure and universality, such as efforts to treat social sustainability as a "stand-alone pillar" in relation to the three pillars (i.e., environmental, economic, and social) of sustainability (Boyer et al. 2016: 4) that has "one-size-fits-all" (Boyer et al. 2016: 11) applicability. Instead they argue for a view of sustainability as "an integrated, process-oriented, and place-based concept [that] shares the challenges of solving so-called 'wicked problems': problems that are unprecedented and context-specific, with oppositional problem framings, and solutions that cannot be tested at low-cost" (Boyer et al. 2016: 12).

Strategic ambiguity, continuing the network

Although it was not apparent to me at the time that I was preparing presentations for the SSRCN conferences and for the steering committee, as I was still trying to make sense of the definition talk and feeling frustrated by the difficulty in not being able to offer a more detailed synthesis of members' contributions, I have since come to realize that the unfinalizable definition discussions that I observed in the breakout session corpus were, perhaps, uniquely useful for the continuation of the network. In my presentation to the membership at the Year 2 conference, I commented on the ambiguous quality of the terms that members associated with social sustainability such as *well-being, values, needs,* and *equity* (see Table 3.3) and other characterizations such as "something for the common good" as found in Excerpt 1 above. The generic quality of these proposed attributes of social sustainability was undoubtedly unavoidable given that the discussions were rarely structured around a particular project, site, or community, but I flagged this ambiguity as something that might be problematic for the SSRCN's goal of arriving at a definition for sustainability.

In retrospect, I now view members' language choices as cases of "strategic ambiguity" (Eisenberg 1984; Leitch and Davenport 2007) that can enable a group of participants to construct "agreement on abstractions without limiting specific interpretations" (Leitch and Davenport 2007: 44). Research on how group members use ambiguous key terms in a discussion situation shows that it can enable participants with different perspectives to rally around a point of shared concern and thus to stay active in the discussion (Leitch and Davenport 2007; Wexford 2009). Menz (1999: 112), for example, has argued that ambiguity can be quite useful in organizational discourse when the goal is to generate new ideas and "preserve various options" in the process of arriving at a shared understanding. While Scandelius and Cohen (2016: 3489) outline some of the pitfalls of strategic ambiguity in organizational discourse, such as the construction of false consensus or indecision and passivity among stakeholders, they also argue that it can be enormously useful in allowing "for sense-making among a diverse audience." In the case of the SSRCN, it seems that one effect of members voicing ambiguous attributes such as "well-being" or "quality of life" when discussing social sustainability is that it enabled and implicitly demanded further discussion. In other words, without closure on the topic, there was always more networking needed. As Wexford (2009: 65) argues, the "motive for mobilizing strategic ambiguity is not to get negotiations done," rather it is to create "shared membership" and "willingness to talk." Although the emergence of strategic ambiguity was not planned, the emergence of ambiguous qualities for social sustainability along with the lack of closure on definition talk might well have contributed to members' ongoing pursuit of new ways to think about and work toward implementing social sustainability, such as the publication by core members of the steering committee noted earlier (Boyer et al. 2016).

Although the SSRCN organization has curtailed much of their formal, organized activities, it did remain active for over a year after the NSF funding expired. In the last four years of the organizations' formal networking activity (three of which were funded), they altered their primary focus and the kind of networking activity that they promoted. They moved, for example, toward a more traditional conference format of individual presentations and panel sessions, but the conferences were structured as simultaneous, multi-sited events with a mix of local activity and joint engagement via Internet connectivity. Keynote presentations were broadcast (streamed) to all sites while the individual sites focused on the social sustainability priorities that were relevant to their local concerns. They shifted from working to attain a singular "universal" understanding of the social component of sustainability to promoting sustainable activities locally. As an example, at the most recent "Sustainability Summit," the Charlotte, North Carolina, chapter of the SSRCN invited members of the local Food Policy Council to talk about how local food systems impact food quality and access for low-income residents of the city. They also invited a local African-American pastor to address the topic of racial equity as well as a former city mayor and current city council members to discuss their efforts to promote environmental sustainability through transportation and housing initiatives, among many others. Although the network's formal activities, such as organized conferences, have now ended, the relationships that were nurtured through the network continue to lead to new collaborations among subgroups of members, and their efforts, though now more diffuse, continue to promote social sustainability (e.g., Gagné et al. 2019; Hollander et al. 2016).

Coda: Ending participation

My decision to step away from the SSRCN after three years coincided with the steering committee's emerging shift away from emphasizing the need for a definition for social sustainability to prioritizing other concerns. It is also true that during my active participation with the network, I felt persistent frustration at not having sufficient time to produce more nuanced evaluations of the talk, while at the same time I was reluctant to direct all of my research time to such analysis and away from my then ongoing work exploring agency and language learning among adult immigrant small-business owners in the US (e.g., Miller 2014, 2016). With the clearer vision of hindsight, I now recognize that my participation in the SSRCN gave me a more concrete awareness of how applied linguists can contribute to social impact work in diverse spaces. During my time as a participating member, I was able to supply feedback to the network on the discourse topics that emerged in the breakout session talk that focused on defining social sustainability. I was able to offer some insights into why the sessions had not led to a clearer and/or a shared understanding of the same, through making use of corpus analysis tools and corpus-assisted discourse analysis. I also learned how important it is to enter into such collaborative work with eyes wide open, anticipating the need for flexibility, being ready to change plans and approaches as needed, while also evaluating the effectiveness of one's ongoing participation.

Note

1 The appearance of *sustainability* as a collocation indicates that this word was repeated within the 5-word windows to the left and right of *sustainability*.

References

Anthony, L. (2019), *AntConc* (Version 3.5.8) [Computer Software], Tokyo, Japan: Waseda University. Available from https://www.laurenceanthony.net/software.
Baker, P. (2006), *Using Corpora in Discourse Analysis*, London: Continuum.
Boström, M. (2012), "A Missing Pillar? Challenges in Theorizing and Practicing Social Sustainability: Introduction to the Special Issue," *Sustainability: Science, Practice and Policy*, 8(1): 3–14.
Bourgeois, W. (2014), "Sustainable Development: A Useful Family of Concepts After All," *Environmental Ethics*, 36(3): 259–82.
Boyer, H. W. R., N. D. Peterson, P. Arora, and K. Caldwell (2016), "Five Approaches to Social Sustainability and an Integrated Way Forward," *Sustainability*, 8(9): 878–96.
Bracken, L. J., and E. A. Oughton (2006), "'What do you Mean?': The Importance of Language in Developing Interdisciplinary Research," *Transactions of the Institute of British Geographers*, 31(3): 371–82.
Chen, S. (2016), "Language and Ecology: A Content Analysis of Ecolinguistics as an Emerging Research Field," *Ampersand*, 3: 108–16.
Colantonio A. (2007), "Social Sustainability: An Exploratory Analysis of Definitions, Assessments Methods, Metrics and Tools," *Working Paper Series,* n.p. Oxford Institute for Sustainable Development (OISD), Oxford, UK.
Cuthill, M. (2010), "Strengthening the 'Social' in Sustainable Development: Developing a Conceptual Framework for Social Sustainability in a Rapid Urban Growth Region in Australia," *Sustainable Development*, 18(6): 362–73.
Dempsey, N., G. Bramley, S. Power, and C. Brown (2011), "The Social Dimension of Sustainable Development: Defining Urban Social Sustainability," *Sustainable Development*, 19(5): 289–300. https://doi.org/10.1002/sd.417
Eisenberg, E. (1984), "Ambiguity as Strategy in Organizational Communication," *Communication Monographs*, 51: 227–42.

Gagné, S. A., K. Bryan-Scaggs, R. H. Boyer, and W. N. Xiang (2019), "Conserving Biodiversity Takes a Plan: How Planners Implement Ecological Information for Biodiversity Conservation," *Ambio*, 1–16.

Gilligan, J. M. (2019), "Expertise across Disciplines: Establishing Common Ground in Interdisciplinary Disaster Research teams," *Risk Analysis*, https://doi.org/10.1111/risa.13407

Gotti, M. (2016), "Collaboration Between Applied Linguists and Professional Experts: An Interdisciplinary Perspective," *Journal of Applied Linguistics & Professional Practice*, 13(1–3): 78–96.

Gotti, M. (2018), "Interactions Between Linguists and Legal Practitioners Within and Across Professional Contexts," in G. Tessuto, V. K. Bhatia, and J. Engberg (eds.), *Frameworks for Discursive Actions and Practices of the Law*, pp. 1–22, Newcastle upon Tyne: Cambridge Scholars Publishing.

Griessler, E., and B. Littig (2005), "Social Sustainability: A Catchword between Political Pragmatism and Social Theory," *International Journal for Sustainable Development*, 8(1/2): 65–79.

Hollander, R., A. Amekudzi-Kennedy, S. Bell, F. Benya, C. Davidson, C. Farkos, and D. Quigley (2016), "Network Priorities for Social Sustainability Research and Education: Memorandum of the Integrated Network on Social Sustainability Research Group," *Sustainability: Science, Practice and Policy*, 12(1), 16–21.

Leitch, S., and S. Davenport (2007), "Strategic Ambiguity as a Discourse Practice: The Role of Keywords in the Discourse on 'Sustainable' Biotechnology," *Discourse Studies*, 9(1): 43–61.

LeVasseur, T. (2015), "Defining 'Ecolinguistics?': Challenging Emic Issues in an Evolving Environmental Discipline," *Journal of Environmental Studies and Sciences*, 5(1), 21–8.

Macpherson, S. (2012), "From Neo-liberal Ideology to Critical Sustainability for Language Policy Studies in the PRC," in G. H. Beckett and G. A Postiglione (eds.), *China's Assimilationist Language Policy: Impact on Indigenous/Minority Literacy and Social Harmony*, pp. 190–206, London and New York: Routledge.

Menz, F. (1999), "'Who am I Gonna Do this with?': Self-organization, Ambiguity and Decision-making in a Business Enterprise," *Discourse & Society*, 10(1): 101–28.

Miller, E. R. (2010), "Agency in the Making: Adult Immigrants' Accounts of Language Learning and Work," *TESOL Quarterly*, 44(3): 465–87.

Miller, E. R. (2011), "Indeterminacy and Interview Research: Co-constructing Ambiguity and Clarity in Interviews with an Adult Immigrant Learner of English," *Applied Linguistics*, 32(1): 43–59.

Miller, E. R. (2012), "Agency, Language Learning and Multilingual Spaces," *Multilingua* 31(4): 441–68.

Miller, E. R. (2013), "Positioning Selves, Doing Relational Work, and Constructing Identities in Interview Talk," *Journal of Politeness Research*, 9(1): 75–95.

Miller, E. R. (2014), *The Language of Adult Immigrants: Agency in the Making*, Bristol: Multilingual Matters.

Miller, E. R. (2016), "The Ideology of Learner Agency and the Neoliberal Self," *International Journal of Applied Linguistics*, 26(3): 348–65.

Mühlhäusler, P. (2003), *Language of Environment, Environment of Language: A Course in Ecolinguistics*, London: Battlebridge Publications.

Munroe, J. (2008), *Gender and the Garden in Early Modern English Literature*, London and New York: Routledge.

Munroe, J., and E. J. Geisweidt (2016), *Ecological Approaches to Early Modern English Texts: A Field Guide to Reading and Teaching*, London and New York: Routledge.

Munroe, J., and R. Laroche (2017), *Shakespeare and Ecofeminist Theory*, London: Bloomsbury.

Munroe, J., and R. Laroche (eds.) (2011), *Ecofeminist Approaches to Early Modernity*, Cham: Springer.

Murphy, K. (2012), "The Social Pillar of Sustainable Development: A Literature Review and Framework for Policy Analysis," *Sustainability: Science, Practice and Policy*, 8(1): 15–29.

Partington, A., A. Duguid, and C. Taylor (2013), *Patterns and Meanings in Discourse: Theory and Practice in Corpus-assisted Discourse Studies*, Amsterdam: John Benjamins.

Phillipson, R. (2008), "The Linguistic Imperialism of Neoliberal Empire," *Critical Inquiry in Language Studies*, 5(1): 1–43.

Phillipson, R., and T. Skutnabb-Kangas (1996), "English Only Worldwide or Language Ecology?" *TESOL Quarterly*, 30(3): 429–52.

Priem, R. L., D. A. Harrison, and N. K. Muir (1995), "Structured Conflict and Consensus Outcomes in Group Decision Making," *Journal of Management*, 21(4): 691–710.

Raworth, K. (2012), "A Safe and Just Space for Humanity: Can We Live within the Doughnut," *Oxfam Policy and Practice: Climate Change and Resilience*, 8(1): 1–26.

Sarangi, S., and C. N. Candlin (2010), "Applied linguistics and professional practice: Mapping a future agenda," *Journal of Applied linguistics and Professional Practice*, 7(1): 1–9.

Scandelius, C., and G. Cohen, (2016), "Achieving Collaboration with Diverse Stakeholders—The Role of Strategic Ambiguity in CSR Communication," *Journal of Business Research*, 69(9): 3487–99.

Stanford, J. N., and L. J. Whaley (2010), "The Sustainability of Languages," *International Journal of Environmental, Cultural, Economic, and Social Stability*, 6(3): 111–22.

Steffensen, S. V., and A. Fill (2014), "Ecolinguistics: The State of the Art and Future Horizons," *Language Sciences*, 41: 6–25.

Stibbe, A. (2015), *Ecolinguistics: Language, Ecology and the Stories we Live by*, London and New York: Routledge.

Stoddart, D. R. (1987), "To Claim the High Ground: Geography for the End of the Century," *Transactions of the Institute of British Geographers*, 12(3): 327–36.

Thompson, J. L. (2009), "Building Collective Communication Competence in Interdisciplinary Research Teams," *Journal of Applied Communication Research*, 37(3): 278–97.

Vallance, S., H. C. Perkins, and J. E. Dixon (2011), "What is Social Sustainability? A Clarification of Concepts," *Geoforum*, 42(3): 342–8.

Wexford, M. N. (2009), "Strategic Ambiguity in Emergent Coalitions: The Triple Bottom Line," *Corporate Communications: An International Journal*, 14(1): 62–77.

4

Finding Answers within the Story: The Transformative Potential of Translanguaging Praxis

Obed Arango
Holly Link

Revolución Arte

> El innombrable's administration and its nationalistic, fundamentalist discourse equates the word *immigrant* with that of *criminal,* which legitimates the mistreatment, oppression, incarceration and abuse of immigrants' human rights. How do I respond to this treatment? How do I humanize myself y mi comunidad?
>
> Obed, February 6, 2020

During the 2020 US presidential election, questions around immigration, dignity, and humanity continued to circulate on many levels and across many spheres. For communities in the United States, like Marshall, Pennsylania, with a large and growing population of Mexican immigrants, these questions reverberate and resonate, but also hold great weight and consequence. In Marshall, we (Obed, Holly) respond by engaging in continual dialogue about such issues at Revolución Arte (RevArte), the nonprofit where we work y dónde convivimos con familias latinx.[1] We also respond by working with community members to find answers in the stories we collectively co-create using both Spanish and English. In this chapter, we use Obed's questions and the real-life consequences they index as a rationale for developing what we refer to as a *translanguaging praxis* and its transformative potential. Following Avineri et al. (2019: 1), we explore "how language provides a crucial vantage point from which to (re)imagine, understand, and contribute to the achievement of social justice." We do so by discussing ethnographic research we conducted at RevArte on a workshop where a group of Mexican and Mexican-American boys co-constructed a bilingual counter-story that challenged and reframed dehumanizing narratives about who they are, can, and should be. We show through the process of co-creating and performing a translanguaged counter-story that young people from Mexican immigrant households not only resisted the ways they and their families were positioned in mainstream media and within immigration policy debates, but they also affirmed their bilingual identities, and developed critical stances from which to read the word and the world (Freire and Macedo 1987). We explore how this process involved critical, creative, and humorous use of forms and features in both Spanish and English evident in the creation and performance of, and reflection on, the story and its co-construction. We argue that arts-based, performative forms of narrative are key components of generative sites like RevArte for translanguaging praxis and working toward social justice for immigrant families. We end by addressing implications of our work at RevArte for research in the field of applied linguistics with a social justice orientation.

Revolución Arte and our roles there

RevArte is located in Marshall, the county seat of Millers County, one of the wealthiest counties in the state of Pennsylvania. However, in Marshall about 22 percent of the population, including many Latinx families, live at the poverty rate or below. Between 1990 and 2010 the Latinx, primarily Mexican, population in Marshall grew from under 5 percent to almost 30 percent (U.S. Census Bureau 2010). Obed, Mexican anthropologist, artist, and educator, founded RevArte in 2009 as a nonprofit, community-based organization with educational programming for young people and adults that would embrace the language(s) and cultural practices of its participants, and provide a space where they could identify and develop their talents, goals, and dreams. Since opening, RevArte's mission has come to include the empowerment of the Latinx community and the collective creation of spaces for individual growth, community engagement, and social justice. By social justice, we mean more equitable treatment of individuals and groups who have been minoritized based on their socioeconomic, racio-ethnic, linguistic, and/or cultural backgrounds, as well as more equitable distribution of opportunities and privileges for them.

Obed

Obed came to the US as an international student and, because of personal circumstances, stayed. Over time, he began to see himself as an immigrant and to reflect on what this meant. This was through experiencing prejudice and discrimination based on his marked accent (en inglés), dark skin color, and rostro tosco (rough facial features). Estas partes de su identidad were often related with foolishness (accent), and ugliness and machismo (appearance), a racism that made his life difficult as an individual, a foreigner, and as an immigrant. This was a continual process of humillación y deshumanización, a process that so many immigrants in the US experience every day. At the same time, he sees how his comadres y compadres have suffered harsher forms of discrimination and racism than he has, based on their social class, documentation status, and level(s) of formal education. RevArte provides a space for its participants to reflect on these issues, and para la comunidad inmigrante to dream and exist, and to see their faces, skin color(s), and ways of speaking as integral to their identidades y dignidad. Within this space, while Obed's official role is Director at RevArte, families are the motor of the center and its programming.

Holly

Holly grew up surrounded by Spanish in Miami, learning it from a young age, studying it through college and using it in the classroom as a bilingual teacher. For her, as White and non-Latinx, studying and speaking Spanish was seen as an asset. En contraste, her Latinx classmates were taught from an early age que hablar español would impede their academic growth y contaminar su inglés. Such ideologías raciolingüísticas (Zentella 2003; Flores and Rosa 2015) are prevalent today in Marshall schools where Holly conducted her doctoral research. She began as a volunteer at RevArte in 2014, and in 2016 became the center's Education Director. As her role there evolves, she continually questions what it means to be a líder as a White, non-Latinx cisgender woman who wields great privilege, not just in terms of race and class, but also in terms of citizenship status and university affiliation. There are no easy answers to this question, but she has learned to acknowledge more explicitly and en diálogo with RevArte participants how her privilege is implicated in social hierarchies and power relationships in and outside of RevArte, and more broadly in the very structures she works to change (cf., Ellsworth 1989; see also Link 2018, Link and Arango 2019).

La teoría que nos guía: Developing a translanguaging praxis

At RevArte, we frame education as a community-led, collective endeavor in which families are positioned as having a wealth of expertise, talents, and goals that can be drawn upon to shape teaching and learning, and to promote positive social transformation en y para la comunidad. This stance is part of what Obed describes as una rebeldía epistemológica de la comunidad, which takes place when a community co-constructs knowledges, discourses, and narratives based on their own forms and definitions. This rebellious vision is rooted in Zapatista notions of community-led social change from the ground up (cf., Stahler-Sholk 2010). In the US context, Critical Race Theory (CRT) enriches this rebellious epistemological stance as it helps emphasize the racialized nature of how Mexican immigrant families experience life in the US (Yosso 2006). CRT is also useful in how it centers the experiential knowledge of Mexican immigrant families and frames this knowledge as critical to understanding, analyzing, and responding to the daily oppressions they face (cf., Yosso, Smith, Ceja, and Solórzano 2009). One way we do this is through working with young people and families to co-create narratives and representations of Mexican immigrants that serve as what Solorzano and Yosso (2002) call counter-stories that resist and challenge the dominant, widely circulating discourses in the US about Mexican immigrants, discourses that portray Mexicans in a racist and negative light. We believe such resistance is a form of what Tara Yosso (2005) refers to as *transformative resistance capital*, a critical form of capital in her discussion of community cultural wealth para la comunidad latina. Such capital is transformative when individuals and groups activate "their cultural knowledge of the structures of racism" and are motivated to transform them (Yosso 2005: 81).

At RevArte we link the creation of counter-stories to Freirean notions of community-led social change from the ground up and from collective action based on praxis, or the "reflection and action directed at the structures to be transformed" (Freire 1970: 126), in our case the structures being the kinds of schooling and educational opportunities available in Marshall for young people and their families. Such reflection and action take place through continual dialogue, both informal (in daily interactions with young people and adults at the center) and formal (in classes and workshops). Another integral part of our praxis at RevArte has involved acknowledging the many ways its participants creatively and critically use different varieties of Spanish and English, and drawing on these language practices to teach and learn from and with each other through the lens of translanguaging.

As we embrace translanguaging as theory and concept, and practice and pedagogy, we acknowledge Williams (1994) and Baker (2003), the scholars who first brought the concept of translanguaging into the field of applied linguistics, as well as those who have continued to elaborate, review, and debate theory and research on translanguaging (cf., Canagarajah 2011; Creese and Blackledge 2015; García 2009; García and Wei 2014; Jaspers 2018; Lewis, Jones, and Baker 2012; MacSwan 2017). As we have discussed previously (Link and Arango 2019), this scholarship aligns with an asset-based view of multilingualism stemming from Grosjean's (1982) notion of holistic bilingualism, as well as on heteroglossic views of language which characterize the speech of bilinguals as consisting of multiple, coexisting norms and forms (Bakhtin 1981; Bailey 2007). We define translanguaging as "the deployment of a speaker's full linguistic repertoire without regard for watchful adherence to the socially and politically defined boundaries of named (and usually national and state) languages" (Otheguy, García, and Reid 2015: 281). At RevArte we use translanguaging as theoretical lens to reframe the mono- and racio-linguistic ideologies underlying the ways in which the language practices of Mexican families are positioned in local schools. We also consider translanguaging as a pedagogical tool that helps open space for RevArte participants to draw on their full linguistic repertoires while affirming their identities and ways of knowing (cf., García, Ibarra-Johnson, and Seltzer 2017: ix).

In recent years, we have begun to link our understanding and use of translanguaging to Freirean praxis as this helps us emphasize and focus on "how language can serve as a critical resource in achieving social justice" (Avineri et al. 2019: 5). In what follows, we explore how Obed engaged in translanguaging praxis with a group of boys in a workshop at RevArte as they co-constructed a counter-story to respond to the current anti-immigrant context in the US.

Methods: Una etnografía de la clase de Kamishibai

The data we discuss in this chapter come from ethnographic data collected during a 7-month period (fall of 2018 to spring of 2019) during a weekly, hour-long Kamishibai workshop. Kamishibai, or paper theater, is a form of Japanese theater and storytelling that was popular in 1930s and post-war Japan. In its early form, traveling narrators set up a miniature stage in a public space, using illustrated boards placed within it to tell a story. It has become a popular form of storytelling in educational spaces.

At RevArte we were introduced to this form by Tara McGowan, a Kamishibai scholar and performer, and after a workshop she led at RevArte, we began a class in the fall of 2018. As a multimodal form of storytelling that bridges connections between oral and written language, we thought it would provide the opportunity for children of different ages to engage with literacy and language in new and creative ways that had little to do with their schoolwork and homework revolving around test preparation that turns them off reading and writing. We wanted to explore how children and maestrxs, including ourselves, used Spanish and English while teaching and learning, and how to more explicitly affirm and draw upon such practices to read (and write) the word and the world together (Freire and Macedo 1987). Fifteen students participated in the class and, during seven months, they co-wrote and performed six Kamishibai stories. Data we collected included twenty-five sets of fieldnotes on weekly classes, ten recordings of class conversations, and the stories themselves.

In this chapter, we discuss the data from one small group of students, a group of four boys aged 10–12, all from Mexican immigrant families with mixed documentation status, who created a Kamishibai story involving lucha libre, Mexican wrestling, and the topic of immigration in the US titled, "El Santo versus Trump, Jr." To supplement this data, we also include fieldnotes from the story's performance for families as well as follow-up interviews with these boys, and discussion of a second theater piece they continue to work on, "El Santo versus Trump, Jr., Part 2."

El Santo versus Trump, Jr.

"El Santo versus Trump, Jr." begins with Donald Trump watching a World Wrestling Entertainment (WWE) championship match between El Santo, Mexican folk hero and one of the most iconic, masked wrestling figures of lucha libre, and John Cena, a White professional wrestler for the WWE. Trump has bet one million US dollars on Cena and when Cena loses, a furious Trump publicly challenges El Santo to a match against a wrestler called Trump, Jr. Trump threatens to deport all immigrants in the United States if El Santo declines the offer, and promises "free papers and tacos" to all immigrants if El Santo wins the match. The story ends with El Santo winning, and the *New York Times* announcing, "Free papers (and tacos) for all!"

In what follows we first explore the story's co-construction and translanguaged text, focusing on the process of reflection and action and how this was deepened through translanguaging praxis. We then discuss the performance of the story para las familias de RevArte. Throughout we highlight how the group used critical, creative, and humorous forms and features in both Spanish and English.

In particular, we focus on the significance of humor in translanguaging praxis at RevArte, showing its significance in relationships among teachers, students, and parents, as well as how it can be used to collectively respond to the dehumanizing treatment and oppression of Latinx immigrants in the US, and more broadly, commenting on it. We also comment on the boys' reflections on the process of the story's co-creation and what they are currently working on in the Kamishibai workshop. We end the chapter by sharing some sugerencias preliminares about translanguaging praxis within this context and how, through this work, the group collectively resisted and reframed racist portrayals of Mexicans by el innombrable, and opened up pathways to justicia social para familias inmigrantes.

La co-construcción del cuento

Co-creating the Kamishibai story involved an iterative and reflexive process of continual reflection and action through dialogue among Obed, its four young authors, Ramiro, Alejandro, Carlos y Francisco, as well as María and Mauricio, parents, teachers, and volunteers at RevArte. Figure 4.1 illustrates this process and the three phases of the story's construction. These phases were not entirely linear, nor completely discrete, as the group continued to explore the world of wrestling and lucha libre, Donald Trump, e inmigración.

Phase 1: Constructing the storyline

The first phase, constructing the storyline, involved reflection and research on Donald Trump, his immigration discourse policies, y los efectos de estas polizas en sus familias. In the first two sessions the group brainstormed "issues affecting

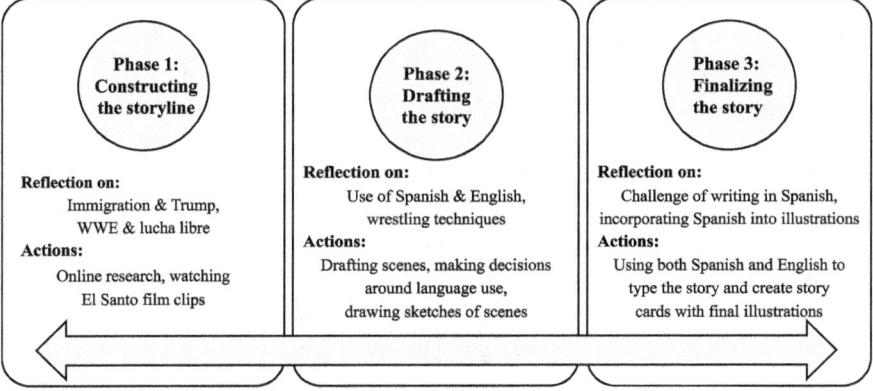

Figure 4.1 Story co-construction based on continual reflection and action

their lives that they wanted explore" (Fieldnote September 24, 2018). De mayor interés fue Deferred Action for Childhood Arrivals (DACA), a US immigration policy in danger of being terminated under Trump's administration. With family members who would be affected by these changes, los chicos wanted to talk about this issue, and more broadly on why "Trump hates immigrants and wants to build a wall" (Fieldnote September 24, 2018). During these early sessions, Ramiro was vocal about how these issues were affecting his family. He commented, "I have papeles, mi hermano doesn't, neither mi padre, ni mi madre" (Recording October 1, 2018). He expressed sadness that his brother specifically did not have papeles, continuing, "after High School things will be tough for him. Why Trump does not understand that? What kind of bad things we do to him or the United States?" Alejandro dijo, "we need to show him who we are" (Recording October 1, 2018). This response shows not just resistance but motivation to contradict Trump's negative portrayal of Mexicans, and affirmation de sus identidades mexicanas. This kind of critical reflection and proposal also illustrates the development of transformative resistant capital para los chicos.

During these initial sessions, they shared what they had heard around town, that Immigration and Customs Enforcement (ICE) agents had been tracking and picking up young men as they went about their day. They also talked about how one went about getting papeles, which led to questions and conversations about reforma migratoria (immigration reform) and why it hasn't succeeded (Fieldnote October 8, 2018). Again, este diálogo opened up a space for the boys to think critically about their lived realities and respond to it creatively. For example, Carlos suggested, "We need a story and in it we have papeles, but how we get Trump to give us papeles?" (Recording October 8, 2018). While the group reflected on these issues, the boys primarily in English, and Obed primarily and purposefully in Spanish, boys used certain words and phrases in Spanish, particularly those related to their families and immigration like "papeles." One of Obed's fieldnotes from the early sessions speak to how he drew the boys' attention to language use (October 15, 2018, translated from Spanish).

> I explain to them the importance to interact in Spanish, to write in Spanish, in order not to lose that important part of their identity, roots and cultural heritage, also I mentioned to them to feel free to use English when necessary. We have a small reflection in how some words work better in Spanish and some other in English, including some expressions. They ask me an example, I said, "La chancla de mamá," everybody laughs and Alejandro says, "yeah, la chancla de mamá... you're right, tenemos miedo de la chancla, but we are not afraid of the flip-flop."

For Obed, humor is a pedagogical tool to connect with young people and engage them in Freirean dialogue (cf., Shih 2018). And through humor, Obed helps them develop increased awareness about language use and about the value of Spanish for expressing certain terms and ideas. As Gallo discusses, the use of humor in this instance also "illustrates the rich traditions of Mexican humor as a vehicle to develop linguistic dexterity" (2016: 282).

These reflections led the group to do online research on Trump. Early on, they became curious about Trump's love of TV and Twitter, and specifically his connection to the world of wrestling and WWE. Wrestling aficionados themselves but in the US context, los chicos also began researching the Mexican luchadores que sus papás, mamás y abuelxs had grown up with. As they found fotos y videos de superhéroes/luchadores mexicanos, their interest in lucha libre grew. In response, Mauricio, a parent volunteer, proposed the group watch video clips on YouTube from El Santo films, El Santo being one of his, Obed's, and many other parents' childhood superheroes. They did this for the next three weeks and los chicos began to connect with this icon of Mexican pop culture. They were initially surprised to see that they were in black and white, and "películas viejas" as they referred to them. As they watched and reflected on the clips, they began to incorporate more Spanish words into the conversation. For example, Alejandro shared, "Yes! I saw El Santo in Cinco de Mayo (a local store)! They have alcancías y juguetes de luchadores (piggy banks and wrestler toys)" (Recording October 15, 2018). Again, humor was a continual part of the dialogue, los chicos laughing and joking with Obed, Mauricio, and María (a RevArte mother and teacher), as they noticed Spanish terms for El Santo's different wrestling moves like "la llave Nelson," and the strange-sounding words in the films such as "terrícolas (people from Earth)," "atemorizados (afraid)," "desintegrarlos (disintegrate them)" (Fieldnote October 22, 2018). This kind of humor also shows how bilingual children can draw upon language-based humor and word play to explore and affirm their cultural identities and affiliations (Martínez and Morales 2014). Critical to note here, too, is that humor helped the group develop intergenerational comradery and collaboration as Obed, Mauricio, and María were part of the film viewing, and the laughing and joking with the boys.

During these viewing sessions, los chicos decided they wanted lucha libre to be the storyline. When Mauricio and Obed reminded them of their interest in addressing Donald Trump and immigration issues, the group agreed to include these issues in a story of a wrestling match (Fieldnote November 5, 2018). They agreed that putting these elements together would make for a good story, the confrontation of a superhéroe mexicano and a "bully president," as Ramiro called Trump (Fieldnote November 5, 2018). Esta decisión, motivada por Mauricio y Obed, illustrates their pedagogical work in guiding the group and reminding them of their initial concerns, pedagogical work based on praxis. This kind of collaboration in the story's co-construction also involved continual reflection on issues that affected theirs and the RevArte community's daily lived realities.

Phase 2: Drafting the story

The second phase of the story's co-creation involved drafting and sketching each scene. During this phase, Obed served as the primary note-taker, jotting down the scene descriptions the narrated by los chicos, the boys drawing and drafting illustrations. Obed writes how this pedagogical move was strategic on his part (Fieldnote November 12, 2018, translated from Spanish):

> It is important for me to keep the boys motivated in the story, and I worry that asking them to write at this stage would re-focus them on the process of writing itself and "doing it right," which is usually what I see when kids have to write at RevArte. They become overly concerned with spelling and grammar because this is often the main focus in writing at school. Also, I want to keep motivating them to use Spanish and can better do this if I serve as the primary writer for now.

Obed's words illuminate una praxis de translenguage at the level of theory and practice. This kind of praxis is akin to the *language experience approach* method in the teaching of English as a Second, a method that within formal school contexts often loses the social justice framing of its origins in the teaching of Sylvia Ashton-Warner (1963) and Paulo Freire (1970).

The work during this phase took place at two levels, the drafting of the story itself, and reflections on Trump and wrestling. Los chicos, while certain that they wanted the story to be about El Santo versus Trump, they decided that Trump was "bien viejito (too old)" to fight El Santo. Ramiro proposed that the story be about El Santo against "luchadores gringos," Francisco chiming in that he knew them all, mentioning John Cena and the Rock (Fieldnote November 12, 2018). When Francisco remembered hearing about how Trump once challenged a rival businessman to a bet on a wrestling match, los chicos made a decision (Fieldnote November 12, 2018):

> **Alejandro** What about if El Santo defeats the favorite wrestler of Donald Trump?

Carlos Pero ¿quién? ¿y si inventamos un luchador llamado Trump, Jr.?

Francisco Oh yeah!

Here, they agreed to invent a wrestler named, "Trump, Jr." who would symbolize Donald Trump, the primary villain and a dangerous figure para familias inmigrantes.

At the same time, drafting the story itself led to interesting linguistic moves and conversations about language use in the story's narration and dialogue. For example, when los chicos decided that in the opening scene El Santo would defeat John Cena, the wrestler referred to by Francisco as "el más gringo de los luchadores de aquí," an interesting conversation around language occurred (Fieldnote November 12, 2018, translated from Spanish):

> The boys discussed how Trump is surprised and furious when El Santo defeats John Cena. They began to laugh as they described his "orange Cheetoh face" turning "red-hot." I began to laugh and commented, "¡se enchiló (a term indexing what happens when one eats too much spicy food or chiles, and the often resulting red, sweaty face)!" As all laugh, Carlos yelled out, "red-hot, peppery mad," and the group decides that this term, translated into English into a funny-sounding word is best to describe Trump's anger.

These examples show how, in the creation of the story, the boys in dialogue and reflection with each other and Obed, develop creative and humorous, but critical ways to tell the story. Their choice in the first scene, to have El Santo beat John Cena, "el más gringo de los luchadores," shows their assumption that Trump would place his bet on the "most gringo" of the WWE wrestlers in a match against the most iconic Mexican luchador, El Santo. While in earlier sessions the boys openly identified with John Cena and other WWE wrestlers, in the conversation about Trump's immigration policies along with his strong affiliation with these figures, the boys identify them as gringos, oppositional characters for los chicos y sus familias through Francisco's framing of Cena in Spanish. This new way of identifying WWE wrestlers suggests they are developing a critical lens on this sport. At the same time, it shows the tensions in the experiences of many young people from Mexican immigrant families in the US who grow up with multiple and often contradictory affiliations and identifications. Attending English Only schools where Whiteness and monolingualism prevails, families often express these tensions through their frustration with their children's preference not only for speaking English, but also for adhering to other standards of Whiteness. In this context, their initial preference for WWE wrestling is turned on its head when they distance themselves from this group through their use of the Spanish term, "gringo."

In addition, their use of a Spanish verb, "enchilarse," to develop an adjective clause in English, "red-hot peppery mad," shows a kind of linguistic inventiveness and word play that we often hear at RevArte among young people and adults. At the same time, we believe that flipping this typically-used Spanish term back into English is another way the group translanguaged together through dialogue. Such inventiveness and word play speak to Li Wei's (2011) point that translanguaging can foster creativity and criticality. In this instance, it fostered creativity by providing opportunities to challenge, play with, and even change the norms for language use for and the boundaries of defined languages. In terms of criticality, translanguaging here promoted exploration of issues related to language and power, especially in communities that have been minoritized based on their cultural and linguistic backgrounds (Wei 2011). Once again, humor, involving young people and adults, is pivotal to the expression "red-hot peppery mad" and the image it provokes. This speaks to the importance of verbal artistry in Mexican culture as a coping mechanism in adverse circumstances (Limon 1996). Being able to creatively and humorously label Trump in this way when he continues to use derogatory terms for Mexicans and Mexican immigrants allowed los chicos to resist and reframe this kind of racist identification, turning Trump's labeling on its head. Opportunities like these link to the social justice agenda activated early on in translanguaging scholarship with Baker's framing of the translanguaging pedagogies discussed by Williams (1994, as cited in Baker 2003) as empowering, liberating tools for speakers of minoritized languages (Baker 2001, 2003).

Phase 3: Finalizing the story

While the first draft wasn't finished until January of 2019, in December Carlos decided to challenge himself by starting to type up the story on the computer, mentioning that it was his first time writing in Spanish (Fieldnote December 3, 2018). This provoked discussion about what many young people at RevArte tended to say about literacy in Spanish, that they spoke and understood it, but didn't know how to read or write it. Obed pointed out to them that they likely could do both (read and write in Spanish) even though they didn't get the opportunity to do this in school. Carlos' challenge to himself became a challenge to the rest of the group as they were finalizing the story and deciding what words they would include in the story card illustrations, and in what language (Fieldnote December 3, 2018).

In early December the group began to brainstorm the story's climax, Ramiro suggesting it revolve around an attempt by Trump, Jr. to rip off El Santo's mask. The group discussed how El Santo would feel if the mask were ripped off, Ramiro commenting, "si El Santo pierde la máscara, it's the end of him" (Fieldnote December 3, 2018). As in many of their conversations, they began to focus on Trump and his anti-immigrant sentiment, especially against Mexicans. Carlos commented, "Trump wants to shame us! We are NOT rapists, we are NOT bad people como él dice" (Fieldnote December 3, 2018). El diálogo continued the following week, as Obed led the group to reflect on Trump's discourse equating Mexicans and Mexican immigrants with criminals (Fieldnote, December 10, 2018). As they drafted and finalized the scenes, the group continued to reflect on Donald Trump, and their commentary about him as when Alejandro said, "I think [Donald] Trump is a racist person, I think he does not think before he acts" (Recording December 10, 2018). Such descriptions of the "real-life" Donald Trump seem to blend into the ways they portrayed Trump, Jr. in the wrestling match, allowing the group to turn a real-life villain into a storybook character they could control and defeat.

For example, the group decided that El Santo would not win in the way Trump, Jr. did, Alejandro comentando, "El Santo always wins the good way, he does not use dirty tricks like Trump, Jr." (Recording December 10, 2018). In this session el grupo reflected on how El Santo always used his experience to think through every move like a chess game, always staying one step ahead of the villains. One of the final scenes of the story illustrates this reflection:

> Scene 6: Trump, Jr. pelea usando todo tipo de trampas incluso le quiere arrancar la máscara a El Santo pero El Santo que tiene mucha experencia peleando contra vampiros y momias y zombies y el diablo no se deja de las artimañas de Trump, Jr. Trump, Jr. finally takes him from behind thinking that he will win, however what he doesn't know is that what El Santo wanted porque podria usar la misma "llave Nelson" que usó contra John Cena para ganar.
>
> Translation: Trump, Jr. fights using every kind of trick, including wanting to rip off El Santo's mask. But El Santo has a lot of experience fighting against vampires, mummies and zombies, and the devil. So he doesn't let himself be taken by Trump, Jr.'s dirty tricks.
>
> Trump, Jr. finally takes him from behind thinking that he will win, however what he doesn't know is that is what El Santo wanted because he wanted to use the same "llave Nelson" move he used against John Cena to win.

As the group finalized the story, Carlos mentioned that El Santo could defeat Trump if he kept "la llave Nelson" move until the end saying, "El Santo needs to be smart so he won't lost his mask" (Recording December 10, 2018). Obed comentó that this would amount to losing his dignidad, which led to a discussion about what dignity meant to each of them. This included, "ser inteligente," "go to college," and "not let anyone tell us different things than we are" (Recording December 10, 2018). For Obed the issue of dignity is integral to affirming Mexican immigrant families' identities, and connects directly to the Zapatista movement and community-led change (cf., Holloway 2002). El concepto de dignidad basado en zapatismo, and his prompting of the boys to reflect on it, was part of his translanguaging praxis. In the final two scenes, Donald Trump is forced to acknowledge El Santo's victory over Trump, Jr., but barely able, spitting out the words, "you win." The story ends not just with a double defeat of Trump and his proxy. El Santo's victory also signifies, "papeles y tacos para todos." The last scene of the story shows a newspaper column with this as a headline. On a symbolic level, it represents the restoration of dignity and justice for Mexican immigrant families. Humor, here, is critical, too, as since the 2016 US presidential campaign, the "threat" of "taco trucks on every corner" stated by leader of Latinos for Trump, Marco Gutierrez, had become a running joke, with a number of RevArte members buying and wearing T-shirts with this slogan during the afterschool program.

Preparing for the story's performance and the performance itself

Once the story was finalized the group continued to type up the text and complete sketches for the story card for each scene. Between mid February and May, in the weekly, hour-long classes, the group drew, redrew, and completed the story cards, and eventually printed out the finalized text for each scene, affixing it to the back of the appropriate card. They also practiced performing the story, which involved learning about and exploring the different positions storytellers could take as they told the story behind or to the side of the miniature wooden stage where the story cards were inserted and changed. Los chicos reflexionaban mucho on the finished text, the incorporation of both Spanish and English, and the significance that this kind of language use had for them. Alejandro provided an insightful comment (Recording March 25, 2018):

> I think it's a nice way to put a story, to mix, and it comes also in itself against Donald Trump's plan that he wants only English. I can't really explain it, but to use both languages in itself makes the case for the story.

His insight illustrates his critical awareness of the language use in the story in relation to the topic of immigration and immigration policy. This awareness shows a deep level of thinking that is often set up as a standard for literacy both in reading and writing. Here, this was accessed by Alejandro through translanguaging praxis.

The group went on to discuss, using both languages was a significant part of the story and the process of creating it. Carlos explained, "Que no solo nos desenvolvemos en un idioma, sino que nos desemvolvemos en dos idiomas y podemos expresarnos más (we didn't only navigate in one language but in two and we could express ourselves more)" (Recording March 25, 2018). As many scholars point out, allowing young people to draw on their full language repertoires is an important way to motivate fuller participation in educational spaces and is wrapped up in issues of equity and empowerment for linguistically minoritized groups (Avineri et al. 2019).

In early June, the group performed their story para las familias de CCATE en la fiesta del fin del año escolar. Los chicos decidieron que Carlos should be the primary narrator as he was the best reader in Spanish. Francisco volunteered to read Donald Trump's lines. Obed introduced the theme, and when he mentioned El Santo, parents sat up in their seats and began to pay close attention (Fieldnote June 5, 2019). Families laughed throughout the performance, but there were also momentos de silencio, especialmente when Donald Trump announced he would deport all immigrants if El Santo refused to fight against Trump, Jr. Many parents laughed and applauded when El Santo used "la llave Nelson" on Trump, Jr. to win the fight, a father later commenting on this signature move of El Santo and how it was the best way to make Trump think he was going to win until the last moment (Recording March 25, 2018).

The audience together applauded los chicos, a mother commenting on the importance of Spanish and how in school there was no opportunity to learn it (Recording March 25, 2018). Manny, el padre de Carlos, dijo a todxs that he knew that in many families, kids asked questions about immigration that they didn't know how to answer, but that "ellos podrían encontrar algunas de las respuestas dentro de la historia (they could find some of the answers within the story)." Important to note here is that Manny located these answers within a fictional and humorous account of a very serious topic that affected families' lives in countless ways. In this way, humor can be seen as a "key narrative device" for marginalized groups "to break silences and resist oppressive forces" (Gallo 2016; Carpio 2008; Carrillo 2006; Limon 1996). At the same time, such playful and humorous narrative construction and language use in the story itself show how the group reimagined what could be and developed their own cues for addressing injustices (e.g., "being intelligent," "going to college," and "not let[ing] anyone tell us different things than we are").

"El Santo versus Trump, Jr., Part 2" y reflexiones de los chicos

We want to end our analysis by commenting on the boys' current Kamishibai project. In the late fall of 2019, they began planning a sequel to the El Santo story, "El Santo versus Trump, Jr., Part 2." They are currently finishing this story and have identified a local setting, Philadelphia, for the story to take place. In November of 2019, the group traveled together to the historic center of Philadelphia for inspiration for the story. Esta decisión fue basada en una serie de conversaciónes they had about the use of the terms "legal" and illegal," which are so often wrongly used to refer to those who are undocumented, and their relation to papeles and citizenship. Alejandro had begun learning about the US Constitution and was curious about how the term "citizen" is used and what it meant in this document in relation to the current immigration debate. Based on his interest and the boys' increased awareness about issues around documentation, they decided that for their story, they wanted to have another epic fight between Trump, Jr. and El Santo, and it would take place in the historic center and setting of Philadelphia.

In interviews with the boys, Obed asked them to reflect on the making of the original story. Their reflections illuminate their critical awareness of and interest in issues around immigration and how they can respond to it. Ramiro, in response to Obed's question, "What can you tell me about the story you wrote?", said (Interview January 20, 2020):

> The story is something that happens a lot, where people have died for it, I mean immigration, I know about many people that could not cross the border. Also, I think it's cool, they're no stories like the one we shared where a Mexican superhero defeat a bad person like Trump who only likes White people. He also does not respect woman. It's cool that El Santo defeats him.

Ramiro recognizes that the dominant stories circulating in the US are "majoritarian stories of racial privilege" and in this way implicitly recognizes that the counter-story he was involved in co-constructing helps to expose and challenge such myths (Solórzano and Yosso 2002: 32). Alejandro's response to Obed asking him how he felt, como mexicano, about the story the group wrote also speaks to his awareness about the significance of counter-stories "stories of people whose experiences are often not told" (Solórzano and Yosso 2002: 32). He said, "Sientes como tu voz ha sido escuchada (You feel as if your voice has been heard)" (Interview January 21, 2020).

Like Alejandro, Francisco also spoke to the value of using both Spanish and English (Interview January 21, 2020):

Writing the story in English and Spanish was very cool, because there are barely books written in both languages that combine both languages, we liked to do it in English and in Spanish, because we can actually do it! Also, it was very fun to do it with my friends, I think we are a great team!

His awareness of the kind of texts he has access to and his recognition and embracing of his and his compañeros' language skills suggest that translanguaging praxis helped him affirm his identity as a bilingual, which in the Marshall school context is seen as a problem to be fixed. Moreover, his comments show the value he assigns to collaborative, team-based modes of literacy engagement and narrative development.

Translanguaging praxis and pathways to social justice: Unas sugerencias preliminares

As we have discussed, engaging in a translanguaging praxis was key to how the group co-created "El Santo versus Trump, Jr.," a counter-story that challenged and reframed dehumanizing narratives about Mexican immigrants, who they are, and who they can and should be. The process of co-creating this counter-story involved a base of continual dialogue, reflection, and action through which the boys affirmed their bilingual identities and developed critical stances from which to read the word and the world (Freire and Macedo 1987). This process involved creative and humorous use of forms and features in both Spanish and English that were key not only to the development of these stances and the counter-story itself, but also to the development of transformative resistant capital. By this we mean: 1) the boys began to recognize the racist framework underlying how they and their families and positioned and treated; and 2) they become motivated to transform this kind of oppression. Moreover, humor was integral to the development of this kind of capital, and promoted intergenerational collaboration and solidarity. We see the development of their transformative resistant capital as part of RevArte's rebeldía epistemológica de la comunidad and as a further opening of pathways to social justice. The words of former Zapatista leader and spokesperson, Subcomandante Marcos, help illustrate this kind of rebellious opening (Muñoz Ramírez 2002: 244): "Rebellion in the world is like a crack in a wall: its first aim is to peek over to the other side. But later, this little glance weakens the wall and ends up breaking it down completely."

To end this chapter, we return to its beginning and Obed's own questions around how to respond to the racist and dehumanizing treatment of Mexicans and Mexican immigrants by el innombrable and in the dominant discourse on US immigration. To describe how we feel and react to such treatment, we draw on the boys' translanguaged phrase, "red, hot-peppery mad," as we balk at the humiliation and deshumanización of Latinx immigrants. The ethnographic research we have discussed in this chapter is motivated by emotion that can be likened to the Zapatista's *dignified rage,* which involves feeling with the head and thinking with the heart (Subcomandante Insurgente Marcos et al. 2018). Such dignified rage is also evident in the comments and reflections of the boys as they co-created their story. Con este grupo, and more broadly at RevArte, we are theorizing the kind of "thinking with the heart and feeling with the head" that we do through the lens of translanguaging praxis. Acknowledging this dignified rage and acting on it, by encouraging and exploring humorous and creative narrative expression, is one way we do this at RevArte. As we work on developing our translanguaging praxis, continued dialogue will be the base for not just reflecting and acting, but also for future research on how arts-based, performative forms of communication help us find answers in the stories we co-construct, as we work toward social justice.

Hacía un enfoque en multimodalidad: Limitations and directions for future research

We conclude by acknowledging the limitations of our work and how they point to future research in the field of applied linguistics. Our primary focus in our research study was on translanguaging praxis in the story and its co-construction, and our main data were fieldnotes from this process. We are grateful to reviewers who encouraged us to address both the story's performance and the boys' reflections, and we were able to do so by collecting some additional data and returning to our limited fieldnotes on the story's performance. We are also grateful to Ellen Skilton who recommended we incorporate multimodal analysis of both the performance and the story illustrations (Skilton personal email April 17, 2020). Although we were unable to do so due to limited performance data and no current access to the illustrations, as we continue to engage in translanguaging praxis through arts-based, performative forms of narrative at RevArte, we look forward to drawing on multimodal analysis. In addition to expanding the analytic focus of our future research, we are in the process of formalizing our commitment to participatory research methods. For the past two years at RevArte, we have formed a team of parent and teacher researchers through el círculo de investigaciones participativas comunitarias cuya misión es promover transformación social. While we have conducted several research projects together, we have not yet focused on language per se outside of naming the importance of bi- and multilingualism for Latinx families. As we continue this work, we would like to explore more in depth the concept of translanguaging with this research circle and to directly involve members in developing our translanguaging praxis at RevArte. We imagine the kinds of research we will conduct as we do so will help us connect with other scholars and community-based researchers in the field of applied linguistics who are also working toward social justice. We look forward to these collaborations and imagine many new co-constructed counter-stories that will provide answers to some of the questions we seek to answer, and to help us ask new ones.

Acknowledgments

We thank the RevArte community for helping us develop a translanguaging praxis, and in particular, Ramiro, Alejandro, Carlos, Francisco, Mauricio y María (nuestra co-instructora). We also thank Doris Warriner, Elizabeth Miller, and Ellen Skilton for their feedback on earlier drafts.

Note

1 We use pseudonyms for names of locations and names of research participants. We use the sign "x" as a gender-neutral alternative to such as "Latino" and "maestros." In addition, in the spirit of translanguaging we do not distinguish between the two named languages of English and Spanish, and thus do not use italics for Spanish.

References

Ashton-Warner, S. (1963), *Teacher*, New York: Simon & Schuster.
Avineri, N., L. R. Graham, E. J. Johnson, R. C. Riner, and J. Rosa (eds.) (2018), *Language and Social Justice in Practice*, New York: Routledge.
Bailey, B. (2007), "Heteroglossia and Boundaries," in M. Heller (ed.), *Bilingualism: A Social Approach*, pp. 257–76, Basingstoke: Palgrave.

Baker, C. (2001), *Foundations of Bilingual Education and Bilingualism*, Clevedon: Multilingual Matters.

Baker, C. (2003), "Biliteracy and Transliteracy in Wales: Language Planning and the Welsh National Curriculum," in N. Hornberger (ed.), *Continua of Biliteracy: An Ecological Framework for Educational Policy, Research, and Practice in Multilingual Settings*, pp. 71–90, Clevedon: Multilingual Matters.

Bakhtin, M. (1981), *Dialogic Imagination: Four Essays*, Austin: University of Texas Press.

Canagarajah, S. (2011), "Translanguaging in the Classroom: Emerging Issues for Research and Pedagogy," *Applied Linguistics Review*, 2: 1–27, Berlin: De Gruyter Mouton.

Carrillo, R. (2006), "Humor Casero Mujerista: Womanist Humor of the Home," in D. Delgado Bernal, A. Elenes, F. A. Godinez, and S. Villenas (eds.), *Chicana/Latina Education in Everyday Life*, pp. 181–95, Albany: State University of New York.

Carpio, G. (2008), *Laughing Fit to Kill: Black Humor in the Fictions of Slavery*, Oxford: Oxford University Press.

Creese, A., and A. Blackledge (2015), "Translanguaging and Identity in Educational Settings," *Annual Review of Applied Linguistics*, 35: 20–35.

Ellsworth, E. (1989), "Why Doesn't This Feel Empowering? Working Through the Repressive Myths of Critical Pedagogy," *Harvard Educational Review*, 59(3): 297–324.

Flores, N., and J. Rosa (2015), "Undoing Appropriateness: Raciolinguistic Ideologies and Language Diversity in Education," *Harvard Educational Review*, 85(2): 149–71.

Freire, P. (1970), *Pedagogy of the Oppressed*, New York: Herder and Herder.

Freire, P., and D. Macedo (1987), *Literacy: Reading the Word and the World*, South Hadley: Bergin and Harvey.

Gallo, S. (2016), "Humor in Father–Daughter Immigration Narratives of Resistance," *Anthropology & Education Quarterly*, 47(3): 279–96.

García, O. (2009), *Bilingual Education in the 21st Century: A Global Perspective*, Malden: Wiley-Blackwell.

García, O., S. Ibarra Johnson, and K. Seltzer (2017), *The Translanguaging Classroom: Leveraging Student Bilingualism for Learning*, Philadelphia: Caslon.

García, O., and L. Wei (2014), *Translanguaging: Language, Bilingualism and Education*, Basingstoke: Palgrave Macmillan.

Grosjean, F. (1982), *Life with Two Languages*, Cambridge MA: Harvard University Press.

Holloway, J. (2002), "Zapatismo and the Social Sciences," *Capital and Class*, 78: 153–60.

Jaspers, J. (2018), "The Transformative Limits of Translanguaging," *Language and Communications*, 58: 1–10.

Lewis, G., B. Jones, and C. Baker (2012), "Translanguaging: Developing its Conceptualisation and Contextualisation," *Educational Research and Evaluation*, 18(7): 655–70.

Limon, J. (1996), "Carne, Carnales, and the Carnivalesque: Bakhtinian Batos, Disorder, and Narrative Discourses," *The Matrix of Language: Contemporary Linguistic Anthropology*, 1: 182–203.

Link, H. (2018), "¡Luego, luego! [Right Away!]: The Urgency of Developing and Exploring Translanguaging Spaces for Immigrant Students and Families," *Translation and Translanguaging in Multilingual Contexts*, 4(3): 405–21.

Link, H., and O. Arango (2019), "La Vida Tiene Muchas Curvas [Life Has Many Curves]: Contemplating a Translanguaging Praxis," *Translation and Translanguaging in Multilingual Contexts*, 5(1): 29–48.

MacSwan, J. (2017), "A Multilingual Perspective on Translanguaging," *American Educational Research Journal*, 54(1): 167–201.

Martínez, R. A., and Z. Morales (2014), "¿Puras Groserias? Rethinking the Role of Profanity and Graphic Humor in Latin@ Students' BilingualWordplay," *Anthropology and Education Quarterly*, 45(4): 337–54.

Muñoz Ramírez, G. (2002), *The Fire and the Word: A History of the Zapatista Movement*, San Francisco: City Lights Press.

Otheguy, R., O. García, and W. Reid (2015), "Clarifying Translanguaging and Deconstructing Named Languages," *Applied Linguistics Review*, 6(3): 281–307.

Shih, Y. (2018), "Rethinking Paulo Freire's Dialogic Pedagogy and Its Implications for Teachers' Teaching," *Journal of Education and Learning*, 7(4): 230–35.

Solórzano, D., and T. J. Yosso (2002), "Critical Race Methodology: Counter-storytelling as an Analytical Framework for Education Research," *Qualitative Inquiry*, 8(1): 23–44.

Stahler-Sholk, R. (2010), "The Zapatista Social Movement: Innovation and Sustainability Alternatives: Global, Local, Political," *Indigenous Politics: Migration, Citizenship, Cyberspace*, 35(3): 269–90.

Subcomandante Insurgente Marcos (2018), *The Zapatistas Dignified Rage: Final Public Speeches of Subcommander Marcos*, N. Henck (ed.) and H. Gales (trans.), Chico: AK Press.

U.S. Census Bureau (2010), Data for Marshall Borough, Pennsylvania. Retrieved from http://factfinder2.census.gov

Wei, L. (2011), "Multilinguality, Multimodality and Multicompetence: Code- and Mode-Switching by Minority Ethnic Children in Complementary Schools," *Modern Language Journal*, 95(3): 370–84.

Williams, C. (1994), "Arfarniad o Ddulliau Dysgu ac Addysgu yng Nghyddestun Addysg Uwchradd Ddwyieithog [An evaluation of teaching and learning methods in the context of bilingual secondary education]," Doctoral Thesis, Bangor, University of Wales.

Yosso, T. J. (2005), "Whose Culture Has Capital? A Critical Race Theory Discussion of Community Cultural Wealth," *Race Ethnicity and Education*, 8(1): 69–91.

Yosso, T. J. (2006), *Critical Race Counterstories along the Chicana/Chicano Educational Pipeline*, New York: Routledge.

Yosso, T. J., W. E. Smith, M. Ceja, and D. G. Solórzano (2009), "Critical Race Theory, Racial Microaggressions, and Campus Racial Climate for Latina/o Undergraduates," *Harvard Educational Review*, 79(4): 659–91.

Zentella, A. C. (2003), "'José, can you see?': Latin@ Responses to Racist Discourse," in D. Sommer (ed.), *Bilingual Games: Some Literary Investigations*, pp. 51–66, New York: Palgrave Macmillan.

5

Being, Seeing, and Hearing White: When Theater Arts Interrogate and Make Visible the Power of the Elephant in the Room

Ellen Skilton

Introduction

Drawing on the linguistic concepts of markedness and performance, LangCrit's (i.e., Critical Language and Race Theory's) analysis of the subject-as-seen/subject-as-heard, and raciolinguistics' emphasis on indexical inversion, this chapter engages in cross-site analysis of community, university, and arts festival performances to make a theoretical and empirical contribution to studies of embodied and artistic forms of meaning-making, and the necessity of embodied analysis that investigates more than words and more than acontextual racial and linguistic categories. The data come from three main sources, each of which address the broader theme of interrogating Whiteness in the US in the twenty-first century: 1) the ongoing work of a local Theater of the Oppressed (TO) "arts-based catalyst for change" organization called *Just Act* that uses community-based applied theater to rehearse for reality to disrupt oppressive systems; 2) the author's undergraduate course entitled *Power of Play* in which students create scenes from their own experiences of inequity; and 3) the script, video of performance, and reflections on the artistic and performative process of the author's one-person show *Reality in Retrograde* in the 2017 Philadelphia Fringe Festival. This chapter looks at how applied linguists who utilize ethnographic methods and focus on semiotic rather than purely linguistic repertoires have particularly useful tools of inquiry and analysis to bring to understanding embodied, aesthetic communication that attempts to disrupt the status quo.

Freeman (1996) once said in exploring the intricacies of bilingual education, and I have often repeated this as a mantra in much of my applied linguistics scholarship: "It's much more than language" (Skilton-Sylvester 2011). More recently, Heller, Pietikainen, and Pujolur (2018: 6) concur about the value of moving beyond language itself in the introduction to their new book on critical sociolinguistic research methods: "Our research is not about language per se. It is about the conditions and consequences of language for people." There are two ways that this "more than language" orientation is important in this chapter. First, there are the ways that the context and content of language-in-use are essential components of any language study in the real world. And second, communication itself involves much more than language. As Blackledge and Creese (2017: 252) explain, "The way people walk, stand, and sit, the way they tilt their head, the gaze of their eyes, the shrug of their shoulders, the movement of their hands and fingers, their smile or frown, all are part of the semiotic repertoire ... Embodied communicative practice is not in any way separate from linguistic communicative practice."

The critical turn in applied linguistics (see Pennycook 2010) over the past thirty years has made it commonplace to assume that applied linguistics research takes us to many places beyond the language classroom and that it assumes attention to "the embodied (somatic, sensory), contextualized (ecological, spatial) and political (decolonial) social practices that bring [language] about" (Pennycook 2010: 8). In fact, one of the key benefits of utilizing language as a component of analysis in social science research is the way in which it can often illuminate differences in status among speakers, listeners, and observers that are not clearly visible or audible in the moment communication occurs. In this chapter, like Friedrich (2019: 5), I am arguing for "an applied linguistics that goes everywhere and forges alliances with many disciplines in its search for expansion and further meaning."

Applied linguistics that goes everywhere: Interrogating the performance of Whiteness

In the US, there is perhaps nothing more powerful and yet hidden in plain sight than Whiteness and its ongoing impact on social structures and multiracial relations. Over the past three decades, White studies and the analysis of White privilege have become common, but traditional multicultural education in K-12 and university settings often remains a study of "the other" without a comprehensive structural analysis of inequality. For White people, this often allows our own racial identity and racialized experiences and the privilege they experience within this system to be nearly unseeable because they are framed as the unmarked norm.

It is not a coincidence that the data for this chapter come from applied theater performances (particularly TO) because these kinds of theatrical engagements allow participants to imagine, disrupt, remake, and practice alternative futures. *Performance* (and not just the notion of a static ideal) is an essential aspect of everyday uses of language as well as in the applied theater contexts investigated in this chapter (see Chomsky 1965; Osipovich 2006 for discussions of performance in all social language use and theater). Any linguistic utterance has an element of performance associated with it. In the case of this chapter that explores applied theater, however, we are adding another layer of performance that is valuable to address and define. Many people, when they hear the word "theater" automatically assume a play, a stage, an audience that sits quietly, and (often) a desire on the part of the actors, playwright, stage crew to entertain. The definition of theater at the center of this chapter is connected to the definition Michael Rohd (2011) proposes for artistic practice that engages in "collaborative civic imagination" for "building a healthy society." Critically, in his work, and in the work of most applied theater, performance is usually engaged in with people who do not see themselves as stage actors. Just as Chomsky defined performance for linguistics, theater scholars have also attempted to define theatrical performance. In a theatrical performance of any kind, two key elements are essential, "liveness" and "enactment" (Osipovich 2006: 469). It is a process of creating "an alternative reality out of [participants'] co-presence."

In the case of TO, which frames much of the data for this chapter, performances are all based on real-life experiences participants have had when they have experienced or witnessed inequality or oppression (see Cahnmann-Taylor and Souto-Manning 2010; Dias 2018). These experiences are then the kernel at the center of fictionalized dilemmas with inequality that allow audience members—called "spect-actors"—to take the place of the protagonist to attempt a different strategy for addressing a social dilemma. The point, according to Boal (2002), is not to find a solution but to have an opportunity to "rehearse for reality" so that new actions might be taken in future encounters with oppression in the real world. These performances typically don't happen on an official stage, but more often in community centers, church basements, classrooms, student centers, etc.

In the TO examples in particular, it is also important to remember that the line between actor and what Boal calls "spect-actor" is fluid, interactive, and proactive. Both the linguistic and theatrical orientation to performance are important to hold onto—we are talking not about the ideal, but the real, everyday ways we perform, communicate, and build and imagine community. In fact, this is the very reason that analyzing these kinds of applied theater is so ripe for interrogating Whiteness—they, too, are always "much more than language," both in the ways that these theatrical interactions create a particular kind of context—what Osipovitch (2006) calls an "alternative reality" and in the ways that the communication is necessarily embodied, gestural, multimodal, and shaped by the people and environment in which that communication takes place.

Interrogating the invisible visibility of gendered Whiteness, politeness, and niceness

Whiteness, particularly for women, is often inextricably linked to niceness, politeness, and ironing out discomfort (see Castago 2019 and Galman 2019). In September of 2017, in the final talkback session for my one-person show *Reality in Retrograde* at the Philadelphia Fringe Festival, Monica Day, who had co-produced the show, said: "And you know, this is basically a story of a White woman's journey ..." and suddenly everything shifted. It is not as if I was a stranger to discussions of race and racism in this country. My doctoral research investigated the experiences of Cambodians in Philadelphia and analyzed the dangerous power of the model minority myth. I have thought deeply about the impact of race and racism on my biracial daughters and my inherent blind spots as a White woman in parenting them. What shifted was the lens of seeing my experience of this show that I didn't think was about race as a White one.

Along a somewhat parallel path, I have spent the last six years working with a theater-based nonprofit called *Just Act* that uses applied theater approaches—particularly TO—to engage diverse participants in exploring and unpacking day-to-day experiences of oppression and trying on new ways of engaging with community members to address inequity in our quotidian interactions. In this work, the words "As a White woman ..." have become a more and more natural way for me to think and speak about myself. During this same time period, I also began teaching a course called *The Power of Play: Improvisation and Learning* with teacher education students and others. In this work, we also explored issues of race class and gender utilizing Augusto Boal's TO approach (Boal 2002). Because the majority of students in the classes are White, direct discussions of Whiteness are also common and I find myself utilizing language to address what was a notable silence in much of my own education. And then last year in my Cultural Foundations of Education class, I organized it so that it was centered on race and the invisible power of White supremacy in schools and communities in the US. We have been reading *White Fragility* (DiAngelo 2017), listening to the *Seeing White* podcast (2017), and utilizing Mica Pollack's book *SchoolTalk* (2017) to frame the ways that school language about difference plays a powerful role in shaping students' experiences. These explorations of difference, race, Whiteness, and social change are the sources of data for this chapter.

In this applied theater/applied linguistics inquiry, I have found three-dimensional forms of engagement, often wordless to start, that involve the body (and not just the mind) as a fundamental source of knowledge, insight, and possible action to dismantle White supremacy in our everyday lives. There are three "stages" I investigate in this chapter: 1) community-based uses of TO techniques in a 5-day workshop facilitated by a social justice arts organization called *Just Act*; 2) campus-based uses of TO as performance and pedagogy in classroom and university-wide contexts to explore everyday inequality; and 3) autoethnographic performances of a scene from a White American girlhood by the author (Skilton 2017). The applied linguistic lenses that I bring to the analysis of these three stages center on understanding the dynamics of power, hierarchy, and perception in interrogating the communication and visible invisibility of Whiteness in embodied, arts-based forms.

Utilizing theoretical frameworks from applied linguistics to interrogate Whiteness: Markedness, subject-as-seen/ subject-as-heard, and indexical inversion

There are three key tools of analyzing language I highlight in this chapter and in my analysis of the applied theater examples that follow: 1) structural linguistics' concept of markedness; 2) LangCrit's notion of subject-as-seen and subject-as-heard; and 3) raciolinguistics' conception of inverted indexicality. Each of these tools provides particular insights that are useful in understanding the hidden-in-plain-sight and unequal power relations inherent in looking at Whiteness in the US. The use of these applied linguistics tools can also play a key role in either maintaining or disrupting some ideologies of Whiteness: niceness (Castagno 2019), comfort (DiAngelo 2017), and control (Duncan, personal communication) alongside what DiAngelo (2017) calls "White solidarity." In each case, it is my applied linguistics lens that influences my systematic and close analysis of practices that hide Whiteness. Even when I am not focused specifically on texts or talk per se, I (and other applied linguists) are focused on meaning-making more broadly and semiotic repertoires that include text, talk, gesture, gaze, movement, etc. (Blackledge and Creese 2017; Heller, Pietikäinen, and Pujolar 2018).

Structural linguistics' and White studies' conceptions of markedness

The concept of markedness originated in the 1920s and 1930s as a way that the Prague School of Structural Linguistics began to identify asymmetry in language (see Trechter and Bucholtz 2001 for an overview). The concept of "markedness" was originally used to describe words that in sound or meaning were binary opposites—where one form (the unmarked one) was seen as more basic, natural, and frequent (see Zhang and Tian 2015). Although originating in linguistics, the application of this concept to social life is very common, particularly in relation to conceptions of Whiteness:

> As a cultural sign, Whiteness works much like a linguistic sign, taking its meaning from those surrounding categories to which it is structurally opposed, such as Blackness, Indigenousness, and foreignness. As an element in each of these binaries ... Whiteness is not opposite and equal, but opposite and unequal. It is in its unmarked status that the power of Whiteness lies ... [We must ensure] that Whiteness, in all its diverse manifestations, *is not only seen but also heard*.
> Trechter and Buchholtz 2001: 5–6, emphasis in the original

The unmarked nature of Whiteness—and the process of engaging with White students as they see their own unmarked race, often for the first time—is both a common and profound experience. It is typical for White students in my class to say something like "race didn't exist in my neighborhood growing up," illustrating that this racially unmarked category feels only relevant in relation to more marked categories of race. In fact, most of my White students, when asked to describe their own race, had an eerie discovery that they, in fact, never really realized they had one. It is important to note that although gender is not a primary focus in this chapter, the majority of my students (especially in teacher education and including the one cited above) are both White and female. As such, there is a particular form of gendered Whiteness that is connected to being nice, being good, and not making anyone uncomfortable.

A new volume on the dangers of niceness in education further reinforces this point by explicitly outlining the dangers of unmarked "nice" Whiteness by connecting it to the often-unexamined orientations of White, middle-class, (largely) female teachers and maintaining inequity (Castago 2019). In the same volume, Galman (2019: 80) speaks specifically about White, female teachers and the widespread, normative constricting and damaging commitment to niceness that can actually be "doing evil in the service of nice." There is no neutrality, only clinging to an image of unmarked niceness/good girl-ness (fearful of the alternative—nasty), while protecting the status quo. In the analysis that follows, I make visible the ways that applied theater can unmask the hidden potency with which Whiteness (and at times, particularly female niceness) functions as unmarked in insidious ways that maintain and obscure inequality and diminish the understandings, analyses, and actions of White social actors in working toward more just and equitable futures. In addition to markedness, the distinction between "subject-as-seen" and "subject-as-heard" is particularly useful in interrogating Whiteness in embodied practice.

LangCrit's concept of subject-as-seen/subject-as-heard

At the intersection of Critical Race Theory and Language Studies is a stance Crump (2014) calls LangCrit (Critical Language and Race Theory). This orientation attempts to analyze language, power, and social structures—especially in relation to race and racism—that are often hidden from view at the surface. For our purposes in this chapter, the idea of subject-as-seen/subject-as-heard is particularly valuable for two reasons: 1) this perspective invites us to decenter language as the solitary focus so that the racial identities and ideologies of speakers and listeners are also seen and addressed and not obscured by less politicized concepts like culture and ethnicity; and 2) the LangCrit orientation toward analysis asks us to look beyond the static notion of marked and unmarked outlined above and pay attention to how particular micro contexts and interactions both shape and are shaped by macro identities and ideologies. First, the LangCrit perspective invites us to not just pay attention to what is heard in linguistic analysis, but also what is seen, particularly for interlocutors whose linguistic landscapes and bodies are marked by marginalized racial categories so that "it becomes possible to theorize the intersections of seen and heard" (Crump 2014: 219).

In addition to paying attention to the unmarked nature of Whiteness, this chapter addresses not just White ways of speaking/being heard, but White ways of being seen, and embodied forms of Whiteness (and non-Whiteness) in action.

By exploring the multimodal communicative repertoires in applied theater, this aspect of both seeing and hearing Whiteness is more possible. Whereas the direction of the applied linguistics research gaze has often been toward minoritized others, this chapter invites the reader to view the often hidden-in-plain-sight ways of speaking and moving that can keep those hegemonic words and actions unexamined, unquestioned, and invisibly shaping power dynamics and opportunities for change.

Second, critical to the study of subject-as-seen and subject-as-heard is a commitment from the point of view of linguistic anthropology to pay close attention to the nuances of what happens in the moment in local contexts and not just macro-level analysis of patterns of speaking, acting, and believing. It is not just the subject-as-seen/subject-as-heard in the moment that is important, however, but also their relationship to wider macro ideologies and macro structures (e.g., income inequality and White privilege). Making Whiteness visible is not enough; this analysis requires attention to the dynamic interplay between micro and macro levels of analysis and the ways that language, identity, and embodied action intersect. Crump (2001: 16) argues that this kind of analysis problematizes "a simple model of marked versus unmarked ... while its hegemonic influence is simultaneously exposed. This is accomplished by highlighting the indexical connections between linguistic practice and social identity, between discursive performance and cultural ideology in different contexts." This focus on seen/heard and micro/macro dimensions builds on the idea of markedness and performance as mentioned above and indexicality as discussed below.

Raciolinguistics' concept of indexical inversion

Beginning in 2015 with the coining of the term "raciolinguistics," there has been a new thread of scholarship cutting across anthropology, linguistics, education, and race studies that looks both at how language is raced and race is "languaged." From the point of view of raciolinguistics, decisions about "appropriate" forms of language need to be interrogated and decolonized. As Rosa (2019: 7) explains:

> Rather than starting from the vantage point of always already constituted racial categories (e.g., Black, Asian, Native American, White) and linguistic varieties (e.g., Standard English, African American English, Spanglish), *a raciolinguistic*

approach considers the joint production of these categories and varieties across institutional and interactional scales. This approach involves accounting for the *modes of perception* through which bodies are parsed in relation to racial categories and communicative forms are construed in relation to named language varieties."

emphasis mine

There are two ways that this raciolinguistic approach matters for this chapter: 1) this approach requires analysis across institutions and types of interaction to see how modes of perception and the contexts/interactions produce racial and linguistic categories; and 2) this approach shifts the emphasis from the minoritized bodies/speakers and toward those who often control perceptions of what is seen and heard. The changes that need to happen to create spaces of freedom and possibility require changes in the perceptions and practices of what Rosa calls "racially hegemonic perceiving subjects" (in this case those who carry the mantle of "Whiteness") rather than "modifying the embodied communicative behaviors of racially minoritized individuals" (Rosa 2019: 6). Of particular value for our purposes in this chapter is the notion of "inverted indexicality." Rosa (2019: 6) suggests a shift in focus:

> ... From modifying racially minoritized subjects' linguistic practices to *contesting hegemonically positioned subjects' modes of perception* ... A raciolinguistic perspective must be informed by a theory of change that is focused on reconstituting or eradicating systems of domination ... and the normative modes of colonial subject formation that organize these systems ...
>
> emphasis mine

Through the lens of inverted indexicality, this chapter pays closest attention to the perceptions and hegemonic assumptions of those who have the most linguistic and social power in the situation and attempts to interrogate and disrupt those assumptions.

Adapting language tools to interrogate Whiteness in applied theater contexts

In the preceding discussion of linguistic (and theatrical) performance, markedness, subject-as-seen/subject as heard, and indexical inversion, I have outlined particular linguistic tools that are particularly well suited for interrogating Whiteness in applied theater contexts. Each of these tools asks us to shift our gaze from analyzing the marginalized other and toward examining what looks and often feels like the norm, but is hegemonically and socially constructed. Next, this chapter delves into three different applied theater contexts and a variety of theatrical performances. I am calling each of these contexts/sets of performances a "stage." Drawing on these tools from language study, in each set of analysis below, I 1) work to disrupt the unmarked nature of Whiteness (especially in relation to unexamined normalization of "generic" White behavior, niceness, politeness, goodness); 2) take into consideration not just language/communication but also the ideologies and moving bodies (subject-as-seen) at play in the interactions/performances; 3) highlight the importance of the interaction between micro-level and macro-level analysis and not relying on static decontextualized racial, social, and linguistic dimensions; 4) foreground the importance of looking at racial categories across institutional contexts and types of interactions; and 5) turn the gaze toward the actions and perceptions of those in power rather than only on "minoritized subjects"; and 6) ensure that recommendations for change also disrupt the status quo rather than asking others to conform to normalized racial ideologies, practices, and ways of interacting. These frameworks and lessons from language study—particularly when used to investigate applied theater performances from the lived experiences of participants—illuminate often unseen and unheard dimensions of Whiteness in order to move toward the possibility of change.

Stage One: Centering the body and using specific pronouns that index the speaker

My work with *Just Act* began in the Spring of 2014 as I participated in a workshop entitled "Flip the Script" with Just Act's Artistic/Managing Director, Lisa Jo Epstein. Since that spring, I have participated in four other trainings about how to utilize TO in educational and social justice contexts. Since joining the board in 2015, I have also participated in many community events where Boal's idea of "rehearsing for reality" has been a key part of the evening. In these "Jams on Justice" and the annual "People's State of the Union" events (a national event to create story circles sponsored by the US Department of Arts and Culture) *Just Act* has created spaces for participants of many ages, races, genders, and socioeconomic statuses to tell their own stories of both oppression and belonging and then, working with ensemble members from *Just Act*, perform what Boal would call "Forum" pieces in which audience members are able to participate in them as spect-actors, trying out new possibilities for disrupting the status quo.

As an educational anthropologist and teacher educator, my participation in trainings and events (as well as board meetings) has included multi-year and multi-context opportunities for participant observation—in churches, Head Start centers, neighborhood festivals, Get Out the Vote events, and living rooms. In this chapter, however, I focus on a training that happened in June of 2019 in which I had permission to document the work of the group. This was *Just Act*'s annual 5-day summer Forum Theater (FT) workshop that has been happening for fifteen years. It drew a set of teachers, social activists, community organizers, nonprofit directors, students, and professors. Although the workshop ends with a set of FT performances around particular scenes of oppression fictionalized from the experiences of the group,[1] my focus is on the first few days of the workshop and the ways that the embodied practices of TO create opportunities to interrogate Whiteness in the context of what Boal (2002) calls "gamesercizes" and the oral unpacking of these small-scale, informal theatrical performances that involve a focus on the body first. As Lisa Jo says to the assembled group on this first day of the workshop:

> How does it feel in your body? It's so hard to name feelings. TO gives us an opportunity to do that. [This was a] physical conversation where we had to navigate and negotiate with others, suspending our brains and doing what we want with our bodies ... At the root of it all, we are all actors, and each body part has a purpose ... Our bodies are involved in the reproduction of power. We are participating in systems of oppression. We make social systems happen. We have to re-find ourselves. Spect-actors have the responsibility for acting in the context of oppression. We want to cultivate and encourage curiosity, courage, compassion, care. Invite possibility, not problem-solving. Practice undoing; living into the situation. We do the non-verbal work first.
>
> Fieldnotes June 15, 2019

The embodied work of TO is a central component of being able to imagine change can happen, that action in the context of oppression is possible.

One of the ways that Whites collude in maintaining the status quo is to remain focused on intellectual arguments that are disembodied, analytical, and without overt emotion. In this early activity below (after some introductory activities), two participants are asked to shake hands and then others comment on what they have seen:

Excerpt 5.1 Handshake Activity: Theater of the Oppressed Training Day 1

Facilitator What did you notice showing up in their bodies as they had that exchange?

Participant 1 Distance, arm extended to make contact, but definitely more rigid, straight up and down.

F ... Distance, up and down, A kind of rigid up and down, other things?

P2 There was still like a willingness and an interest in the interaction.

F How did that show up, interest, physically in the interaction?

P2 You know how when you extend your arm ...

F *You mean, when you saw P6 or P7 extend their arm? Just so you know, I'm just going to coach you a little bit, because when you start using you, you know I might not have seen that, so honoring what YOU saw, practice it.*

P2 So when she extended her arm to [her friend], she met midway or vice versa. Now I forgot ... (laughs)

P3 I also think ... you also saw certain signs and that's why you approached her that way ...

P4 I also felt it like, energetically from you too. Right. You know, physically, like "I don't know what you're into." (Leans back, laughter) Energetically, I feel that more.

P5 I also saw you get closer in eye contact. With the hand, but then the eyes really came close. And with curiosity and openness to each other ...

In the following paragraphs we return to our central analytical question: How do the concepts of markedness, subject-as-seen/subject as heard, and indexical inversion help us to see and hear what's important to understand in this interaction?

This example, in one of the very first activities of the workshop, addresses an unmarked but problematic use of language that is very common—a generic you. A participant begins by saying, "You know how when *you* extend your arm ..." as if everyone has had that common experience and the facilitator stops her right away asking her not to use the generic you but to focus on her own experiences. Often, this is a shift toward using "I" (although not in this case), but always a reminder to pay attention to the experiences of the particular people in the room and not gloss over possible differences in experiences. This reminder happens throughout these community workshops (and also in my classroom now) until participants are able to practice speaking directly from their own point of view, and acknowledging the specific perspectives in the room.

As an activity that involves not just talking but also movement and analysis of movement as well as a claiming of particular in-the-moment identities, it is also a good example of not just focusing on what is heard but also what is seen by racialized subjects in the interaction. There is much description of what is seen in the analysis of these particular moments and always, an attention to power and privilege. As Lisa Jo says, as she starts to write down reflections from the group, "I'm going to write down exactly what you say, not paraphrase in my White, privileged voice." Making Whiteness marked, seen, embodied, and articulated is a powerful way that this work invites participants to name and deconstruct normative patterns of interaction that are often very powerful and yet also invisible to the naked eye. In terms of indexical inversion, we see the emphasis not on trying to change minoritized communities but rather on the hegemonic perceptions and actions of White actors.

Later in the workshop (on day three), pairs of participants utilized image theater (wordless sculptures made from the gestures, stances, and stature of the bodies of participants). These particular body sculptures asked participants to first sculpt "fear" and then "healing." Throughout it all, the emphasis was not only on macro processes, but on the very specific experiences of those in the room in building these particular paired sculptures. In her introduction, Lisa Jo talked about "decolonizing our bodies and minds" (Fieldnotes June 27, 2019). As people discussed their experiences, an African-American male participant said, "when I was in the fear position, I didn't look at others" (Fieldnotes June 27, 2019). An Asian-American woman in the group said, "Looking down illustrated loneliness and wasn't present in other sculptures. When we moved from the fear to healing position, it felt good not to be stuck, but the number of steps it took to go from fear to healing was really apparent and longer than I expected" (Fieldnotes June 27, 2019). Finally, an African-American woman explained, "Our bodies can send a message to our minds, just as our minds can send messages to our bodies. If you can't mentally get there, you could get there physically first" (Fieldnotes June 27, 2019). By taking each of these experiences and vantage points seriously, these perspectives are not asked to be generalizable to all people of a particular racial category but allow all participants to be individuals—at the micro-level—operating in the context of those wider societal macro structures.

In these preparatory phases of TO described above, it is possible to see how theatrical performance in informal spaces that center embodied experiences of participants (even outside of a particular scene) can be a generative space for seeing and hearing Whiteness in the context of micro and macro dynamics. In what follows, the analysis shifts toward more narrative representations of particular instances of oppression, sometimes with audiences of spect-actors who have not been part of the original preparation for the scenes. As we shift to a different stage of the processes involved in utilizing TO, we also shift from a community workshop context, to a course at a university.

Stage Two: Tableau and Forum Theatre performances in a university context

When I first started thinking about this chapter, there were two FT scenes that came immediately to mind: 1) *Driving While Not White*; and 2) *Class and Race in Racial Profiling*. The first, *Driving While Not White*, was a very early scene in the spring 2019 semester that some of my students created and really stayed with me as a key example of how this work could help us interrogate Whiteness in powerful ways. Students were randomly put in small groups of four and asked to think of a time when they had personally witnessed or experienced inequality or oppression. Each student in each of the groups told a quick version of their story and then, as a group, they chose one to turn into a wordless tableau.

Driving While Not White

The groups were mixed racially—in this particular group, there were two White women, one Black woman, and a mixed-race person who is gender fluid. The particular tableau that they enacted took place in a car with the mixed-race person who is gender fluid in the driver's seat, a White woman in the front passenger seat, and a Black woman in the back seat. A White woman was outside of the car and represented a police officer.

Before analyzing the work that this group did—particularly after they added words and actions to the scene—I want to mention a few aspects of the way we look as a group at these images. We create a kind of museum for each one and participants are asked to describe what they see without interpretation. Just like with beginning attempts at ethnographic fieldnotes, participants usually begin by saying things like "Person in the back looks happy" and they are pushed to describe instead what they see: "Person in the back is smiling and making eye contact with the person next to her." All of this work is honing participants' tools for observation without initial interpretation, working toward being able to see what's there and not what we assume to be there. Sometimes, participants (as in Banscombe and Schneider 2013) were asked to step out and speak from the point of view of the person they were representing in the wordless tableau.

In this particular group, we tapped the driver on the shoulder and they explained that they and their brother were always getting pulled over in this small town for "driving while not White" and that this time the police officer had said they were speeding (which they were not). It was early in the semester, and students were just getting to know each other and I could feel the tension rise a bit in the room. One White student from a different group talked about her uncle being a cop and how hard a job it is (with a bit of defensiveness). When we tapped on the shoulder of the White woman who was portraying the police officer, she (after sensing the tension in the room from White participants not used to discussing racial profiling in such a direct and personal way) immediately offered that she was planning to just give him a warning and tell him to have a good day. The person whose story it was that was being represented said during the debrief, "But that's not what happened to me." It created a moment to discuss one of Boal's rules for FT, and that is that you can't create magic solutions to problems (Boal 2002). As the woman who was playing the police officer talked about her decision to change the story, she said, "It wasn't fair. I didn't want him to feel targeted." This was a really important moment in the classroom—both for students of color and White students.

Because we were not talking in the abstract about something that happened, but enacting it, students were in a position to have to feel the discomfort in more of a visceral way and were asked not to "fix it" but to imagine possibilities for how different people in the scene might be able to try out different actions that might lead to different outcomes. The idea that the person being the cop could magically change the situation was a very appealing option to alleviate the tension in the room about this injustice. What TO allowed in this situation, however, was a chance to feel and sit with the discomfort, live into the possible thoughts and feelings of particular characters in the scene without being able to save the day—in fact, in order to honor their classmates' experiences, they needed to try to accurately represent their peer's story—even if it was uncomfortable. This illustrates the power of the subject-as-seen and subject-as-heard in applied theater approaches. The point was not about debating the issue, it was about seeing, hearing, and attempting to represent the experience of another—and they were directing the show. It also allowed for a chance to experience firsthand indexical inversion. Whereas the problem is framed by the cop as an issue of speeding, enough members of the class were able to see that the issue was actually one of racial profiling where the locus of the problem shifted from the driver to the officer and societal perceptions, fears and attitudes toward people of color.

Class and Race in Racial Profiling

This particular FT scene was from a different semester in a class that had a higher than usual percentage of people of color in the group. In this particular group of five, all of the participants were women of color. Unlike the tableau scene described above, this one was worked on over several weeks, full characters were developed, dramatic action was increased, dialogue was added, etc. Although the initial kernel of an idea for the scene had come from the same exercise (a student's individual experience), at this point in the process students were encouraged to fictionalize the account in ways that helped them to convey something honest and true, but not necessarily a verbatim representation of what had happened in their classmate's experience. The scene took place in a hair supply store in which the owner and worker suspected the less well-dressed customer who was listening to music on headphones of shoplifting and asked to search her bag, while the more middle-class-looking customer (who had actually shoplifted) was able to leave the store. The last participant was a security officer from the mall where the incident took place.

Because all of the members of the group were people of color and because it was performed for a wider campus audience at the end of the semester, it played a really different role than the first scene in our engagement around the issues presented. Also, because those who were doing the profiling were also women of color, it created an opportunity to talk not just about individuals but also about social structures and how they shape participant actions—even for people of color. That is, racist and classist policies affect different people of color unequally. This scene created especially rich opportunities when others entered the scene as spect-actors to try out possible ways to handle the situation differently. When another person would take the place of one of the original actors, if they were White, I would say, "We now have a White woman taking the place of an Asian-American woman so that will shift the scene in some ways." That created new forms of visibility about how racial profiling is enacted at the intersection of structural and individual forces.

On a campus that is predominantly White, it also provided opportunities for students of color in the audience to speak with authority and their own authorship about their own experiences of being profiled. This scene made visible the differentially marked/unmarked hierarchy of race and class in this context, created complex and nuanced opportunities for seeing the subject of the scene as both seen and heard, and the opportunities for White participants from the class and in the wider campus audience to observe and hear their peers of color discuss their racialized experiences with each other in ways that allowed them to see quite clearly how their (White students') perceptions of the situation were sometimes in conflict with their peers of color. If, as Rosa (2019) suggests in his discussion of indexical inversion, the goal is "shifting focus from modifying racially minoritized subjects' linguistic practices to *contesting hegemonically positioned subjects' modes of perception*, this scene and the wider university context in which it happened allowed for those hegemonic perceptions to be highlighted for White students as they heard their peers of color discuss their own experiences and perceptions. In much the same way that a fishbowl discussion might allow for hearing the perceptions of others different than oneself—although this scene included not just talk but also movement, action, and the taking on of a particular character's point of view—this scene and the parameters for engaging in FT created relatively safe structures for privileging minoritized subjects embodied/enacted perceptions.

In the final piece of data analysis in this chapter, I engage with a scene from my one-person show, *Reality in Retrograde*. Whereas the other two stages focused on TO in community workshop, university classroom spaces, this one is quite different in the ways that it focuses on a single performer in the context of the Philadelphia Fringe Festival. Some would call it an autoethnographic performance of a White girl/woman's experiences growing up.

Stage 3: What justice requires of White women and girls

Reality in Retrograde is a 50-minute one-person show that was performed at the Philadelphia Fringe Festival in 2017. It consists of several scenes from birth through the present that are autobiographical but not a literal representation of what happened in the past. For example, in several short interludes between scenes it appears that I am being pulled around the stage by the forces of retrograde while talking about astrological and scientific explanations of the planetary phenomenon of retrograde. In the first scene I analyze below, called "Fighting" (the sixth of twelve scenes in the show), I dramatize perhaps the only time in my childhood that I was a fiercely active agent, defying White nice/good girl stereotypes and invisibility.

Excerpt 5.2 "Fighting" scene from *Reality in Retrograde* (Skilton 2017)

Announcer   Good evening ladies and gentlemen and welcome to the notorious RED DOG HILL. On this legendary hill where sledding in the winter is not for the faint of heart and where sometimes children get buried in snowdrifts until spring, we have an epic fight in the making. It's the Thursday before Easter 1976—the night of the last supper in the Christian tradition—hoping for something more interesting than an outright crucifixion. This afternoon we have two prepubescent girls facing off after school.

In one corner, we have defending champion, manipulative bully, and popular girl, Sue Petuchnig, and in the other, we have Ellen Skilton, awkward, conflict-avoidant fourth grader who thinks fist fights are morally wrong. I can't see how Skilton has a chance.

"Can you tell us how you ended up here on the eve of Easter weekend, fighting defending champion, popular girl, and bully Petuchnig?"

Ellen   "Well, she made Lori and Paula cry at recess today and I just can't take it anymore."

So you said, "Sue, meet me on Red Dog Hill after school and I'll pummel you, smash your face in."

Ellen   "What?"

Announcer   "OK Skilton, best of luck." And here we go, folks, first round. Petuchnig and Skilton charge at each other and then try to topple the other. Skilton goes for Petuchnig's hair! Petuchnig counters with some hair-pulling of her own. The crowd is cheering but it's hard to tell who for. Someone pulls them apart. And they're back at it. A shove from Petuchnig almost knocks Skilton over, but Skilton steadies herself. Looks like it's a draw. Petuchnig starts to walk away. Ladies and gentlemen, this fight is OVER!

Ellen   I remember being completely out of breath and surprised to still be standing. The whole thing felt a little embarrassing. What was I really trying to accomplish anyway? It's not going to change anything and was just completely out-of-control in front of friends and strangers. I should have just kept my mouth shut and we could have all avoided her at school. I'm relieved it's over, I guess I need to go home and tell my mom before she hears it from someone else.

And then, as we both walked away, I heard Sue say something under her breath that no one else could hear: "Losers!"

Announcer   WAIT A MINUTE. Skilton is suddenly running toward Petuchnig. Skilton has pounced on her back knocking her over!! PETUCHNIG DOWN, DOWN GOES PETUCHNIG, DOWN GOES PETUCHNIG ON **RED DOG HILL**! SKILTON IS THE VICTOR ON RED DOG HILL!

Ellen   I cried all the way home, walking down the railroad tracks. I had just hurt someone, committed violent acts. What I did was wrong. But strangely, my mom wasn't mad. In fact, she seemed kind of proud of me. Ladies and gentlemen, I think this may have been my first sweet taste of justice. I did the wrong thing for the right reasons and maybe that's what retrograde really is.

This scene plays with the style of a sporting event with an announcer in ways that did not literally happen, but that augment the dramatic moments of the fight—in what almost feels to me like a good dream. The reality of what happened and the staging of this particular scene come together to show a very early moment in a young White girl's life when she acts in not-nice/not-good-girl ways to go after a bully. What is most noticeable to me when watching a recording of the scene are the outrageously varied emotions, volumes, tones, and body movements that help convey meaning throughout. This interruption to the White good girl trope also creates some foreshadowing of adult willingness to seek discomfort in spite of the costs.

The performance itself, and the voicing of a single actor across many roles, illustrates, too, the marked nature of these actions (with an announcer more likely to be part of a boxing match between two adults)—illustrating, too, that an understanding of these words requires analysis beyond language and subjects that are both seen and heard.

Table 5.1 Snapshot of dimensions of visual/aural/gestural analysis of marked subject-as-seen/subject-as-heard at start of "Fighting" scene (adapted from Blackledge and Creese 2017)

Role(s) All Played by Ellen Skilton	Staging	Verbal Action	Gesture/Other Forms of Action	Tone/Volume
Announcer	Standing on boxes	Announcing fight on Red Dog Hill	Using microphone, arms above head. Arm out toward eye chart	Formal, like TV announcer at sporting event
Sue as child	Off to one side for interview with announcer	Says hello to audience	Moves body toward audience (coy)	Speaks in a sultry tone
Ellen as child	Off to one side for interview with announcer	Says hi to audience	Moves body away from audience (shy)	Speaks with a questioning tone (rising intonation)

Conclusion

The final scene of the show is called "Coda," and comes after what feels like a triumphant ending where I'm running around the room to the theme of *Rocky*. I address the audience directly in what feels more like the familiar genre of an academic talk.

> **Excerpt 5.3** "Coda," *Reality in Retrograde*
>
> Earlier this summer, I participated in a workshop with the *Center for Performance and Civic Practice*. On the final day, we were asked about how we might take this work into the world to use the arts and performance in and with communities to build connection and change. We were asked to dramatize our answer and others could join us to respond. I laid down on the floor in a fetal position. Another participant came out into the circle and encouraged me to get up: "Just take one step," he said. And I said, "But I don't know if it's the right step and the problems of the world seem so big and intractable." He continued, "Just take a step. If it's the wrong one, you can take another step. The system wants you to stay immobilized. Just take a step." Whoa. The system wants me to stay immobilized. Wants me not to see. Wants me not to fight. Wants me to remain comfortable in my privilege, in my good-girl orbit. To pretend that things are fine . . .
>
> When Donald Trump said that both sides were responsible for the conflict between White supremacists and counter-protesters in Charlottesville, I wanted to lie on the floor again. But this time, the talking heads saw it, even Miss Texas saw it, didn't pretend. The ugly, racist system was too visible to ignore. The emperor had no clothes and we didn't act like he did. And even though it is terrifying to see the truth in the light of day, it was also a relief to be awake with so many others. No more pretending. No more standing alone. Just one step together and then another.

As I analyze my show now—as a part of a "White woman's journey"—my ability to see what is visible but that we pretend is not true (e.g., the opportunity gap, the White supremacist structures of society, etc.) feels particularly important. In fact, practicing the discomfort of naming it and making mistakes is one of the key suggestions DiAngelo makes for White people seeking equity and justice—noting that one participant of color said White people beginning to hear feedback with grace would be "revolutionary" (Biewen and Kumanyika 2017). Trechter and Bucholtz's (2001) discuss the fact that making Whiteness visible is not enough. I agree.

What the analyses in this chapter show, however, are that utilizing embodied movement and action in a theatrical performance can create opportunities for practicing for reality, for practicing the discomfort of shining the light on Whiteness and then working to take action to interrogate it and create change. The theoretical frames from linguistics utilized in this chapter provide a starting point for making visible both Whiteness itself and how to dismantle some of its power.

Note

1 This group of ten included White, African-American, Asian-American and Latinx participants: nine women and one man.

References

Alim, H. S., J. R. Rickford, and A. Ball (2016), *Raciolinguistics: How Language Shapes Our Ideas About Race*, Oxford: Oxford University Press.

Biewen, J., and C. Kumanyika (2017), *Seeing White* Podcast. Scene on Radio, Duke University Center for Documentary Studies. http://www.sceneonradio.org/seeing-white/

Blackledge, A., and A. Creese (2017), "Translanguaging and the Body," *International Journal of Multilingualism*, 14(3): 250–68.

Branscombe, M., and J. J. Schneider (2013), "Embodied Discourse: Using Tableau to Explore Preservice Teachers' Reflections and Activist Stances," *Journal of Language and Literacy Education*, 9(1): 95–113.

Cahnmann-Taylor, M., and M. Souto-Manning (2010), *Teachers Act Up! Creating multicultural learning communities through theatre*, New York and London: Teachers College Press.

Campbell-Galman, S. (2019), "Nice work: Young White Women, Near Enemies and Teaching Inside the Magic Circle," in A. E. Castagno (ed.), *The Price of Nice: How Good Intentions Maintain Educational Inequity*, pp. 70–90, Minneapolis: University of Minnesota Press.

Castagno, A. E. (ed.) (2019), *The Price of Nice: How Good Intentions Maintain Educational Inequity*, Minneapolis: University of Minnesota Press.

Chomsky, N. (1965), *Aspects of the Theory of Syntax*, Cambridge MA: MIT Press.

Crump, A. (2014), "Introducing LangCrit: Critical Language and Race Theory," *Critical Inquiry in Language Studies*, 11(3): 207–24.

DiAngelo, R. (2018), *White Fragility: Why It's So Hard for White People to Talk about Racism*, Boston MA: Beacon Press.

Dias, A. (2018), "Decolonizing 'Diversity' on Campus Using Applied Improvisation," in T. R. Dudeck and C. McClure (eds.), *Applied Improvisation: Leading, Creating and Collaborating Beyond the Theatre*, pp. 221–44, London: Bloomsbury.

Duncan, L., and N. White (2018), "Interrupting Racism through Movement and Story," *Friends General Conference*, Toledo OH.

Freeman, R. D. (1996), "Dual-language Planning at Oyster Bilingual School: It's Much More Than Language," *TESOL Quarterly*, 30: 557–82.

Friedrich, P. (2019), *Applied Linguistics in the Real World*, New York: Routledge.

Heller, M., S. Pietikainen, and J. Pujolar (2017), *Critical Sociolinguistic Research Methods: Studying Language Issues that Matter*, New York: Routledge.

Osipovich, D. (2006), "What is Theatrical Performance?", *The Journal of Aesthetics and Art Criticism*, 64(4): 461–70.

Pollack, M. (2017), *SchoolTalk: Rethinking What We Say About—And To—Students Every Day*, New York: The New Press.

Rohd, M. (2011, May), "Civic Theater," *Howlround: Theatre Commons.* https://howlround.com/civic-theater.

Rosa, J. (2019), *Looking Like a Language, Sounding Like a Race: Raciolinguistic Ideologies and the Learning of Latinidad*, Oxford: Oxford University Press.

Skilton, E. (2017), *Reality in Retrograde*, Philadelphia Fringe Festival, Philadelphia PA.

Skilton-Sylvester, E. (2011), "Continuing the Continua: Why Content Matters in Biliterate Citizenship Education," in F. M. Hult and K. A. King (eds.), *Educational Linguistics in Practice: Applying the Local Globally and the Global Locally*, pp. 68–79, Clevedon: Multilingual Matters.

Trechter, S., and M. Bucholtz (2001), "White Noise: Bringing Language into Whiteness Studies," *Journal of Linguistic Anthropology*, 11(1): 3–21.

6

Language as a Social Determinant of Health: Partnerships for Health Equity

Emily M. Feuerherm, Rachel E. Showstack, Maricel G. Santos, Glenn A. Martínez, and Holly E. Jacobson

Introduction

The idea that good health starts with good individual choices is a widely accepted assumption. While this emphasis on individual choices—such as the choice to eat well, exercise, not smoke, or follow screening guidelines—may not seem controversial, it fails to account for the broader social, economic, and physical environmental conditions that may influence our health. In other words, where we are born, live, work, go to school, or raise our families can make a significant difference in our health outcomes, quality of life, access to healthcare resources, risk for disease, and even our sense of safety. In US public health and in social and behavioral sciences more generally, these social and physical conditions are referred to as "social determinants of health" (Irwin and Scali 2007). Research indicates that individuals and communities living even a few miles from one another can experience vastly different health outcomes, with minoritized communities[1] disproportionately affected (Chetty et al. 2018).

The populations we focus on in our research experience serious *health disparities*, or unfair differences in health outcomes that can be traced to a history of social and linguistic segregation, discrimination, and weak investment in the neighborhoods where they live. Social conditions that are associated with negative health outcomes for individuals are often accompanied by other coexisting conditions and multiple illnesses; patients who encounter language difficulties in healthcare contexts may also experience socioeconomic disparities and participate in diverse cultural practices related to health and illness to which their healthcare providers may not know how to respond (Briggs and Mantini-Briggs 2016; Martínez 2018; Singer et al. 2006). In response, the US public health system has prioritized the advancement of *health equity*, which encapsulates the ideal that "everyone has the opportunity to attain their highest level of health" (American Public Health Association, or APHA). In this chapter, we highlight our efforts to respond to the call of APHA Executive Director Georges Benjamin: "Health equity is a goal we can achieve, and it's within our power to do so. *We have the tools and the knowledge to make health equity happen, but it's up to all of us to use them*" (our emphasis). What "tools and knowledge" can we, as applied linguists and language educators, harness to advance health equity in our local communities? We address this question through a discussion of three partnerships:

- Feuerherm describes her work with community partners to develop a community-based English as a second language (ESL) health literacy program in response to the Flint water crisis.
- Showstack and Martínez describe the process of developing a patient-centered outcomes project to address the language barriers that limit Spanish-speaking patients' access to quality healthcare.
- Santos describes a health literacy partnership that aims to position ESL learners as critical interpreters of public health messages.

By exploring the intersections between language and health, we demonstrate the potential of interdisciplinary research with partners in the classroom, the community, and the clinic.

Partnerships between applied linguistics and public health: Domains of intersections

Language and health is an interdisciplinary line of inquiry between the fields of applied linguistics, public health, nursing, linguistic anthropology, and communication studies, among others. Researchers from these disciplines alongside language educators, healthcare providers, language minority patients, and interpreters should (and do) develop interdisciplinary ties to optimize their potential to impact individuals, communities, and health outcomes. This chapter begins by theorizing the domains and intersections of partnerships between applied linguists and those working on public health challenges from a variety of disciplinary perspectives and areas of expertise. We begin with a metaphor to explain *why* such partnerships are valuable:

> Next fall, when you see geese heading south for the winter, flying along in V formation, you might consider what science has discovered as to why they fly

that way: As each bird flaps its wings, it creates an uplift for the bird immediately following. By flying in V formation the whole flock adds at least 71% greater flying range than if each bird flew on its own.

People who share a common direction and sense of community can get where they are going more quickly and easily because they are traveling on the thrust of one another.

Stoecker 2005: 24

Stoecker's (2005) "goose metaphor" helps us characterize the promise of community-based partnerships between applied linguistics and public health, two fields acutely familiar with the challenges of meeting the complex needs of socially disadvantaged language minoritized communities. When our flocks work together, we can do better to define and overcome barriers to health equity. By building a shared set of flight patterns with public health and minoritized communities, we expand our capacity and sphere of influence as applied linguists.

The value of partnerships between applied linguistics and public health is being recognized at national policy levels (e.g., National Action Plan for Health Literacy). Language policies that intersect with issues related to health equity are a robust space for research and action. Approaches such as conversation analysis, discourse analysis, and critical discourse analysis can all be useful to examine the processes of positioning and negotiation that occur in health interactions (Jacobson 2009; Raymond 2014). Work that addresses diverse practices of communication about health and illness within different types of healthcare and community settings is needed to understand the types of communicative disjuncture that can occur (Guzman 2014; Harvey 2008). Also critical are analyses of intercultural pragmatics, specifically the study of communicative practices in healthcare contexts which can provide valuable insights into a range of cultural misunderstandings and negotiations of meaning between diverse cultural groups (Cohen 2012). This work can also provide valuable material for educational programs, especially for interpreters and providers, that address intercultural communication. In addition, rigorous interdisciplinary research in translation and interpreting testing and assessment is needed to assure quality of services provided to patients and healthcare providers (Angelelli and Jacobson 2009). This research can inform the policies and practices in the field of public health, leading to more equitable healthcare practices.

Figure 6.1 outlines intersections of language and health across various domains. It identifies where partnerships between applied linguists and health professionals might contribute to improving health outcomes for individuals historically left on the margins of healthcare access. On the left, the diagram shows the macro, meso,

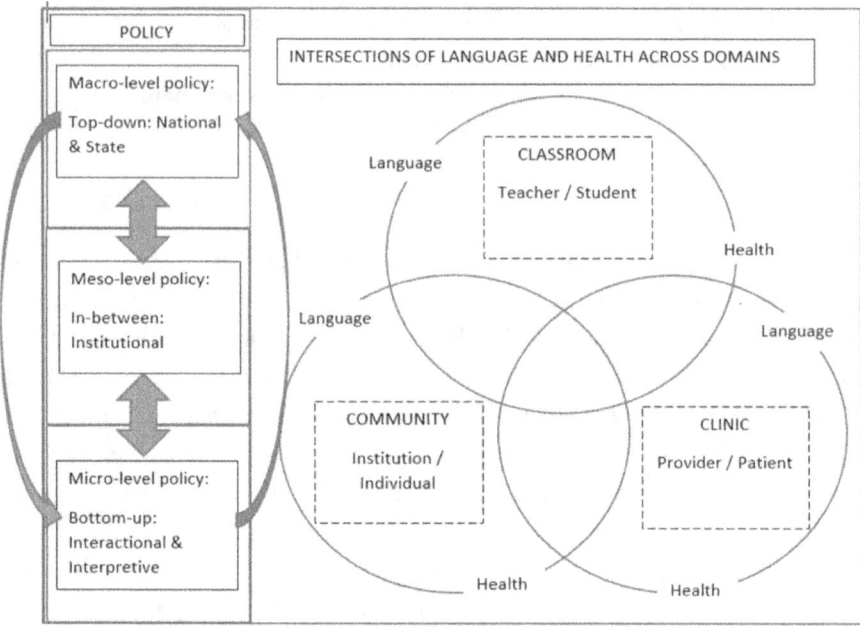

Figure 6.1 Intersections of language and health across domains

and micro levels of policy with bidirectional arrows to indicate the influence that each level has on the other. The arrows are bidirectional to indicate both the top-down and bottom-up nature of health policy interactions. On the right of the diagram, the three circles represent the overlapping and intersecting nature of language and health across the classroom, community, and clinic.

This framework allows us to explore the various domains in which linguistic marginalization undermines meaningful access to health services and health information (cf., Nielsen-Bohlman et al. 2004). It also helps us identify lines of research on the relationship between linguistic differences and health disparities, which remains largely under-theorized and under-researched (Sentell and Braun 2012).

Exploring intersections with the community domain: Responding to a public health crisis

Applied linguists extend innovations in health science to culturally and linguistically diverse communities by building partnerships to involve those communities in public health research. *Translational research* seeks to identify and implement the best strategies for the adoption of evidence-based interventions in community settings (Madon et al. 2007; McNulty et al. 2019; Rubio et al. 2010). To determine how language practices function in specific communities, there is a need to include community voices in the conversation. This "emic" (or insider) perspective on language access has the potential of opening up new areas of inquiry that intersect with applied linguistic interests in areas such as translation and interpreting, second language studies, and language ideologies. Community-centered approaches can make a significant contribution to determining future directions for research on language barriers and health equity, and funding for these types of research projects has increased at the national level (Tendulkar et al. 2011). Applied linguists can draw on their expertise to engage the voices of linguistically minoritized patients and their communities in translational research and implementation science (cf., Showstack, 2019).

Feuerherm's research in Flint, Michigan, provides an example of a partnership for such impactful translational research in the wake of a public health crisis. Flint, Michigan, made international headlines in January 2016, when President Obama declared a state of emergency for the city because of toxic levels of lead in the drinking water system. Despite international attention to this public health crisis, information was only distributed in English and efforts to spread information and bottled water were hampered by a lack of linguistic and cultural sensitivity. According to the US Census, the percentage of Flint residents who do not speak English in the home is 3.6 percent out of a total population in the city of about 102,434 (Quick facts Flint, MI, 2010). The most common immigrant language in the city is Spanish, although Arabic, American Sign Language (ASL), and other languages can also be found. During the crisis, grassroots organizations—new and old—stepped in to advocate for minoritized language speakers and translate or interpret information for widespread distribution. Representatives from these organizations traveled to Michigan's state capital, Lansing, and Washington DC to advocate for relief funding and policies to protect communities from lead exposure. The repercussions continue to be felt, and the role of grassroots organizations continues to be essential in continuing to address the life-long symptoms of lead poisoning as the (inter)national focus on Flint has dwindled.

Research in Flint following the water crisis has shown that residents are untrusting of national and state government representatives, the Environmental Protection Agency and the Department of Environmental Quality (Carrera et al. 2019). They also feel resentment toward local higher educational institutions

(University of Michigan, Michigan State University, and Kettering University) because they felt people there knew about the crisis but were late to address it. However, community nonprofit and faith-based institutions consistently received high levels of trust. For academics and policymakers who wanted to address the effects of the water crisis, partnering with local organizations provided a means to support community public health.

In order to address this public health crisis, Feuerherm partnered with two community organizations and organized a community advisory board for a health literacy program called Health and English as a second language Literacy Program (HELP) to prevent lead exposure. Feuerherm and the two community partners, Genesee County Hispanic Latino Collaborative (or *La Placita* as it's known locally) and Attentive Committed Expertise (ACE) Community Health provided complementary expertise to the program:

- Feuerherm offered expertise in language teaching and pedagogy, along with university resources and grant funding for the partnering organizations. Grants included the Michigan Institute of Clinical Health Research (NIH)[2] and Flint Truth and Action Partnership Project grants (from the Kellogg Foundation).[3]
- *La Placita* provided expertise in community organizing, translation, and interpreting, and deep local knowledge of the lives and experiences of the target participants.
- ACE Community Health provided expertise in community-based research for health.

Feuerherm's relationship with *La Placita* began when the organization gained its 501c3 nonprofit status in January of 2016 and she has served as the Board of Directors Secretary since its establishment. In 2016–17, Feuerherm and *La Placita* collaborated in surveying and holding focus groups with Latino residents in English and Spanish about their needs and experiences (Feuerherm and Oshio 2020). The results showed that Latino residents needed more ESL instruction, more information on and access to safe drinking water, and more health resources for those with lead exposure. In direct response to this need, Feuerherm and *La Placita* began working on HELP, a program that would use a translingual approach[4] to support Latino participants' English and health knowledge. Then, in October 2017, Feuerherm met the president of ACE Community Health, Bonnie McIntosh, a public health researcher and consultant. Together, they reviewed the health literacy project and outlined the gaps that ACE Community Health could fill in order to increase the impact of the research. ACE Community Health contributed by writing grants, navigating the clinical trial processes, and building the digital tools to support community-based research (e.g., a website and social media campaign).

In addition to the partners listed above, a community advisory board was established with local stakeholders from other Latino organizations and representatives from the fields of health and education. The advisory board recruits participants, advises on the health and cultural components of the curriculum, and disseminates information back out to stakeholders in the community. The first meeting of the advisory board was held in February 2020 and the ESL health literacy program will begin as soon as is safely possible under the coronavirus pandemic.

Although the relationships between each of these partners has remained strong since their establishment, there have been several sets of challenges that have tested that strength. The primary issue has been that university processes slowed the collaboration's response to an urgent community issue. It has taken nearly three years for this project to come to bear because of lengthy funding applications with slow turnaround, institutional review board (IRB) approval, and other organizational structures for a clinical trial,[5] and now restrictions on in-person research because of the coronavirus. At each stage the process took longer than expected, partly because of the university's increased rigor and oversight when working with multiple community partners (ensuring no conflicts of interest) and a particularly vulnerable population (undocumented immigrants). Because of the delays, one of the partners was nearly unable to participate: *La Placita* had run out of grant funding for their work and both of the staff members left for other positions (causing another delay). Luckily, *La Placita's* President, San Juana Olivares, returned after only a couple of months away, and because the grant funding for this project was finally accessible, she was able to pick up where she left off. The setbacks to timely implementation of this project demonstrate the issue described by Carrera et al. (2019)—that academic institutions are slow to respond to the needs of their community. During these three years, community members have been asking *La Placita* for the program's start date and are eager for it to begin. We had to delay our start (scheduled for mid March 2020) because of the coronavirus pandemic, Michigan's stay-at-home order, and the university's restrictions on face-to-face research. With this new delay, we are exploring all options for alternative modalities and other forms of support.

Despite the difficulties, each group has benefited from these relationships. The funding included compensation for the President of *La Placita* to become a certified medical interpreter for Spanish. Local hospitals require certification, which can be acquired from a couple local training programs offered through universities. The grant funding compensated for her time and paid for the certification training. Additionally, this meets a need expressed by local hospitals and free clinics for more local interpreters while simultaneously increasing financial support for *La Placita*.

ACE Community Health and the academic partner have benefited from the support of graduate research assistants who have contributed their knowledge of social media, technology, and Spanish to produce additional means of dissemination for the project, thus increasing its potential impact. This includes development of a website and YouTube videos in English and Spanish, plus a Facebook and Twitter page in English for the community advisory board.

The community advisory board brings additional recruitment support by distributing HELP's recruitment flyers to their clients. The advisory board also shares information with HELP about community resources for Spanish-speaking residents such as local free clinics, food pantries, and other opportunities to improve health outcomes. At the same time, *La Placita*, Ace Community Health, and Feuerherm can use their resources to advocate for better representation of Latino residents' needs and experiences in community policies, services, and outreach by informing the advisory board members when HELP participants experience barriers to their services, such as being asked for identification when attempting to access a food pantry or free clinic.

The effectiveness of any language-assistance policy arguably depends on an expanded, strengths-based appraisal of the rich linguistic repertoire that minoritized patients bring to healthcare interactions (Santos, Jacobson, and Manneh 2017). For HELP this means developing the program with input from all stakeholders, teaching using a translingual pedagogy, and making all of HELP's health resources available in English and Spanish. Federal, state, local, and institutional language policies, and the implementation of such policies, play an important role in access to quality healthcare for minoritized patients. Partnerships across several sectors of a community cause ripple effects for patients who can find new advocates in healthcare, education, and nonprofit organizations.

Exploring intersections with the clinical domain: Building trust between patients and healthcare providers

In the clinical setting, interdisciplinary research collaborations between applied linguists and public health researchers offer ways to explore how a patient's language interacts with their health and healthcare, as well as other aspects of their life and background, to lead to particular health outcomes. Wide-ranging studies on language concordance (LC) have uncovered that a shared language shapes healthcare encounters on multiple levels. LC providers ask more questions and are less concerned about medical malpractice complaints than providers who work through an interpreter. Patients with LC providers, moreover, display greater trust, show more agreement, and are more likely to follow doctor recommendations, although research has shown that this depends on clinician proficiency (cf., Lion et al. 2012; Diamond et al. 2012). Patients with type 2 diabetes, for instance, have been found to have better health outcomes, including glycemic control and medication adherence, when their provider speaks their language (Traylor et al. 2010; Fernandez et al. 2011; Parker et al. 2017).

Another aspect of communication in healthcare contexts that has been examined is the role of healthcare interpreters in the doctor-patient-interpreter triad (Angelelli 2004; Dysart-Gale 2005, 2007; Hsieh 2006, 2009; Showstack, 2020); ethical guidelines stipulate that interpreters serve as patient advocates, clarifiers, and cultural brokers, but understandings of these roles often vary, and development and validation of the guidelines often fail to take into account patient preferences and perspectives (Angelelli 2004). Although the use of ad hoc interpreters, such as a patient's family member or the administrative staff at a hospital, remains common in many facilities (e.g., see Benda et al. 2019), this practice has been associated with clinically significant errors in communication and reduced health outcomes for patients with limited proficiency in the dominant language (Flores et al. 2012). Applied linguists can help to illuminate and address these issues of healthcare and inequity by engaging in research on language policy in healthcare contexts, such as requirements for interpreter competency, policies for reimbursement of healthcare facilities for the use of interpreters, and the implementation of such policies (e.g., Showstack et al. 2019; Youdelman 2017). In addition, it is important to examine the nature of nonprofessional interpreting practices and the experiences and perceptions of nonprofessional interpreters, especially child language brokers, children who interpret for family members and often provide mediation between the healthcare system, the broader community, and their families (Green et al. 2005; Katz 2014; Reynolds and Orellana 2015). Explorations of these communication issues, however, must move beyond the prescriptive, top-down formulation of standards of practice driven exclusively by healthcare providers and interpreters that have prevailed in the literature. Instead, we must bring in multiple voices including those of patients who need language assistance and their caregivers, and other stakeholders in the healthcare delivery system.

To bring the voices of multiple stakeholders into the conversation on language access, Martínez and Showstack are engaged in a translational research project in Ohio and Kansas. They are collaborating with Spanish-speaking patients and their family members, healthcare interpreters and interpreter service provider agencies, and bilingual clinicians to address the language barriers that limit access to quality healthcare in Latino communities in the US. Spanish-speaking patients obtain language access to the health delivery system through multiple modalities. Communication is facilitated through bilingual healthcare providers, face-to-face and remote healthcare interpreters, bilingual caregivers, and family networks. While quantitative research has compared the accuracy of remote and face-to-face modalities, Martínez identified a need for a comprehensive approach to determine how to provide the most appropriate language access services in specific contexts for specific patients and their families.

Initially, the collaborations in Ohio and Kansas developed separately. In Wichita, Kansas, safety-net clinics reached out to Showstack, who was the coordinator of a Spanish for the Professions program at her university, to request volunteer student interpreters for patient–physician encounters. Knowing that it was not ideal for students with limited training to serve as interpreters in healthcare contexts, Showstack began to develop a program of teaching and research to improve language access for Spanish speakers in the region and developed collaborations with health professions faculty. She created a healthcare-themed advanced Spanish language course, invited volunteer interpreters and medical students to visit her class to simulate interpreting scenarios for her students, coordinated with the school of nursing to facilitate interprofessional interpreter-meditated patient care simulations that her students and the nursing students participated in together, and offered lectures on working with interpreters for groups of students in various health professions. When she sent selected students to interpret at the safety-net clinic to meet a service-learning requirement for her course, she conducted case studies on the students' experiences, illuminating significant ethical questions about the role of the healthcare interpreter (Showstack 2020). Simultaneously, she collaborated with colleagues from the Department of Public Health Sciences to investigate Kansas's language access policies and provide recommendations for improvement (Showstack et al. 2019).

Meanwhile, in Columbus, Ohio, Martínez obtained a "Pipeline to Proposal" award from the Patient-Centered Outcomes Research Institute (PCORI) to build capacity for patient-centered research on language access for patients with type 2 diabetes. Patient-Centered Outcomes Research (PCOR) is a translational approach to public health research that involves patients, patients' family members, healthcare providers, and other stakeholders in determining which aspects of healthcare should be investigated and how a research project should be designed, and in conducting the research and analyzing the findings (e.g., Martínez 2018). PCOR is structured in various phases, starting with capacity building and stakeholder engagement, followed by a research project with quantitative comparisons (e.g., a comparison of the effectiveness of different interventions in healthcare). The diabetes project (A Tu LADO: Language Access in Diabetes for Ohio) allowed for the formation of an initial group of stakeholders (primarily patients and caregivers) based in Columbus, and the development of an approach to stakeholder engagement.

In 2018, Showstack and her colleagues joined forces with the Ohio team, and together they obtained an engagement award from PCORI. In the current stakeholder engagement phase, Showstack, Martínez, and their collaborators in the health professions have engaged bilingual healthcare providers, healthcare interpreters, patients, and caregivers in order to explore the challenges and opportunities for improving healthcare among Spanish-speaking patients. Facilitated in the Spanish language by applied linguists, stakeholder meetings are structured to encourage the sharing of stories and perspectives among patients and caregivers, and to coordinate contributions in a way that respects all perspectives. The process of "systematic perspective sharing" includes a bid to share stories, elicitation of successes and challenges, a bid to reflect on stories, and the identification of factors contributing to successes and challenges. In these meetings, sensitivity to stories elevates narrative as the most salient discourse type in patient and caregiver engagement. Patients' stories of their experiences with an illness or the illness of a loved one were intertwined with experiences of (mis)communication with, and (dis)trust of, healthcare providers and interpreters. After each stakeholder meeting, a team of language researchers reflected on salient themes and stories that needed to be shared more broadly, such as interpersonal communication with audio and video remote interpreting (a salient theme in Ohio) and the medical errors and the psychological effects resulting from situations in which facilities did not offer a professional interpreter at all (a major topic in Kansas). The patients' experiences allowed the language researcher team to identify areas that needed to be further investigated and addressed through action.

Applied linguists have held key leadership roles throughout the different phases of the project. Martínez was the project initiator, principal investigator, and grant writer. The language researcher team (which included Spanish professors from Ohio, Kansas, Texas, and California) prepared themes and questions for stakeholder discussions, and facilitated those discussions, taking care to ensure that all voices were recognized and heard. In one case, a linguist shared her own experience with caring for a family member who encountered language and cultural barriers in healthcare. Recognizing that applied linguists comprehend aspects of communication that may not be understood by healthcare providers and public health researchers, one of the objectives of the language researcher team was to engage more applied linguists in patient-centered research.

Although moving forward from the project pipeline through patient engagement and toward the development of a research project can be described in a linear fashion, the process of engaging stakeholders in Ohio presented some challenges, which prompted a reformulation of the engagement format to a less linear model. Initially, patients and caregivers viewed themselves as "subjects" of research rather than as "agents" of research, and there was a need to support the development of their researcher identity. This was achieved through a two-step process that included active listening and participatory reimagining. We began each meeting by providing participants a platform to discuss key focal topics related to language access. We allowed participants to talk uninterrupted and then posed questions about the experiences narrated. In subsequent sessions, we shared our own stories and encouraged participants to pose questions about our experiences. Over time, participants became accustomed to the format of narration followed by critical questioning. This was a first step in the development of researcher identity. A second step emerged when we were trying to divide the group in a series of subcommittees that included evidence gathering, question formation, study design, and dissemination. In defining and describing these various subcommittees, participants began to relate these activities to their own cultural mores and to reimagine themselves in these roles. For example, the evidence-gathering group referred to themselves as "los metiches" or the nosy group; the question-formation group referred to themselves as "los preguntones" or the questioners; the dissemination group referred to themselves as "los chismosos" or the gossipers. In these ways, participants began to develop researcher identities by engaging in sustained critical practice and by relating critical practice to known cultural identifiers. In addition to the need to develop a researcher identity, we also discovered a need to adopt a braided engagement strategy that simultaneously addressed both the long-term research goals of the group as well as the more immediate needs that emerged in conversation. For example, through our conversations we found that patients and caregivers desired a space to share their concerns and struggles in managing type 2 diabetes, greater knowledge of good eating habits, and practical strategies to promote physical activity. Our braided engagement approach integrated research engagement with these challenges and concerns, and resulted in the formation of a diabetes support group, the development of healthy eating classes, and what we called "mobile" meetings—where instead of meeting in a fixed location sitting around a table we met in the park and walked and talked together.

Throughout the project, each group of collaborators benefited in different ways. Benefits to the patients included stipends and meals, an opportunity to share their perspective with providers, administrators, and policymakers and have a voice in how the project's response to language barriers is structured, and an opportunity to learn about the structure of the healthcare system. The braided engagement approach also allowed patients to benefit from activities dedicated to improving their own health and the health of their families.

Healthcare providers benefited from learning about patients' experiences. They learned how to best address patient and caregiver needs and developed a deeper understanding of the context of their own experiences providing healthcare to Spanish speakers. As applied linguists, we benefited by experiencing a feeling of satisfaction from the sense that the team was drawing on our expertise in linguistics to make a difference in their lives and their professional practice. In addition, we obtained greater social capital in our communities and publication opportunities. Finally, for those whose university adopts the UniSCOPE system for evaluating scholarship, community engagement is also valued for tenure process (Hyman et al. 2001). The researchers hope that the healthcare system will benefit by developing more effective and efficient processes for providing language access, and ultimately, improved health outcomes for speakers of minoritized languages.

Exploring intersections in the classroom domain: "Re-storying" public health messages in ESL classrooms

For Santos, interdisciplinary partnerships with public health partners and local ESL programs have provided a platform for interrogating local gaps in health equity. Two core assumptions lie at the heart of this interdisciplinary work. First, collaborations that work directly at the point of contact with immigrants are critical for building capacity, improving communication and comprehension in healthcare, and advancing health equity in under-resourced immigrant communities. Second, the adult ESL classroom is an ideal space for health literacy interventions that harness immigrant learners' own interpretations of health data which can then be translated into improved health messaging—for both patient-focused care and community health.

When people think about "health research data," images of numbers and dense hard-to-decipher jargon often come to mind. Many immigrant and refugee adults struggle to sync existing public health messages with their own understandings of the healthcare system and their everyday healthcare stories (Handley, Santos, and McClelland 2009). Rarely are they given tools to draw connections between evidence of how social determinants of health impact the health of their communities and lead to widening health disparities (Ferrer 2019). These disconnects have serious health consequences for US immigrant and refugee adults with low basic skills, who, according to recent international survey data, are four times more likely to report poorer health than adults with stronger literacy skills (OECD 2013).

The role of ESL learners in participatory research has not received attention proportional to the growing concerns about the links between low literacy and poor health outcomes and the urgency around chronic disease prevention and management to achieve population health goals. This gap in immigrant learner engagement persists despite the fact that adult ESL learners comprise about 40 percent of the nation's adult basic skills population in federally-funded programs (U.S. Department of Education, Office of Career, Technical, and Adult Education 2016).

How can the adult ESL classroom provide a meaningful context for empowering learners to access research about health problems affecting their own communities, and affirm their role as viable partners in health disparities research and outreach efforts? To many academics and researchers, it may be difficult to imagine adult ESL learners as appropriate research partners, particularly if they lack formal research training, have limited literacy skills, or little schooling. Over the past twelve years, Santos has collaborated with Margaret Handley, a public health epidemiologist, and several adult ESL teacher partners in the Bay Area of Northern California to interrogate this logic: What are the benefits of including adult ESL learners as "expert interpreters" in the process of translating health research into information their own communities can understand?

Santos, Handley, and a network of adult ESL teachers have developed a participatory research approach—the "learners as interpreters" model (Handley et al. 2009; Santos et al. 2011)—which aims to transform the way immigrant learners access, adapt, and question health information, and use the information to alter their own health actions. The "learners as interpreters" model initially grew out of an adult ESL curriculum project on prevention of lead poisoning associated with contaminated foods from Mexico. In 2008 and 2009, with intramural funding from San Francisco State University, Santos and Handley teamed up with Jeff McClelland, an adult ESL teacher based at an Oakland-based family literacy program, to create curricular materials that integrated English teaching/learning with critical interpretations of lead information (e.g., toxicity statistics on the learners' own communities and excerpts of focus group data with Mexican immigrants that members of our team previously collected to investigate risk factors).

The team's focus on lead contamination was significant because of an ongoing lead problem in California, for which food sources of lead feature prominently. Of particular concern for transnational Latino communities were findings that show elevated lead concentrations in some foods that are regularly sent from Mexico to California, including toasted seeds, herbs, or grasshopper snacks called *chapulines* (Handley et al. 2007). Handley's prior research indicated that these lead risks needed to be presented within the positive cultural connectedness made possible by the transnational flow of goods, not merely as a threat to public safety. A community strengths-based approach would convey a respect for cultural practices around food and support immigrants in their efforts to stay connected to their communities of origin (Handley and Grieshop 2007). Together, Handley, Santos, and adult ESL teachers began exploring how ESL learners' own interpretations of these known lead risks could spark new, more resonant environmental health messaging.

Drawing on critical reading frameworks (Ada 1988; Wallace 2006; Wallerstein 1983), this collaborative team developed a series of pedagogical tasks and activities that gave learners multiple opportunities to "re-story" the public health messages about lead risk found on official brochures and posters (also see Fiddian-Green et al. 2019). Dialogic reading protocols (Ada 1991; Beck and McKeown 2006) and role-plays cultivated a culture of critical questioning in the classrooms. Lessons on question formation in English (e.g., *What is a poison? Who likes chapulines? Who sells chapulines? Why do we talk about Mexico only?*) were more than just contextualized grammar instruction: in addition, the lessons also reinforced the act of questioning in healthcare as a "public, literate act" (Peck et al. 1995) that validated the learners' right to question whose worldview is allowed to shape public health recommendations, and perhaps more profoundly, to affirm their own contributions to the public deliberation of risk messaging.

This work demonstrated that the learners' interpretations could educate the public health profession about the kinds of lead poisoning messaging that could help learners preserve transnational food identities, while reducing health risks. The learners' sharing of the "re-storying" activities beyond the classroom (with co-workers and family members back in Mexico) also helped to validate the learners as a powerful link in environmental health information dissemination networks (cf., Briggs 2003). Since 2008, Santos and Handley have continued to develop the model with a diverse network of ESL partners, with a focus on a range of healthcare issues, such as family nutrition, type 2 diabetes, including gestational diabetes, stress, and chronic depression. This "re-storying" work enabled the teachers to develop their own collections of critical reading activities suitable for beginning-level learners, and more powerfully, new stories that learners are motivated to share with others in their local communities.

Thus far, documenting the impact of the "learners as interpreters" model has largely relied on classroom observation, learner self-report, and ongoing reflective conversations as an interdisciplinary team. However, for community-engaged models to gain traction in the broader scientific community, we need to be able to combine the professional wisdom of interdisciplinary partners with meaningful empirical evidence. Widely used measures that narrowly define health literacy, such as using a word-pronunciation task like the Rapid Estimate of Adult Literacy in Medicine (REALM) or a cloze passage with the Test of Functional Health Literacy for Adults (TOFHLA), are insufficient for capturing changes in engagement with health information in populations with low literacy or limited schooling. Santos and Handley's work in the adult ESL classroom has pointed to the urgent need for the health literacy world to develop measures that reflect meaningful changes at the classroom level and community level, such as *collective efficacy* (Hohn and Rivera 2019), expansion of *social networks*, increased access to *social support*, and changes in role, from adult learner to community advocate (Sarkar et al. 2019).

Since 2008, Santos and Handley have secured funding periodically to support their work on the "learners as interpreters" model, from intramural grant programs at their respective universities, as well as extramural funds from The Public Trust Fund[6] and the National Institutes of Health.[7] Notably, adult ESL teachers have chosen to work with Santos and Handley because of a shared commitment to health equity and community engagement, not in response to a funding requirement. The curricular work on learner empowerment, "re-storying," and social action reflect what the adult ESL teachers already do on a regular basis. At the same time, the ability to provide teacher honoraria, gift cards for the learners, classroom supplies, and food cannot be underestimated: these small gestures enable Santos and Handley to publicly acknowledge the contributions that teachers and learners make to the health literacy field.

Santos can trace the roots of her interdisciplinary partnership with Handley to a serendipitous meeting at a 2006 immigrant health conference in Berkeley, California: Handley introduced herself to Santos and shared her own experiences teaching French in Canada, which sparked a lively conversation about the rewards of language learning and teaching. The rest, as the saying goes, is history. What are the opportunities we have in our everyday professional lives to explore interdisciplinary connections and relationships? In other words, how, practically speaking, do adult ESL teachers and public health practitioners find each other? Closing the equity gap in healthcare requires that these connections cannot be left up to chance.

Future directions

Martínez (2020) argues for a "syndemic sensibility" when considering the relationship between language and healthcare. This sensibility accounts for the complex interactions between proficiency in the dominant language and other social factors embedded within multiple health conditions. Language researchers are uniquely positioned to highlight processes of intersubjectivity and shared experience in health communication and interaction—leading to better understanding across all stakeholders. These case studies demonstrate that minoritized communities' experiences with systems of healthcare and health information must inform our understanding of the relationship among a patient's language proficiency, disease, health disparities, and health outcomes. To return to Stoecker's (2005) "goose metaphor": we signal our positionality by "honking" at one another as we tell our stories around health and language, whether we are patients, linguists, caretakers, interpreters, or teachers. Even in times of limited resources, we derive a sense of hope that we are able to act on these syndemic sensibilities together—indeed, "flying" in a coordinated formation toward health equity. Our experiences have made us more versed in the language of public health, with new frameworks, methods, and concepts (e.g., "syndemics," "implementation science") for pursuing our interdisciplinary work.

Our role as language researchers is to help these stories become heard by policymakers and to challenge barriers to health equity. Linguists come with privileges of position to legitimize stories by amplifying them, removing the barriers of discrimination, and finding a common language. In clinical practice, the so-called "Limited English Proficiency" (LEP) marker is frequently tied to global assumptions about proficiency and deficit views of language. During patient intake processes, the default measure of English proficiency is *spoken* English proficiency, and literacy level is regarded as literacy in English (Santos et al. 2017). Applied linguists are well-poised to clarify important sociolinguistic realities in healthcare communication, specifically helping to illuminate the relationship between linguistic marginalization and health outcomes for diverse linguistic, racial, and ethnic groups. Furthermore, the multilingual turn unfolding in the field of applied linguistics invites critical reflection about a monolingual bias in public health, and ultimately, opens up new lines of thinking about the relationship between a patient's evolving linguistic repertoire (not just proficiency in spoken English) and healthcare needs over the course of one's life time (Santos et al. 2017).

As teachers we can partner with those in the healthcare field to build interdisciplinary programs or add modifications to existing programs that foreground health equity. All language educators, including but not only ESL teachers, have the capacity to address overlapping issues between language and health. It is important to provide training opportunities for students with personal investment in language and health, such as the program for high school students in Columbus, Ohio that trains Spanish heritage speakers to become medical interpreters. Similarly, educators can provide institutional support to legitimate the role of multilingual community health workers (*promotores de salud*) because there is a need for more LC providers. We also need improved training that goes beyond the notion of "cultural competence" for socially and culturally diverse patients (Fernández and Pérez-Stable 2015; Karliner et al. 2004; Koehn and Swick 2006). As applied linguists and language educators, we can develop training programs to create a workforce of competent interpreters and LC providers, and we can also develop interprofessional programs that allow providers and language professionals to learn together (Showstack et al. forthcoming).

Finally, although the case studies presented here are centered in the US context, language barriers are a significant component of health equity worldwide, and sociolinguistic phenomena may affect health outcomes in different ways in different geographical and sociopolitical contexts. Some interdisciplinary, translational, place-based research has already begun; it extends across a broad range of disciplines, professions, and geographic and sociopolitical contexts and requires a dedication to cooperation and collaboration.

We charge the reader to consider how language and health overlap in your proverbial backyard, and what capacities you have for raising awareness of language barriers. In other words, how can you advocate for health equity through your own research, teaching, writing, clinical work, translation/interpreting work, professional interactions, or other work? How can you find partners in health or applied linguistics? How will you benefit from these partnerships personally and professionally while working toward social justice and health equity for linguistically marginalized groups?

Notes

1. We use *minoritized* here, rather than *minority*, to signal the power imbalances between groups with larger and smaller numbers which contribute to the health disparities we investigate. This term is interchangeable with *marginalized*.
2. Michigan Institute of Clinical Health Research (MICHR) grant number UL1TR002240, funded by the National Institute of Health (NIH), June 2019–July 2021.
3. Flint Truth and Action Partnership Project (FTAAPP), funded by the Kellogg Foundation, July 201 –December 2020.
4. In this approach, all health information is provided in English and Spanish, through oral/aural and written modes. The classes support Spanish-language literacy alongside English literacy and learning. The approach used here recognizes all of the linguistic tools that speakers have and assesses students bilingually.
5. This is a clinical trial under the behavioral category, NCT04125680.
6. Subcontract award from LiteracyWorks, supported by the Public Health Trust Settlement Fund, October 2008–January 2010.
7. Subcontract award from the Center for Health And Risk in Minority youth and adults (CHARM) University of California, San Francisco, supported by the NIH P60 Grant (Bibbins-Domingo, PI), March 2013–March 2017.

References

Ada, A. F. (1988), "Creative Reading: A Relevant Methodology for Language Minority Children," in L. M. Malave (ed.), *NABE 87: Theory, Research and Application: Selected Papers*, pp. 97–111, Buffalo: State University of New York Press.

Angelelli, C. V. (2004), *Revisiting the Interpreter's Role: A Study of Conference, Court, and Medical Interpreters in Canada, Mexico, and the United States* (Vol. 55), Amsterdam: John Benjamins.

Angelelli, C. V., and H. E. Jacobson (2009), "Testing and Assessment in Translation and Interpreting Studies," in C. V. Angelelli and H. E. Jacobson (eds.), *Testing and Assessment in Translation and Interpreting Studies: A Call for Dialogue Between Research and Practice* (Vol. 14), pp. 1–10, Amsterdam: John Benjamins.

Beck, I., and M. McKeown (2006), *Improving Comprehension with Questioning the Author: A Fresh and Expanded View of a Powerful Approach*, New York: Scholastic.

Benda N., R. Fairbanks, D. Higginbotham, L. Lin, and A. Bisantz (2019), "An Observational Study to Understand Interpreter Service Use in Emergency Medicine—Why the Key to Improvement May Lie Outside of the Initial Provider Assessment," *Emergency Medicine Journal*, 36(10): 582–8.

Briggs, C. (2003), "Why Nation-States and Journalists Can't Teach People to be Healthy: Power and Pragmatic Miscalculation in Public Discourses on Health," *Medical Anthropology Quarterly*, 17(3): 287–321.

Briggs, C. L., and C. Mantini-Briggs (2016), *Tell Me Why My Children Died: Rabies, Indigenous Knowledge, and Communicative Justice*, Durham NC: Duke University Press.

Carrera, J., Key, K., Bailey, S., Hamm, J., Cuthbertson, C., Lewis, E., Woolford, S., et al. (2019). Community Science as a Pathway for Resilience in Response to a Public Health Crisis in Flint, Michigan. Social Sciences, 8(3), 94. MDPI AG. Retrieved from http://dx.doi.org/10.3390/socsci8030094

Chetty, R., J. N. Friedman, N. Hendren, M. R. Jones, and S. R. Porter (2018), "The Opportunity Atlas: Mapping the Childhood Roots of Social Mobility." Available online: https://www.census.gov/ces/dataproducts/opportunityatlas.html

Cohen, A. D. (2012), "Research Methods for Describing Variation in Intercultural Pragmatics for Cultures in Contact and Conflict," in J. C. Félix-Brasdefer and D. A. Koike (eds.), *Pragmatic Variation in First and Second Language Contexts*, pp. 271–94, Amsterdam: John Benjamins.

Diamond, L. C., D. S. Tuot, and L. S. Karliner (2012), "The Use of Spanish Language Skills by Physicians and Nurses: Policy Implications for Teaching and Testing," *Journal of General Internal Medicine*, 27(1): 117–23.

Dysart-Gale, D. (2005), "Communication Models, Professionalization, and the Work of Medical Interpreters," *Health Communication*, 17(1): 91–103.

Dysart-Gale, D. (2007), "Clinicians and Medical Interpreters Negotiating Culturally Appropriate Care for Patients with Limited English Ability," *Family and Community Health*, 30(3): 237–46.

Fernández, A., and E. J. Pérez-Stable (2015), "¿Doctor, Habla Español? Increasing the Supply and Quality of Language-Concordant Physicians for Spanish-Speaking Patients," *Journal of General Internal Medicine* 30(10): 1394–6.

Ferrer, B. (2019), "Immigrant Health: Anchoring Public Health Practice in a Justice Framework," *American Journal of Public Health*, 109(9): 1156–7. https://doi.org/10.2105/AJPH.2019.305235

Feuerherm, E., and T. Oshio (2020), "Conducting a Community-Based ESOL Programme Needs Analysis," *ELT Journal, ccaa011*, https://doi.org/10.1093/elt/ccaa011

Fiddian-Green, A., S. Kim, A. C. Gubrium, L. K. Larkey, and J. C. Peterson (2019), "Restor(y)ing Health: A Conceptual Model of the Effects of Digital Storytelling: Health Promotion Practice," *Heatlh Promotion Practice*, 20(4): 502–12. https://doi.org/10.1177/1524839918825130.

Flores, G., M. Abreu, C. P. Barone, R. Bachur, and H. Lin (2012), "Errors of Medical Interpretation and their Potential Clinical Consequences: A Comparison of Professional Versus Ad Hoc Versus no Interpreters," *Annals of Emergency Medicine*, 60(5): 545–53.

Green, J., C. Free, V. Bhavani, and T. Newman (2005), "Translators and Mediators: Bilingual Young People's Accounts of their Interpreting Work in Health Care," *Social Science & Medicine*, 60(9): 2097–110.

Guzman, J. (2014), "The Epistemics of Symptom Experience and Symptom Accounts in Mapuche Healing and Pediatric Primary Care in Southern Chile," *Journal of Linguistic Anthropology*, 24(3): 249–76.

Handley, M. A., and J. Grieshop (2007), "Globalized Migration and Transnational Epidemiology," *International Journal of Epidemiology*, 36(6): 1205–06. https://doi.org/10.1093/ije/dym027

Handley, M. A., C. Hall, E. Sanford, E. Diaz, E. Gonzalez-Mendez, K. Drace, R. Wilson, M. Villalobos, and M. Croughan (2007), "Globalization, Binational Communities, and Imported Food Risks: Results of an Outbreak Investigation of Lead Poisoning in Monterey County, California," *American Journal of Public Health*, 97(5): 900–06. https://doi.org/10.2105/AJPH.2005.074138

Handley, M. A., M. G. Santos, and J. McClelland (2009), "Reports From the Field: Engaging Learners as Interpreters for Developing Health Messages—Designing the 'Familias Sin Plomo' English as a Second Language Curriculum Project," *Global Health Promotion*, 16(3): 53–8. https://doi.org/10.1177/1757975909339773

Harvey, T. S. (2008), "Where There is No Patient: An Anthropological Treatment of a Biomedical Category," *Culture, Medicine, and Psychiatry*, 32(4): 577–606.

Hohn, M. D., and L. Rivera (2019), "The Impact and Outcomes of Integrating Health Literacy Education into Adult Basic Education Programs in Boston," *HLRP: Health Literacy Research and Practice*, 3(3): 25–32. https://doi.org/10.3928/24748307-20190325-01

Hsieh, E. (2006), "Conflicts in How Interpreters Manage Their Roles in Provider–Patient Interactions," *Social Science and Medicine*, 62(3): 721–30. 10.1016/j.socscimed.2005.06.029

Hsieh, E. (2009), "Understanding Medical Interpreters: Reconceptualizing Bilingual Health Communication," *Health Communication*, 20(2): 177–86.

Hyman, D., E. Gurgevich, T. Alter, J. Ayers, E. Cash, D. Fahnline, . . . and H. Wright (2001), "Beyond Boyer: The UniSCOPE Model of Scholarship for the 21st Century," *Journal of Higher Education Outreach and Engagement*, 7(1&2): 41–65.

Irwin, A., and E. Scali (2007), "Action on the Social Determinants of Health: A Historical Perspective," *Global Public Health*, 2(3): 235–56. doi:10.1080/17441690601106304

Jacobson, H. (2009), "Moving Beyond Words in Assessing Mediated Interaction: Measuring Interactional Competence in Healthcare Settings," in C. V. Angelelli and H. E. Jacobson (eds.), *Testing and Assessment in Translation and Interpreting Studies* (Vol. 14), 49–70, Amsterdam: John Benjamins.

Karliner, L. S., E. J. Pérez-Stable, and G. Gildengorin (2004), "The Language Divide: The Importance of Training in the Use of Interpreters for Outpatient Practice," *Journal of General Internal Medicine*, 19 (2): 175–83. doi:10.1111/j.1525-1497.2004.30268.x

Katz, V. (2014), "Children as Brokers of Their Immigrant Families' Health-Care Connections," *Social Problems*, 61(2): 194–215.

Koehn, P. H., and H. M. Swick (2006), "Medical Education for a Changing World: Moving Beyond Cultural Competence into Transnational Competence," *Academic Medicine*, 81(6): 548–56.

Lion, K. C., D. A. Thompson, J. D. Cowden, E. Michel, S. A. Rafton, R. F. Hamdy, . . . and B. E. Ebel (2012), "Impact of Language Proficiency Testing on Provider Use of Spanish in Medical Care," *Pediatrics*, 130(1): 80–7.

Madon, T., K. J. Hofman, L. Kupfer, and R. I. Glass (2007), "Implementation Science," *Science*, 318, 1728–9.

Martínez, G. (2018), "Engaging Language Professionals for Patient-Centered Outcomes Research with Latinos," *Patient-Centered Outcomes Research Institute*. Available online: https://www.pcori.org/research-results/2018/engaging-language-professionals-patient-centered-outcomes-research-latinos

Martínez, G. (2020), *Spanish in Health Care: Policy, Practice and Pedagogy in Latino Health*, New York: Routledge.

McNulty, M., J. D. Smith, J. Villamar, I. Burnett-Zeigler, W. Vermeer, N. Benbow, . . . and H. Brown (2019), "Implementation Research Methodologies for Achieving Scientific Equity and Health Equity," *Ethnicity and Disease*, 29(1): 83–92.

Nielsen-Bohlman, L., A. M. Panzer, and D. A. Kindig (eds.) (2004), *Health literacy: A Prescription to End Confusion*, Washington DC: National Academies Press.

OECD (2013), "Time for the U.S. to Reskill? What the Survey of Adult Skills Says," OECD Skills Studies, Paris: OECD Publishing. http://dx.doi.org/10.1787/9789264204904-en

Parker, M., A. Fernandez, H. Moffet, R. W. Grant, A. Torreblanca, and A. J. Karter (2017), "Association of Patient-Physician Language Concordance and Glycemic Control for Limited English Proficiency Latinos with Type 2 Diabetes," *Journal of the American Medical Association*, 177(3): 380–7.

Peck, W., L. Flower, and L. Higgins (1995), "Community Literacy," *College Composition and Communication*, 46, 199–222.

Raymond, C. W. (2014), "Conveying Information in the Interpreter-Mediated Medical Visit: The Case of Epistemic Brokering," *Patient Education and Counseling*, 97(1): 38–46.

Reynolds, J. F., and M. F. Orellana (2015), "Translanguaging Within Enactments of Quotidian Interpreter-Mediated Interactions," *Journal of Linguistic Anthropology*, 24(3): 315–38.

Rubio, D. M., E. E. Schoenbaum, L. S. Lee, D. E. Schteingart, P. R. Marantz, K. E. Anderson, ... and K. Esposito (2010), "Defining Translational Research: Implications for Training," *Academic Medicine: Journal of the Association of American Medical Colleges*, 85(3): 470–5.

Santos, M. G., J. McClelland, and M. Handley (2011), "Language Lessons on Immigrant Identity, Food Culture, and the Search for Home," *TESOL Journal*, 2(2), 203–28.

Santos, M., H. Jacobson, and S. Manneh (2017), "Limited English Proficiency as a Consideration When Designing Health and Risk Messages," *Oxford Research Encyclopedia of Communication*. Retrieved from https://oxfordre.com/communication/view/10.1093/acrefore/9780190228613.001.0001/acrefore-9780190228613-e-538

Sarkar, J., A. Salyards, and J. Riley (2019), "'Health in the English Language': A Partnership with the Alaska Literacy Program," *HLRP: Health Literacy Research and Practice*, 3(3), 79–87. https://doi.org/10.3928/24748307-20190624-02

Sentell, T., and K. L. Braun (2012), "Low Health Literacy, Limited English Proficiency, and Health Status in Asians, Latinos, and Other Racial/Ethnic Groups in California," *Journal of Health Communication*, 17(3): 82–99. doi: 10.1080/10810730.2012.712621

Showstack, R. (2019), "Patients Don't Have Language Barriers; The Health Care System Does," *Emergency Medicine Journal*, 36(10): 580–1.

Showstack, R. (2020), "Making Sense of the Interpreter Role in a Healthcare Service-Learning Program," *Applied Linguistics*, amz058. doi: 10.1093/applin/amz058

Showstack, R., K. Guzman, A. K. Chesser, and N. Keene Woods (2019), "Improving Latino Health Equity Through Spanish Language Interpreter Advocacy in Kansas," *Hispanic Health Care International*, 17(1): 18–22. doi:10.1177/1540415318818706

Showstack, R., S. Nicks, N. Keene Woods, and G. Martínez, G. (forthcoming), "Interprofessional Simulations for Students of Translation/Interpreting and the Health Professions," *Hispania*.

Singer, M. C., P. I. Erickson, L. Badiane, R. Diaz, D. Ortiz, T. Abraham, and A. M. Nicolaysen (2006), "Syndemics, Sex and the City: Understanding Sexually Transmitted Diseases in Social and Cultural Context," *Social Science & Medicine*, 63(8): 2010–21.

Stoecker, R. (2005), *Research Methods for Community Change: A Project-Based Approach*, Thousand Oaks CA: Sage.

Tendulkar, S. A., J. Chu, J. Opp, A. Geller, A. Digirolamo, E. Gandelman, M. Grullon, P. Patil, S. King, and K. Hacker (2011), "A Funding Initiative for Community-Based Participatory Research: Lessons from the Harvard Catalyst Seed Grants," *Progress in Community Health Partnerships : Research, Education, and Action*, 5(1): 35–44. https://doi.org/10.1353/cpr.2011.0005

Traylor, A., J. Schmittdiel, C. Uratsu, C. Mangione, and U. Subramanian (2010), "Adherence to Cardiovascular Diseases Medications: Does Patient-Provider Race/Ethnicity and Language Concordance Matter?," *Journal of General Internal Medicine*, 25(11): 1172–7. doi:10.1007/s11606-010-1424-8

U.S. Department of Education, Office of Career, Technical, and Adult Education (2016), "English Literacy/English Language (EL) Education in the Adult Basic Grant Program: Fact Sheet." Available online: https://www2.ed.gov/about/offices/list/ovae/pi/AdultEd/factsh/english-literacy-education.pdf

Wallace, C. (2006), "The Text, Dead or Alive: Expanding Textual Repertoires in the Adult ESOL Classroom," *Linguistics and Education*, 17(1): 74–90.

Wallerstein, N. (1983), *Language and culture in conflict: Problem-posing in the ESL classroom*, Reading MA: Addison-Wesley.

Youdelman, M. (2017), *Medicaid and CHIP Reimbursement Models for Language Services*, National Health Law Program. Available online: https://healthlaw.org/resource/medicaid-and-chip-reimbursement-models-for-language-services/

"It Depends Case by Case": Understanding How the Practices of Cultural Health Navigators Impact Healthcare Access and Delivery for Refugee-Background Families

Katherine E. Morelli and Doris S. Warriner

I'm in an exam room with a family from the Democratic Republic of Congo that is new to the clinic. Casey, the Cultural Health Navigator from Burundi, has a number of forms with her including the New Patient Authorization Form. This form is needed to authorize the clinic to treat her child. Casey goes over the form with the mother. They speak back and forth to each other in Swahili as Casey asks questions and marks down responses. The mother is sitting down with her baby daughter in her lap. Suddenly, Casey says something, and the mother stands up. She tells me that the mother needs to sign the form, but she cannot read or write. Not even her name. Casey hands the pen to the mother and points to a line on the document where her signature is required. The mother takes the pen and writes the symbol of a cross where her name should be.

Introduction

Linguistic marginalization is commonly recognized as a major barrier to access health services and information (e.g., Bischoff et al. 2003; Chen 2006; Meeuwesan 2012; Nielsen-Bohlman, Panzer, and Kindig 2004). Despite widespread recognition that linguistic marginalization contributes to health disparities, *how* it contributes remains largely under-theorized and under-researched (Sentell and Braun 2012). A recent AAAL brief (Showstack et al. December 2019) asks how the expertise of applied linguists can make a difference in efforts to reduce health disparities for racial, ethnic, and linguistic minority communities—and how new cross-disciplinary and institutional partnerships might support such efforts. As the excerpt above exemplifies and as our analysis of additional data later in this chapter demonstrates, applied linguists have an important role to play in identifying and examining the complex relationship between linguistic marginalization and health outcomes for diverse linguistic, racial, and ethnic groups. This chapter demonstrates how a collaborative approach to inquiry (involving health professionals and university-based applied linguists) that showcases the experiences and views of *linguistic minority health professionals* (in this case a small group of Cultural Health Navigators working with refugee families at a pediatric clinic in the southwest US) provides an opportunity to identify, document, and analyze the relationship between their "insider" knowledge and the language and literacy dimensions of healthcare access and delivery.

Cultural Health Navigators (CHNs) are typically members of the communities they serve, acting as liaisons, links, and intermediaries between health services and their communities (American Public Health Association 2009). As multilingual "insiders" with an emic understanding of their communities, CHNs can facilitate important connections and relationships to/with the healthcare system and can be powerful sponsors for refugee families' access to and pursuit of literacy in the health context. CHNs offer a distinct category of nonclinical knowledge and skill sets based on life experience or "experience-based-expertise" (Gilkey et al. 2011). In much of the literature on CHNs, their contributions are documented or described in terms of patients' health outcomes, the number of times they returned to the clinic, and/or their ability to use primary or follow-up services (Brownstein et al. 2011; Davis et al. 2007; Satterfield et al. 2002; Thompson et al. 2007; Witmer et al. 1995). However, relatively few studies of the role of CHNs in healthcare access or delivery have examined how they draw on or think about their lived experiences or linguistic resources while working to facilitate refugee families' understanding, communication, and access in healthcare settings. This is where an applied linguistics perspective can be valuable in terms of thinking about and examining linguistic marginalization, linguistic diversity, and multilingualism in healthcare.

The director of the pediatric clinic (who supervised and served as the on-site primary investigator of the study) and the head CHN worked with us to shape the initial focus and design of the study and agreed that current research methods typically fail to account for the dynamic work the CHNs do within the clinic. Together, we agreed on the need for more collaborative approaches to investigating the complementary role the CHNs play in the healthcare of refugee families. We also discussed how findings from such a study might facilitate local understandings of and responses to language, literacy, and communication "barriers" experienced by refugee families with limited access to healthcare services and/or information about healthcare services. The university–clinic partnership described here, which provided an opportunity for participants to collaborate in the design of the study, actively worked to make sense of and respond to questions and concerns (e.g., about the role of language, literacy, and communication in access) shared by the CHNs and the researchers/authors. As a result of the collaborative inquiry, the partnership drew needed attention to related but separate questions about resource allocation, time constraints, and labor relations. In this chapter, we explore some of the ways that the partnership facilitated our (university-based researchers' and healthcare professionals') collective recognition of the language, literacy, and communication dimensions of healthcare access and delivery. We focus in particular on the ways the CHNs as "insiders" provide more culturally and linguistically responsive care and work to support more inclusive practices. Through analysis of specific events and the CHNs' reflections, this chapter offers a nuanced portrait of what linguistic marginalization looks like in one healthcare setting and shows that how we come to understand and theorize the language and literacy dimensions of healthcare access influences what we come to know. By theorizing the CHNs' efforts to improve refugee families' healthcare access and utilization, we demonstrate the role that applied linguists might play in working with community partners to address questions and issues of mutual interest, concern, and priority. We also demonstrate the value of drawing on methods of inquiry from outside the field of applied linguistics to improve what can be learned about language, literacy, and communication in a multilingual setting. We conclude by reflecting on the value of this kind of collaborative partnership and interdisciplinary approach to eliciting insider's knowledge in clinical settings to better inform our emerging understanding of the role of language in healthcare access and delivery.

Research context and background to the study

The refugee pediatrics clinic, the site of this collaborative inquiry, is housed in a comprehensive health center (formerly the County Hospital) in a metropolitan city in the southwest US. The center treats both pediatric and adult patients and provides primary and specialist services. Most of the patients that seek care at this center are low-income. The refugee pediatric clinic offers specialized care to refugee and immigrant children with the assistance of a team of health professionals, including one attending physician, nurse, medical assistant, social worker, care coordinator, and five CHNs. The CHNs who participated in this study are from Burma, Somalia, Iraq, and Burundi. Between them, ten languages were spoken: Arabic, Burmese, Chin, French, Karen, Kinyarwanda, Kirundi, Maay, Somali, and Swahili. Two of the CHN participants are former refugees themselves and had spent considerable time living or working in refugee camps. These five CHNs helped everyone on the team understand how their language proficiencies and lived experiences strengthened the clinic's efforts to provide more culturally and linguistically appropriate care and thereby facilitate families' navigation of the healthcare system.

Through a series of meetings, observations, interviews, and group conversations, the CHNs and university-based researchers worked collaboratively to identify and document the practices and views of the CHNs. Guided by a focus on the language and communication dimensions of healthcare delivery and access, Morelli took the lead in documenting what the CHNs did, how they engaged with that work, and what sense they were making of the practices involved. During meetings with healthcare professionals (e.g., the clinic director and the lead CHN) working at the pediatrics clinic, we established a mutual interest in exploring and understanding how language, literacy, and cultural differences might become major "barriers" to care for refugee families—and what might be done to address these barriers in real time. For instance, refugee families and providers alike seemed frustrated by the ways that restricted communication influenced diagnosis and treatment. Restricted communication contributed to a lack of trust and information sharing (e.g., about symptoms, one's medical history, treatment options) and shaped the quality of care received and therefore health outcomes (see also Ashton et al. 2003; Lawrence et al. 2005; Mirza et al. 2013). We knew (from the literature) and heard (from meetings, observations, and interviews) that more "culturally and linguistically appropriate services and resources" were needed to address language and communication challenges, improve trust, increase independence, and foster agency among families (Donnelly et al. 2011; Feldman 2006; Jatua 2011; Mirza et al. 2013), and believed it would be important and useful to find out more about how this concept was operationalized in practice.

The questions that guided the team's collaborative inquiry included the following:

1. What practices and resources (e.g., languages, artifacts, people) do the CHNs use and consider valuable to assist and support refugee families navigating the healthcare system?
2. How do the CHNs lived experiences as refugees/immigrants influence their work?
3. Do the CHNS talk about their practices in ways that indicate shared experiences and understandings across groups? What do their shared and distinct understandings and experiences reveal about the kinds of knowledge needed to address complex health-related challenges facing marginalized groups?
4. What concepts and understandings of health literacy are circulating the clinic among providers and how do these understandings inform and impact the routine practices of the CHNs?

A collaborative approach to inquiry

With a focus on the role of language, literacy, and communication in healthcare delivery, the collaboratively designed research study explored the nature of the CHN's work in the clinic and how they viewed that work—and their reflections on whether those efforts seemed to be addressing the language and literacy dimensions of access to and utilization of healthcare services. Observations, interviews, and artifact collection (conducted by Morelli) generated insights and questions that were shared with other members of the team (e.g., Warriner, the clinic director, the supervising resident, and the CHNs). All five of the CHNs participated in three semistructured interviews (fifteen in total). The interviews were immediately transcribed and thematically coded as the CHNs were often called upon to explore and help analyze themes or significant moments or situations in prior interviews. Observations at the clinic, which took place over the course of a year, and interviews yielded nuanced accounts of the CHNs' practices, activities, tasks, interactions, routines, and responsibilities. Interviews provided an opportunity for learning more about the views of the CHNs, including how they understood the needs they were meeting and what they thought about the language and literacy dimensions of refugee families' access (or lack of access) to healthcare services and information about health/healthcare. Since neither of us spoke any of the families' primary languages, the interviews were particularly useful for eliciting specifics about the strategies the CHNs used to manage challenges involving language or communication, especially during the clinical encounter where they spent the majority of their time. By involving the CHNs in the analysis of data generated during observations and interviews, the entire team learned a lot about the situated, embodied, and experiential knowledge that informed their practices and views.

To involve the CHNs in the analysis of data generated through observations and interviews, Morelli invited the CHNs to reflect and elaborate on the insights and findings that were emerging from the study via a set of critical incident technique (CIT) interviews. The CIT (Flanagan 1953), which has origins in the field of psychology but has since been used in the field of rhetoric, enables researchers to engage participants in data generation by inviting their reflections on and responses to tentative findings or preliminary data analysis (presented by the researcher). The CIT involves listening for moments where an account or story or response "got traction" or "raised tension" and helps to surface local "funds of knowledge" that directly inform decisions made or actions taken but that typically remain hidden from view (Clifton, Long, and Roen 2016). This technique was used to elicit elaborations and clarifications on issues that emerged during interviews—e.g., any language and communication differences or tensions between healthcare providers (e.g., resident interns, CHNs), medical culture, and refugee families. Drawing on and modifying the CIT, Morelli created three composite "scenes" that reflected recurring incidents elicited across interviews and observations. During a group meeting with the CHNs, Morelli invited them to perform the scenes, which involved enacting their roles in familiar situations and to reflect on the issues they highlighted as well as their decisions and actions. To facilitate this process, Morelli would periodically interrupt the flow of dialogue or action to ask the CHNs participating to offer comments on what was happening (including problems, remedies, and unanticipated consequences of well-intentioned actions). By inviting participants to make their in-process thinking transparent and engage in problem-solving, this way of using the CIT yielded insights that allowed everyone on the team to better understand the kinds of work being done by the CHNs, its affordances and its challenges.

In the remainder of this chapter, we demonstrate how applied linguists might draw on approaches to inquiry from outside their field to make a collaborative, cross-disciplinary community-based research project that is responsive to local priorities and concerns. Together, we (the CHNs and the university-based researchers) reflected on some of the ways that the CHNs drew on their lived experiences and linguistic resources to facilitate refugee families' understanding, communication, and access in healthcare settings. We argue that applied linguistics as an interdisciplinary field of inquiry benefits from the intentional and selective use of theories and ideas from other fields and subfields to understand complex social phenomena. In this case, our efforts to identify, document, and examine the practices and views of the CHNs was improved by using a modified version of the CIT to elicit responses from CHNs that went beyond what they offered during individual interviews. Importantly, our regular presence, genuine interest, and sustained engagement—together with our invitation to revisit key findings from our analysis of data—prompted the CHNs to pay close attention to their own practices and views and ultimately gave the CHNs an opportunity to articulate a nuanced critique of what and how they addressed the language and literacy dimensions of refugee families' access to and use of healthcare services offered by the clinic.

Access to care: Health insurance

One of the greatest barriers to care for refugee families that fell outside the CHNs' official responsibilities was health insurance. When the study began, we were not aware that the CHNs often felt as if they had to assist families with insurance-related paperwork or questions since much of this work was done outside of the clinic (and therefore outside of our observations). However, during interviews and the group performance, the CHNs described in great detail how they support families who do not have health insurance or who don't know how to use/renew it. In this section, we explore the language, literacy, and communication dimensions of health insurance.

According to the CHNs, the very concept of health insurance is new for most of the families they work with. This means they have to figure out effective ways to support understanding without overwhelming families with information. This is often done incrementally during visits to the clinic. Many families also tend not to know *why* health insurance is important and how they might benefit from having it. During interviews, we learned that one of the things the CHNs try to do is to help families understand the *reasons* to apply for and maintain health insurance. They said they try to "create incentive" by talking about the impact of being uninsured—on their children, on their ability to manage unpredictable health-related emergencies, and the likelihood of receiving large bills they cannot afford. While talking with us, the CHNs emphasized how important it is to establish an understanding of what health insurance is before helping families apply for and/or utilize insurance plans. For families with limited to no knowledge of health insurance, this can be very challenging to explain and is often an ongoing effort.

In addition to establishing a rationale for applying for health insurance, the CHNs also often spent a considerable amount of time working with families on how to fill out applications and eligibility forms. The CHNs often mentioned that families frequently come to the clinic without insurance. When this happens, they could send families elsewhere or ignore the issue entirely, but they usually do not. When prompted during interviews to reflect more deeply on why this is, Kriti, the CHN from Burma, explained:

> That's why I say we are not CHN ... a social worker. Without insurance they must pay. They don't have money. So, the doctor need to follow up everything too. So, this is actually, this is social work from outside the clinic. But we still doing everything because we don't want to miss their health. This is related and connected all the health issues with the social work and the medical care is together. So, we cannot ignore it.
>
> Kriti, September 8, 2017

As an experienced CHN, Kriti had seen firsthand how interconnected families' social realities are with their health and access to medical services. She told me that, like a social worker, she often finds herself evaluating and trying her best to respond to both the person (or family) and their current situation as it pertains to medical care and access to resources. Like the other CHNs, Kriti knew that families were unlikely to be able to access insurance without assistance, given the demands of trying to navigate new practices, beliefs, concepts, and contexts that seem to situate them at the margins of the entire system. Kriti told me that while language support certainly helps with understanding how to obtain or use health insurance, additional support and resources are needed to support literacy development and to expand navigational capacities.

During interviews and observations, the CHNs often described how lengthy the application is; how it can only be accessed in places that are challenging for families to access (e.g., the Internet); how the forms only come in English and Spanish; how the application consists of culturally specific information and questions about things such as premiums and copayments that families may be unfamiliar with; how they ask complex questions about things like income and require documentation families may not have (e.g., W-2 forms) to support their responses; and how an interview with a representative is required after all submissions. The application process clearly demands high levels of literacy in English, contextual and cultural knowledge, as well as experience filling out forms. Because the CHNs knew the challenges involved as well as the consequences of being uninsured, they told me that this was a hurdle that must be cleared and that it would be important for them to play a critical role in collecting required information, documenting that information on behalf of families, and facilitating interactions with representatives as needed to complete the application or renewal process.

During interviews, CHNs also described the challenges that remain after families qualify for health insurance. For instance, just because families have insurance does not mean they know what to do with it. Furthermore, most of the resources available to help navigate this system are linguistically inaccessible. The CHNs also pointed out that the "organizational structure" is also challenging to explain but is necessary if families want to use their plans. If time permits, the CHNs work with families to build "structural knowledge" about health insurance. They helped us understand that they are often involved in helping families understand the network of entities that manage their care and how they interact with each other. All the CHNs in this study commented on the fact that many refugee families are unclear about the relationship between their insurance agency and their healthcare benefits—or that important services like transportation to medical visits are covered benefits. As Angela, the CHN from Burundi explained, "we have to go through the structure" but sometimes families want to arrange their own transportation support (which is often covered by insurance), in which case they need to understand how this system works and who to contact. Other ways the CHNs help families utilize their plans is by reminding them of the services available to them while they are in the clinic. Morelli observed conversations in exam rooms while waiting for the doctor to arrive where parents asked the CHN present about what services were available to them and their children under their plans. These side conversations seemed to provide valuable opportunities for parents to ask questions and learn about things that were not always urgent but helped expand their knowledge about health insurance and the broader healthcare system.

The interviews and group conversation—both of which created opportunities for the CHNs to provide additional details and explanations about their experiences and perspectives—also encouraged the CHNs to reflect on the tensions that seem to characterize the work they do involving health insurance. Through interviews and the group performance, their rationales for putting so much effort into helping families obtain insurance and know how to use it became more clear to them and to us. Because there is nowhere else for the CHNs to send families for help and because there are few resources (human and material) to support their independent learning about health insurance, assistance from the CHNs is often needed. The reflections they offered about the reasons for this prompted important questions and insights about time allocation, resources, responsibilities, and the social realities of families that make it so difficult for the CHNs to ignore health-insurance-related issues—much of which was brought to the attention of other health professionals in the clinic. These insights also illustrate some of the challenges that linguistic minority patients face when accessing services and how health insurance is only the beginning of a series of seemingly insurmountable obstacles that push them further to the margins of the entire system.

The clinical encounter

This section is informed by insights gleaned from regular observations of the clinical encounter and from reflections on such encounters that were offered during interviews and the group conversation. The CHNs' translation and interpretation efforts also helped providers understand patient or parent responses, especially when those responses did not seem relevant to the questions being asked. All of this attention to clarifying language and communication across cultural differences helps with trust-building—for providers and families.

Over the course of many months, the CHNs helped us understand the interpretive work they did during the clinical encounter, what that entailed, and what impact they thought such practices might have on the families' experiences. Samira, a CHN from Somalia, responded in a way that echoed what all the CHNs described. As she explained, "The doctor comes in. I do interpretation. If they need clarification, clarify things. If they need advocacy, advocate for them." During interviews, Morelli asked the CHNs to elaborate on what they thought "clarification" and "advocacy" meant during the clinical encounter. While reflecting on such topics, and by exploring what might be contributing to the tension that emerged during certain clinical encounters, the CHNs and the interviewer (Morelli) began to collaboratively construct a clearer picture of the many different ways that the CHNs helped to scaffold the encounter and manage the families' different expectations and overall unfamiliarity with the patient–family interaction. For example, the CHNs talked a lot about how often they needed to interpret questions and how important it was for them to explain *why* providers asked the questions they did. The explanations they provided to families and physicians helped everyone efficiently and effectively communicate about sensitive topics and diagnosis. When the CHNs were not able to be present, they later learned that families viewed some questions as rude, intrusive, or confusing. For instance, Morelli observed a number of examinations where questions about medical histories seemed to confuse families as they did not see the relevance of the question to the visit. The CHNs themselves experienced this in their first encounters with the healthcare system in the US. During an interview Casey, the CHN from Burundi explained, "Yeah, for the first time I was like why all these questions? I didn't know why they are asking, for example, is there any health condition in your family? And I was like, what health condition? Why?"

Another substantial and substantive way that the CHNs helped to support communication and clarify meanings during the parent–provider interaction was by encouraging parents to value and contribute their own understandings and knowledge to the conversation. As Casey explained:

Because sometimes the provider ask questions, and they're like, "No, you are the doctor, you know everything." But I remind them, he's the doctor, yes, he knows, but you help him to know about your kids. If you don't help him, he will not help your kid because you are the mom, you are the dad, you know your kid best than the doctor. It's you who guide the doctor to know your kid and to help your kid.

Casey, September 8, 2017

As this excerpt indicates, the CHNs understood that many parents come to these visits with the idea that the doctor knows best and needed help understanding that they play a vital role in the healthcare delivery of their children.

The CHNs also discussed the work they do to encourage parents to elaborate and expand on their short and minimalist responses to their providers' questions or explanations. As Kriti explained:

Like most of my patients they just say in front of the doctor, yes, yes, yes. So, I explain in more detail. Example, like, iron medication. I told them the baby has to get on the iron medication for six months. She said yes. So, then I have to make sure the right information she get. Okay, she tell me again how you gonna give to your baby. And sometimes they didn't pay attention and then they just say yes, yes, yes. And then they say, what did you say? I said the doctor explain to you that you have to give your baby medication twice a day. And then I ask them again did they get the right information or not and she just says, yes.

Kriti, September 8, 2017

This excerpt demonstrates that parents will often respond to a yes/no question with "yes" even when they mean something else; it also highlights the value of having an engaged and patient CHN present. While one CHN said the parent might have replied this way to "save face," other CHNs thought the response might indicate a lack of understanding. Figuring out what the parent means by "yes" in each situation often involves a lot of back and forth between all parties (the parent, the CHN, and the provider) to assess their comprehension of the question and the intended meaning of their response. For instance, Morelli noticed many parents said "yes" when asked if they understood why a doctor issued a referral even though we later learned that they did not know what a referral was or why it was needed. In situations like this, the CHN may ask them how they understood what the referral was, why it was needed, and what action was required of them as parents.

CHNs are often needed to provide clarification when medical terms have no direct translation in the primary languages. For instance, Kriti once described a situation where she needed to clear up a parent's misunderstanding of the meaning of the term "stone" (a term that was used in the diagnosis):

> I have one patient it was from the hospital. So, the doctor said kidney stone, right? You have a kidney stone, we have to operate, to take it out, the kidney stone. So, the kidney stone, the way you translate is like we call in Burmese it's only one word ... like *kyaut cut* right? So, okay. But some patient, they speak Burmese too, but we have different ethnic groups, right? So, some different ethnic groups do not understand what *kyaut cut* is. So, ok what is *kyaut cut*? What does it mean? So, and then she left from the hospital and she said she couldn't sleep the whole night. The next morning, early morning, she calls me, "Kriti, why I never eat stone? And the body ... if the body or digestion system it can make a stone in your body?" I said what kind of stone? "I don't know. Yesterday I went because I had a hard time to pee and something and they check ultrasound and after everything they say I have a lot of stones in my stomach." Oh my god that's not right! That's not what they mention. Ok so do you understand what is *kyaut cut*? "No." Oh okay, then now I got it. This is not the stone. You know the water sometimes, when you boil water, right? Okay, sometimes you see the white under the boil. If you boil so many times and then it's stinky, white stinky, that's there on the pot. She said "Yes." Okay, exactly like this. You eat and then drink and the water is not clear, it can cause your kidney, kidney is a part of your body. So, I have to explain everything.
>
> Kriti, September 8, 2017

In this example, after Kriti understood what the woman thought was happening, she attempted to provide clarifying information. Observations and interviews made clear that this kind of "in-the-moment" interpretation was necessary but complicated and situated. For instance, when shifting from the families' languages to English, the CHN must imagine multiple potential contexts and audiences. Reem (a CHN from Iraq), for instance, described when and why this typically occurs:

> Yeah, sometimes, in some situations you cannot translate exactly what the patient says because, you know, it depends. As I am an interpreter for all the Arabic speakers so they are from different countries so sometimes even them the patient, herself, she cannot give the exact word for about how she feels. That's why I'm looking for a word which fits that what she is feeling and what she is saying.
>
> Reem, September 8, 2017

The testimonies and elaborations offered by the CHNs during interviews highlighted some of the ways that they shouldered the burden of figuring out the best way or the "right" way to communicate with refugee-background families in the clinical setting and the pressure that often came with this task. These collaborative elaborations also highlight how languages are not all uniform and may include differences based on ethnicity, dialect/accent, or social and/or regional variation—linguistic knowledge that may be significant when working with interpreters and translated documents.

In addition to developing new ways to talk about medical terms and concepts, CHNs also commented on the importance of developing rhetorical skills needed to inform families and persuade them to take action. During the second interview with Casey, she reflected on an incident involving a mother and two children from the Democratic Republic of Congo. One of the children had a hole in their heart and the other had tuberculosis (TB) and both were in need of urgent medical attention and care. However, despite the efforts to get the mother to come to the clinic, she never came. The story Casey told during the interview revealed feelings of frustration, concern, and anxiety. In response to the request for elaboration and clarification, Casey explained the critical role she played in raising the family's awareness of the children's serious medical conditions and of the consequences of inaction:

> Every time I explain to her this situation, they need to see the child, if you don't do this with this condition, you will see one day, they can come to take your kid. And don't think it's me or it's the doctor, because the doctor must report everything, because this is the situation where they must act and now. You can't wait. If they think the baby has TB, they must protect other kids. If she goes to

school, they must protect others at school. If your baby doesn't grow right because the hole in the heart, they must close that. You need to understand that if this is not ... we are not here to play. We are helping you, and if we don't help you, I don't think you will get somewhere that can do everything how we are doing.

Casey, September 8, 2017

In this particular instance, Casey shared her concern that the mother did not know much about mandated reporting and other bureaucratic protocols of seeking care at a clinic. However, even though she had tried to educate the mother and convince her of the urgency of the situation, the mother never made it back to the clinic. During our interview, Casey became more aware of her own frustration and seemed to want to analyze why she was unsuccessful despite all her efforts. It became clear that the interview itself had provided a space for identifying points of critical tension and for thinking through the implications of action and/or inaction. At one point, she even said "we share the same language, but I don't think she gets what we are doing here."

This section has explored how the presence and interest of an informed researcher created opportunities for the CHNs to identify, describe, and reflect on the many valuable ways they draw on their lived experiences to address and support the language- and communication-related challenges that refugee families often face during the clinical encounter. Through our collaborative work to surface and analyze specific examples of the CHNs practices, our team discovered that sharing a language, while helpful, is not always enough to address all communication challenges that emerge during the routine clinical encounter. As this chapter has explored, contextual and specific cultural knowledge is also needed in order to provide adequate support to families new to such interactions. Over time, the research project itself helpfully drew attention to the ways that CHNs support the active participation of families and how that support helped more families feel included, heard, and understood while also promoting advancements in family members' health literacy.

Medication and prescriptions

One challenge that concerned everyone in the clinic involved following treatment plans and obtaining prescriptions for medication and/or filling them. Typically, obtaining medication and following treatment plans are things that happen outside the doctor's visit. However, families attending the refugee pediatrics clinic tended to seek out the support system they found within the clinic, a support system facilitated and strengthened through their interactions with the CHNs. During interviews and the group conversation, we attempted to collaboratively explore the language and literacy dimensions of medication and following treatment plans; the challenges that the CHNs encounter trying to meet the needs of the families they work with; and the ways in which they have come to respond and/or wish they had the time and resources to respond.

One of the problems that frequently came up was the lack of oversight of prescriptions in the home. Another issue that came up is that many immigrant and refugee-background parents tend not to be fully aware of how prescriptions work. For instance, they may not realize they cannot refill a prescription anytime they want because there are a number of entities that manage their prescriptions and dictate when this can happen (e.g., doctors, pharmacies, insurance agencies). The CHNs explained that without careful oversight of prescriptions in the home and without understanding how prescriptions work, medication may get spilled, lost, or shared among family and friends.

We also learned that one of the biggest challenges for families was following instructions and reading prescription labels in large part because all instructions and labels are written in English, making them inaccessible to preliterate and non-English-speaking patients. The CHNs often expressed concern over what might happen after families go home, especially in cases where they do not know what to do or have no one to turn to for help. When asked how they respond and/or aid with comprehension, the CHNs talked about doing what they can to teach families when they are in the clinic. This often involves drawing on multimodal strategies. As Samira described during the group conversation:

> Yeah, like one patient, I think Dr. Day prescribed three medications and he told the mom they could not drink milk. And I tried . . . we tried to draw everything and to show, to put colors on the medication, to put signs like for this medication "eat" or "do not drink milk." We try to do everything.
>
> Samira, September 8, 2017

Families' linguistic constraints make it extremely challenging to follow instructions. Color coding, marking labels and syringes, drawing, providing oral summaries, and asking parents to repeat back what they said are common practices among the CHNs to facilitate comprehension and promote healthy practices. During the group conversation, we learned that the CHNs often have parents take photographs of the label of a prescription bottle when they are home and text it to them. Then, they call the parent back and translate the instructions. They also explained that if it is a really urgent prescription and they have time, they may call the parent and remind them to administer the medication; however, rarely is this possible. Through these conversations they continued to emphasize how stretched they were and how limited their time was.

In addition to the linguistic constraints that families encounter, there are also limited resources to support them beyond the clinic walls; and according to the CHNs, the resources that do exist are not particularly useful. For example, there is a "medication sheet" that providers use in the clinic to help parents understand *when* to administer medication. When asked about the sheet and why it is not useful one of the CHNs explained:

> Because [the medical sheet] was showing morning, evening, afternoon. Some patients don't know. For the morning, they put, what do you call it . . . a chicken. And in the evening, they put the sun going down. But they don't know. It's complicated to say to them. That's why we mark and we tell them "with food, morning" or "after food" or evening "after eating." Things like that.
>
> Casey, September 8, 2017

For the families they work with, terms like "morning," "afternoon," and "evening" as well as the visual aids (e.g., roosters, sunsets) may have no clear meaning, especially for those coming from refugee camps where time was not a mediating factor in their lives. However, following treatment plans correctly requires attention to time. And if the only resources available to them to help them *with timing* have no meaning, it is highly unlikely that they will follow the treatment plan as it was intended.

We learned from many of the CHNs that their efforts to help families with medication are often unsuccessful. Children tend to return to the clinic still sick. When this happens, the CHNs and the doctor try to determine if this is a new development, or if they never received the treatment they needed. To do so, they ask a series of questions and conduct follow-up tests, as relayed in a story told by Kriti:

> The parent said they gave the child the medication. Dr. Day asked what the urine looked like and they said yellow. But if they were giving him the medication, it would be black. We ask questions like what color is the urine and order labs to see. Then we tell them about the disadvantages of not taking the medication. We have to educate them.
>
> Kriti, September 8, 2017

Generally, the CHNs did not try to point fingers or blame parents because they know this may discourage or upset them and/or contribute to them not returning to the clinic. Instead, the CHNs tried to determine whether the treatment plan was followed by asking the parent to explain how they administered the medication and by ordering tests, which is often how they discover a treatment plan was not followed.

Checking up on adherence to treatment plans, however, was only one dimension of a larger problem. The CHNs were concerned that families who visited their clinic also needed to be able to interact with pharmacies and most pharmacies in the local context did not provide much language support (particularly when the patient has limited proficiency or literacy in English or Spanish). We discovered that the CHNs tried to support families who were new to the clinic by addressing the language and literacy issues involved with filling prescriptions, interacting with pharmacies, or taking medication. As valuable and necessary as all of this support is, however, it is exceedingly time-consuming and logistically challenging, compounded by the fact that each CHN needed to keep track of each family's medication and tailor their responses to each situation. Angela explained that:

> It depends case by case. If it is a medication that it has to be picked up at the pharmacy and we know it is long-term, then we educate them on how to save the bottle so they can go get the refills and just bring the bottle, because those bottles for some at the beginning, so many things happening, they will even let the child play with the label. We explain that the information that is on the label will be used later.
>
> Angela, November 13, 2017

Since the CHNs know there is little oversight when it comes to prescriptions, they tried to get parents in the habit of saving bottles and labels and reusing them (to minimize some of the confusion and miscommunication that occurs at pharmacies). As Angela points out, however, when it comes to medication- and prescription-related challenges, there is no single response. It is "case by case." This in many ways characterizes much of their work and the nature of their families' experiences with the healthcare system.

Overall, we found that even though a lot of attention was given to helping families get prescriptions filled and understand the dosage of the prescribed medication, the CHNs noticed that their efforts often did not have the desired impact. Patients often returned sick to the clinic and the CHNs received frequent calls from worried parents at pharmacies. During the group conversation, we asked the CHNs to think about and reflect on this particular problem and one of the CHNs asked a question that captured what we had discovered to be an unresolved frustration and confusion experienced by the rest of the group but which they rarely could express: "How will they understand if they don't understand with us and the doctor together?" The question became central to our analysis as it draws attention to what happens when patients exist at the margins of the healthcare system and lack the resources to support their full participation and inclusion. After this question was spoken, the group engaged in a lively discussion about the strategies they *wished* they had been able to try. One strategy they mentioned was to create translations of the pharmacy prompts in their families' languages. They also talked about possibly collaborating with ESL instructors at the local resettlement agencies. This is where applied linguists can potentially help the field of health by developing pedagogies, building and supporting collaboration, and working toward the creation of more linguistically inclusive practices and material resources (see also Feuerherm et al., this volume).

Conclusion

In this chapter, we have explored how applied linguists might contribute expertise and generate insights and understandings about the role that language, literacy, and communication play in healthcare access and delivery. Our presence, interests, and analysis ultimately facilitated a nuanced, context-specific understanding of how CHNs manage and respond to the language, literacy, and communication dimensions of healthcare access and quality. Through this collaborative investigation, we were able to offer a more nuanced picture of what linguistic marginalization looks like in healthcare and how challenging it can be situated at the margins of the healthcare system—as patients and as health professionals. The findings of this study suggest that more investment in making healthcare linguistically (and culturally) accessible is needed as are efforts to train health professionals (and clinics, health organizations) to work with refugee-background individuals and families. The insights and information generated from this study can be used by this clinic and possibly other clinics or health organizations to increase access to care among communities served.

In the case of the refugee pediatric clinic, this information might impact language policy within the clinic by challenging the dominance of written English. This information also might encourage more investment at the institutional level in making healthcare services and information more accessible to patients and families. Without accessible resources, the CHNs frequently took on responsibilities beyond their professional roles (e.g., helping with insurance) that left them with little time to focus on other important aspects of their jobs like working on projects and developing material resources to support communication and learning (e.g., translated pharmacy prompts, how-to videos). It also limited the time they spent in the community, which each CHN cited as extremely important. The CHNs often mentioned wanting to collaborate with ESL programs in the area to support health literacy development. The conversations that took place during this study were extremely relevant to considering how such an idea might get implemented. Applied linguists might help a clinic and health organization (as well as health professionals) think through other community-based collaborations to support health literacy development. As applied linguists, this study shows one way we can begin to facilitate efforts to understand and address health disparities at a variety of levels—from language policy to institutional practice to the ways in which we theorize, assess, and promote health literacy in our communities.

In this chapter, we have also demonstrated the value of using methods of inquiry that are not typically embraced by applied linguists. Applying a modified version of the CIT, for instance, allowed us to elicit and analyze data that expanded what we had learned from observations in the clinical setting and individual interviews with the CHNs.

The technique helped to elicit the tacit experiential and situated knowledge that guides their practice so that we could document, analyze, and share that knowledge with those who might stand to benefit from it (e.g., the clinic director, the attending physician). We used the tools of rhetorical analysis to make explicit how the CHNs in this study describe and value their own experiences (as refugees/immigrants), expertise, knowledge, and action. Applied linguists or healthcare providers with similar interests and priorities might use similar approaches and tools (theoretical and methodological) to elicit insiders' knowledge in other clinical settings. Such approaches to inquiry might help other health professionals (and organizations) better understand the value of not only hiring but privileging and including the expertise of professionals like the CHNs. Although linguistically marginalized healthcare professionals have historically lacked a supportive infrastructure within the healthcare system, this chapter demonstrates one potential remedy to this problem.

References

American Public Health Association (2009), "Community Health Workers." Available online: https://www.apha.org/apha-communities/member-sections/community-health-workers.

Ashton, C. M., P. Haidet, D. A. Paterniti, T. C. Collins, H. S. Gordon, K. O'Malley, and R. L. Street, Jr. (2003), "Racial and Ethnic Disparities in the Use of Health Services: Bias, Preferences, or Poor Communication," *Journal of General Internal Medicine*, 18(2): 146–52.

Bischoff, A., P. A. Bovier, R. Isah, G. Françoise, E. Ariel, and L. Louis (2003), "Language Barriers Between Nurses and Asylum Seekers: Their Impact on Symptom Reporting and Referral," *Social Science and Medicine*, 57(3): 503.

Brownstein, J. N., G. R. Hirsch, E. L. Rosenthal, and C. H. Rush (2011), "Community Health Workers '101' for Primary Care Providers and Other Stakeholders in Health Care Systems," *The Journal of Ambulatory Care Management*, 34(3): 210–20.

Chen, A. (2006), "Doctoring Across the Language Divide," *Health Affairs*, 25(3): 808–13.

Clifton, J., E. Long, and D. Roen (2016), "Constructions of Critical Incidents." Available online: http://ccdigitalpress.org/stories/chapters/roenlongclifton/ways.htm.

Davis, K. L., M. L. O'Toole, C. A. Brownson, P. Llanos, and E. B. Fisher (2007), "Teaching How, Not What: The Contributions of Community Health Workers to Diabetes Self-Management," *The Diabetes Educator*, 33(6): 208–15.

Donnelly, T. T., J. J. Hwang, D. Este, C. Ewashen, C. Adair, and M. Clinton (2011), "If I Was Going to Kill Myself, I Wouldn't be Calling You. I am Asking for Help: Challenges Influencing Immigrant and Refugee Women's Mental Health," *Issues in Mental Health Nursing*, 32(5): 279–90.

Feldman, R. (2006), "Primary Health Care for Refugees and Asylum Seekers: A Review of the Literature and a Framework for Services," *Public Health*, 120(9): 809.

Flanagan, J. C. (1954), "The Critical Incident Technique," *Psychological Bulletin*, 51(4): 327.

Gilkey, M. E., C. H. Rush, and C. Garcia (2011), "Professionalization and the Experience-Based Expert: Strengthening Partnerships Between Health Educators and Community Health Workers," *Health Promotion Practice*, 12(2): 178–82.

Jatau, M. (2011), "Living Between Two Cultures: A Reproductive Health Journey of African Refugee Women," PhD dissertation, Arizona State University, Tempe AZ.

Lawrence, J., and R. Kearns (2005), "Exploring the 'Fit' Between People and Providers: Refugee Health Needs and Health Care Services in Mt Roskill, Auckland, New Zealand," *Health and Social Care in the Community*, 13(5): 451–61.

Meeuwesen, L. (2012), "Language Barriers in Migrant Health Care: A Blind Spot," *Patient Education and Counseling*, 86(2): 135–6.

Mirza, M., R. Luna, B. Matthews, R. Hasnain, E. Herbert, A. Niebauer, and U. D. Mishara (2014), "Barriers to Healthcare Access Among Refugees with Disabilities and Chronic Health Conditions Resettled in the US Midwest," *Journal of Immigrant and Minority Health*, 16(4): 733–42.

Nielsen-Bohlman, L., A. M. Panzer, and D. A. Kindig (eds.) (2004), *Health literacy: A Prescription to End Confusion*, Washington DC: National Academies Press.

Sentell, T., and K. L. Braun (2012), "Low Health Literacy Limited English Proficiency, and Health Status in Asians, Latinos, and Other Racial/Ethnic Groups in California," *Journal of Health Communication*, 17(3): 82–99.

Satterfield, D., C. Burd, L. Valdez, G. Hosey, and J. E. Shield (2002), "The 'In-Between People': Participation of Community Health Representatives in Diabetes Prevention and Care in American Indian and Alaska Native Communities," *Health Promotion Practice*, 3(2): 166–75.

Thompson, J. R., C. Horton, and C. Flores (2007), "Advancing Diabetes Self-Management in the Mexican American Population: A Community Health Worker Model in a Primary Care Setting," *The Diabetes Educator*, 33(6): 159–65.

Witmer, A., S. D. Seifer, L. Finocchio, J. Leslie, and E. H. O'Neil (1995), "Community Health Workers: Integral Members of the Health Care Work Force," *American Journal of Public Health*, 85(8): 1055–8.

8

Applied Linguistic Anthropology: Balancing Social Science with Social Change

Netta Avineri, Eric J. Johnson, Bernard C. Perley, Jonathan Rosa, Ana Celia Zentella

Introduction

Netta Avineri

This chapter features four applied linguistic anthropology case studies, highlighting how interdisciplinary scholars of language can acknowledge their positionalities, engage in in-depth examination of particular language-related issues, and mobilize to advocate for social change. We will discuss the inherent dilemmas involved in applied linguistic anthropology, including asking who our publics are, what "change" we seek to effect, how identifying the nature of "change" may help us determine if we are "successful" in moving toward social justice, and recognizing that language-related issues are never only about language—they are about ideologies, perceptions, experiences, practices, and histories of both powerful and marginalized groups.

These four case studies stem from collaborative work of the American Anthropological Association's Society for Linguistic Anthropology (henceforth SLA) Task Group on Language and Social Justice (henceforth LSJ), an interdisciplinary group of publicly engaged scholars who collaboratively tackle language and social justice issues. As an applied linguistic anthropologist interested in mobilizing our fields for positive change, I have collaborated with this chapter's coauthors in meaningful ways. The chapter will first provide a critical analysis of the use of linguistically demeaning categories in the US Census to classify groups that speak languages other than English. Second, the use of the word "illegal" immigrant in public discourse is described within the campaign to stop the "I-word" in major media outlets, as an example of broader advocacy focused on language-related issues. Next, the use of Native American symbols and representations in sports team mascot names is critiqued and linked to the ongoing erasure of Indigenous communities and their histories. Last, the misguided notion of a "language gap" between economically privileged families and those living in poverty is outlined in terms of how it has been used to justify disadvantages that academically derail students from linguistically diverse backgrounds. The role of institutions (government, education, media, sports) is central to these case studies and to the lives of marginalized and minoritized[1] groups in the US and beyond.

Highlighting language ideologies around counting, referring, and words as evidence of language, the case studies foreground the notion that simply finding new labels does not address systemic, and the systematic nature of, marginalization. The authors demonstrate how everyday manifestations of socially divisive language cater to culturally unmarked audiences and reify norms of linguistic hierarchies and racial divides. They highlight the role that language plays in structuring social relationships within and between communities and how hegemonic epistemologies impact those with the least advantage. These examples also demonstrate how language is implicated and can be mobilized in creating more just worlds, therefore unpacking both processes and collective impact. Overall, the chapter interrogates what is "known" and seen as "matter of fact" and emphasizes the role of collaboration and criticality in counteracting ideologies and practices that dismiss and erase the experiences of marginalized communities.

Foregrounding a critical, pragmatic, and social change-oriented approach to research in language and society, the authors counteract a positivist view of science anchored in notions of empiricism and truth. This methodological framing balances empiricism with positionality and in-depth description with advocacy for social change. We recognize the complexity of undertaking an applied linguistic anthropology since it involves value judgments and particular worldviews in the service of social justice. In each case study, the author discusses how they navigated a multilayered 5-step applied linguistic anthropological process of:

1. Methods of noticing, in-depth observation, longitudinal reflection, and thoughtful critique
2. Centering the role of language in social justice efforts
3. Recognition of one's positionalities and roles in relation to the topic/issue at hand

4. Processes of collaboration, coalition-building, audience coalescence (Avineri and Perley 2019)
5. Efforts to raise awareness for social change and liberation

These five steps demonstrate a "critical ethnographer's dilemma": the notion that understanding issues and contexts in depth can uncover problems and tensions—which necessitates both collaboration and empathy. As these authors illustrate, one must mobilize the tools and perspectives of various disciplines in order to move meaningfully toward social change.

Who is "linguistically isolated"? Challenging a damaging US census category

Ana Celia Zentella

As the daughter of a Mexican father and Puerto Rican mother and a self-proclaimed anthro-political linguist concerned about the negative impact of misinformation about immigrant family language skills and practices, I was appalled to learn the Census Bureau (CB) classified all members of households where no adult spoke English "Very well" as "linguistically isolated." A bar graph[2] based on the 1990 data—accompanied by troubling drawings of children crouching in shadows—claimed that 6 percent of New York State's children "lived in linguistic isolation," and that 20 percent of them did not speak English at home. If all the adults in a family reported that they spoke English "Well," "Not well," or "Not at all," the entire household was considered "linguistically isolated." This damaging categorization began in 1980. The CB spoke in 2000 of "11.9 million Americans living in 4.4 million linguistically isolated households in the United States" (Soifer 2009). Frantic news stories deplored the threat to the nation and the non-assimilation of immigrants, particularly Spanish speakers. Yet the same report indicated that 78 percent of Hispanics either spoke only English (24%) or spoke English "Very well" (40%) or "Well" (14%); only 8 percent of Hispanics did not speak English at all (Dockterman 2011). But because those who spoke it "Well" were classified as "linguistically isolated" together with those who did not speak English well or at all, the resulting 36 percent heightened unwarranted fears, sometimes leading to verbal and/or physical attacks against speakers of other languages, often Spanish speakers (Zentella 2019). Between 2005 and 2010, "anti-Latino hate crimes rose disproportionately to other hate crimes" (Van Zeller 2011).

It does not require linguistic expertise to see that placing those who speak English "Well" in the same category as those who do not speak English well, or at all, results in unreliable data that impedes adequate educational, medical, legal, and social services. There are only three questions regarding language in the Census:

1. Do you speak a language other than English at home?
2. IF SO—which language?
3. Do you speak English: Very well, Well, Not well, or Not at all.

The answers to these questions determine which families and communities may be provided medical, legal, and social services support in languages other than English. The answers also determine "bilingual election requirements," as well as the "allocation of educational funds to ... teach students with lower levels of English proficiency" (Census Bureau 2010). But there is no question about children's English ability or their use of English at school and with friends. Nor does the Census ask about every resident's ability to read and/or write English. Limited questions, problematic categories, and a disparaging label result in a distorted picture of immigrant homes, encouraging hostility against speakers of other languages. The situation called for an anthro-political linguistic approach (Zentella 1995) that reached out not only to language scholars but to educators and the broader public to unmask the ways in which power—that of the government in this case—uses language to support the dominant group's language (e.g., Why weren't those who spoke only English considered linguistically isolated?) and misrepresents the linguistic abilities of minoritized groups (e.g., Why was there no question about their knowledge of and ability in languages other than English?).

In 2005, I turned to the newly formed LSJ Task Group of the SLA, and together we met challenges, enjoyed some success, and endured major disappointments. In articles, papers, panels, and resolutions over the next six years, we questioned the accuracy and reliability of data resulting from the Census language questions, highlighting their limitations and the implications for social justice of its categorizations (Zentella et al. 2007). Of particular concern was the reliance on assessments of one's own linguistic ability, the lumping together of those who said they spoke English "Well" with those who did not speak it well or at all, and the damaging "isolated" label. In 2008, the members of our parent organization, the American Anthropological Association (AAA), passed a resolution to "urge the Census Bureau to include a question about proficiency in languages other than English, and to stop classifying those who speak

English less than 'Very well'—and all members of their households—as 'linguistically isolated' because the term is inaccurate and discriminatory, and the classification promotes an ideology of linguistic superiority that foments linguistic intolerance and conflict" (American Anthropological Association 2008).

We then reached out to language-related national organizations, to the Latinu[3] community in the US, and to the CB directly. The AAA resolution won the support of the Conference on College Composition and Communication, the National Council of Teachers of English, and the American Association for Applied Linguistics. Latinu organizations included the National Institute for Latino Policy (NILP) and its extensive Latino Census Network, which lobbied the CB's Advisory Committee on the Hispanic Population, and the National Hispanic Leadership Committee. My bilingual editorials in New York's leading Spanish daily and in online newsletters reached the broader public (Zentella 2009, 2011).

Convincing the CB was more difficult; we parried with its directors and their congressional overseers, the House Committee on Energy and Commerce, for three years in letters, meetings, and conference calls, challenging the limits of the questions, the categorization of proficiency levels, and the labeling of households and individuals. The CB insisted there was no federal mandate to ask about languages other than English, and that "irrespective of its label," the category that separated "Very well" from the other levels was useful, based on 1980s research, and "used routinely by researchers, policy makers and practitioners" (David Johnson letter to AAA President Setha Low, 2008). The three alternative proficiency categorizations we suggested—including "emergent bilinguals"— were all rebuffed, and we were told that changing "linguistically isolated" would involve a long legislative process. We were disheartened, given the imminent release of the 2010 data, until our efforts convinced a new CB director to change the title of the category beginning in 2011; he acknowledged it would be "less stigmatizing" to replace "linguistically isolated" with "Households in which no one 14 and over speaks English only or speaks a language other than English at home and speaks English 'Very well.'" The AAA press release (2011) that welcomed this substitution nevertheless continued "to urge the CB to expand its language questions and to acknowledge that those who speak English 'Well' should not be grouped with those who speak it 'Not well' or 'Not at all.'" Celebration over the elimination of the "linguistically isolated" label was short-lived; the cumbersome "Households in which ..." was soon replaced by "Limited English speakers," a discredited label from the early days of bilingual education.[4]

Moreover, the category illogically continues to join many monolingual English-speaking children and adults who speak English "Well" with those who do not know much English.

Obviously, we cannot claim that "we won"; we continue to challenge the CB's policies and statistics. Although a second study by the CB in 2015 reaffirmed the "Very well" cut-off point by comparing self-reports to comprehension of literacy tasks, only adults were tested (Leeman 2018a); households with English monolingual children continue to be categorized as limited English proficient (LEP) if no adults speak English "Very well." As Leeman (2018b) argues, the problematic language questions and categories of the Census reflect and reinforce English-only ideologies and policies that view other languages as problems and deficiencies to be overcome. What should our next steps be, given the numerous language-related problems facing the nation?

Efforts to make English the official language are on the rise, as are verbal and physical attacks on those who speak other languages. This aggression continues despite the fact that 80 percent of people living in the US speak only English at home and 15 percent of those who speak another language also speak English "Very well." The COVID-19 pandemic has exacerbated fears of perceived "foreigners," as the proposed House Resolution 908 "Condemning all forms of anti-Asian sentiment as related to COVID-19" makes clear. Clearly, as language scholars, we must dispel misconceptions about the linguistic strengths of immigrants, challenge the failures in government data collection methods, and address the monolingual ideologies pervasive in an English-only-speaking society. Such formidable tasks are perhaps best tackled by focusing on a target that is highly visible, concrete, and with significant implications, like the CB labels and policies. This requires matching our goals and expertise to pursue research that disproves the usefulness of one category for those who speak English well and those who do not and a multipronged approach that builds supportive coalitions with groups of educators, health officials, and social justice activists, while raising awareness in the broader public. There is a lot more work to do; on inauguration day in 2017, president Donald Trump's administration removed the Spanish links to the whitehouse.gov page, eliminating critical access to information about government programs. Our petition drive to "Reinstate the Spanish Links on WhiteHouse.gov" was ignored by the White House, but our (limited) success in eliminating "linguistically isolated" encourages us to challenge this erasure by reaching out to language scholars and the general public. In addition, we denounce recent attempts to exclude immigrants from the Census and/or from the apportionment of congressional seats as part of our defense of speakers of other languages, in the interest of greater justice in the nation.

Debating the language of migrant "illegality": Connecting linguistic advocacy to broader struggles

Jonathan Rosa

As horrifying images of migrant families separated and detained at the southern US border have been projected globally across digital screens and newspaper pages over the last several years, many people might wonder how we arrived at this moment in which it has become legally possible for children to be ripped out of the arms of their parents and toddlers to appear in court unaccompanied for their deportation proceedings. However, these scenes are not simply atrocities particular to the Trump administration, but rather rearticulations of long-standing histories of Indigenous genocide and African enslavement that founded the US and have been violently enacted and reproduced in colonies and metropoles throughout the world. That is, the separation, containment, exploitation, criminalization, and eradication of families is an all-American practice—with an emphasis on the plural Americas as a politically and economically intertwined territorial expanse superseding and subtending US borders, with historical and contemporary ties to various colonial powers and colonized peoples.

This fraught context is part of the backdrop against which debates about discourses of migrant "illegality" have taken shape. From some perspectives, "illegality" is a straightforward fact of laws stipulating which persons can cross which borders in which times and places. In this view, "illegality" is a politically neutral designation for migrants who enter or remain in a nation's borders without authorization. In contrast, scholars of US immigration history have carefully traced the nation's shifting borders and policies, pointing out that, within the US, the widespread circulation of the concept of "illegality" is in fact a relatively recent phenomenon that corresponds to the nation's efforts to strategically facilitate particular populations' migration and labor participation while maintaining them in a perpetual status of deportability (De Genova 2004). Thus, historically, representations of various populations' migration, particularly the framing of their presence within the US as legitimate or illegitimate, is characteristically less a reflection of migrants' efforts to obtain authorization than of the extent to which they correspond to racially coded models of idealized citizen-subjects.

In solidarity with migrant communities and pro-immigration reform activists, critical language scholars have offered analyses of how discourses of migrant "illegality" erase political and economic structures that produce and depend on migration while subjecting migrants and the broader racialized communities of which they are a part to continued forms of surveillance, containment, and marginalization (Santa Ana 2000). This work has included both conventional academic research, as well as public-facing scholarship that seeks to reframe popular debates about language and immigration (Santa Ana and González de Bustamante 2012). As a linguistic anthropologist who studies language and the racialization of US Latinx populations with a commitment to bridging theory and practice to advocate for racial and linguistic justice, I took particular interest in this issue. It is within this context that I worked with members of the LSJ Task Group of the SLA to advocate in support of the "Drop the I-Word Campaign,"[5] an effort to challenge the use of the term "illegal" and variations thereof in mainstream media representations of immigration. The campaign sought to appeal to humanist sentiments by galvanizing broader publics around the notion that no human is illegal (Ngai 2006). Drawing on frameworks within linguistic anthropology, I drafted and circulated a statement in support of this effort.[6] In the statement, I sought to challenge the notion that "illegal" is somehow an unbiased or neutral term, as had been claimed by influential US media outlets including the *Associated Press*[7] and the *New York Times*.[8] Inspired by the key linguistic anthropological insight that language is not simply a passive way of representing already existing objects in the world but rather a powerful form of social action, I pointed to the stigmatizing functions of discourses of migrant "illegality." This stigmatization includes heightened forms of violence that have increasingly positioned US Latinxs, and others considered "illegal," as targets of hate crimes.

The statement circulated widely, accumulated endorsements from dozens of fellow linguistic anthropologists, and was mentioned in prominent US and international media outlets including *ABC News/Univision*,[9] *CNN*,[10] *NPR*,[11] and the *Guardian*.[12] We were encouraged by the reception of these efforts, which contributed to the decision by outlets such as the *Associated Press*,[13] *USA Today*,[14] and *LA Times*[15] to change their style guidelines regarding the use of the term "illegal" in reference to (im)migrants. Specifically, the influential *Associated Press* decided to amend its Stylebook, which serves as a guide for media outlets throughout the nation. The Stylebook now recommends to drop the use of the phrase "illegal immigrant," as well as the term "illegal" in reference to a person. However, as linguistic anthropologists, we were also sensitive to the importance of emphasizing that this was more than simply a struggle over terminology. In many of the media interviews I gave in conjunction with the public statement, I was often asked for alternative terms that could be substituted for "illegal." While I discussed the politics of terms such as "undocumented" and "unauthorized" (Plascencia 2009) and emphasized the importance of respecting many targeted community members' preference for "undocumented," I also challenged the notion that we could resolve the (im)migration debate by merely identifying a new word. Indeed, as discussed above, contemporary violence at the southern US border is tied to histories that preceded use of the term "illegal" and will continue in its aftermath without a critical interrogation and reimagination of migration as a fundamental human right in the US and across the world. This speaks to a broader challenge for applied linguists who might understandably focus their efforts primarily on language issues. Apparent language-related problems are often rooted in societal structures that cannot be unsettled simply by modifying language policies and practices. Therefore, we must work in critical interdisciplinary solidarity with marginalized communities and social movements to lend our expertise when relevant while also recognizing the importance of linking struggles over language to wider efforts toward envisioning and enacting worlds beyond narrow intellectual, sociolinguistic, and geopolitical borders. In the context of debates surrounding the language of migrant "illegality," this involves shifting from advocacy for discourses that affirm access to citizenship and inclusion into the nation as end goals, to conceptualizing and enacting abolition and decolonization as pathways toward more just and sustainable worlds.

Mascot names and the naturalization of public racism

Bernard C. Perley

The first signs of autumn often include cooler temperatures, shorter days, the leaves changing color, and apple harvests. Fall is also football season. In September 2019, residents in Cincinnati, Ohio saw another sign of autumn: someone had sprayed graffiti on Anderson High School's athletic facilities. The school mascot is the "Redskins" and someone was not happy about the racist moniker and decided to display disaffection (Bogage 2019). Among the graffiti expressions considered *vandalism* was the word "Racists" which was sprayed on the running track and on the back wall of the baseball dugout, the expression

"Redskins? More like Whiteskins" sprayed on the right side of the Indian head logo, and the phrase "Change the name!" sprayed on the left side.

The vandalism that took place in Cincinnati puts on full display the hypocrisy of the school superintendent and the law enforcement agency. According to the *Washington Post* article the officer who discovered the graffiti described it as "profane" with "racial overtones." Yet, the officer does not regard "redskins" as either profane or racist. Again, according to the *Post* article, the school superintendent is quoted as saying, "The graffiti at Anderson High School is deeply disturbing and does not reflect the beliefs of our students nor staff." Yet, the superintendent did not denounce the use of the racist moniker nor the naturalized racism that celebrates the racist mascot. Anderson High School perpetuates one of the most insidious and longest-running practices of social injustice here in the US; namely, White public racism against Native Americans. The reason the school official and law enforcement do not see their actions as hate speech and racist actions against Native Americans is because it has become naturalized, "in which individuals do not consciously realize that these seemingly innocent yet harmful representations of others are socially constructed and learned" (Avineri and Perley 2019: 148). The year-round display of sports mascots that stereotype Native Americans (Cleveland Indians; Atlanta Braves; Kansas City Chiefs; Chicago Blackhawks) is hate speech that inflicts harm to young Native Americans. These displays continue despite over four decades of Native American activism to change racist monikers and logos (King 2016). The push to retire mascots led to the courtroom strategies to further push for the retirement of both racist mascots and racist monikers. Meanwhile, researchers explored the negative psychological impact of these displays (Gambine 2015).[16] The American Psychological Association issued a statement citing a "growing body of social science literature that shows the harmful effects of racial stereotyping and inaccurate racial portrayals, including the particularly damaging effects of American Indian sports mascots on the social identity development and self-esteem of American Indian young people" (American Psychological Association 2018). Scholars from multiple disciplines have drawn upon one another's work to demonstrate in various ways how the harm is real and the need for healing is immediate.

What are the prospects for healing? In any remediation of victim abuse it is not enough for the victim to be treated for the trauma suffered. Comprehensive remediation must also address the pathology of the abuser. In the case of White racism against Native Americans, through the everyday use of mascots and monikers, we must acknowledge that it is not only Native American youth who need healing, but those who perpetuate the hate speech with impunity must also learn that they will suffer from the pathology of bullying. The school superintendent and the law enforcement officer in the Anderson High School case must realize that they are bullying invisible communities of Native American youth. Such naturalized racism continues to be exercised because the victim is invisible. Is there social justice for communities that suffer erasure from public consciousness? Yes. It requires a coalescence of academics across diverse disciplines, educators at all levels, students at all levels, and public and elected officials and representatives to address the harm done to young Native Americans. We propose an active and engaged strategy of public coalition-building through *audience coalescence* (Avineri and Perley 2019) that highlights the hidden racism indexed by ideologies of historical denigration of Native Americans. Each time a mascot is celebrated and a racist moniker is used it perpetuates the semiotics of hate derived from colonial histories and reified in contemporary displays of willful ignorance. Audience coalescence is "an emergent coalition building process that identifies and promotes predispositions and stances toward redressing social injustices" (Avineri and Perley 2019: 149). The process seeks to reveal the naturalized racism toward Native Americans as the insidious normalization of centuries of hatred toward Native Americans. In doing so, unwitting perpetrators like the Anderson High School staff will not only realize that their condemnation of the graffiti reifies White hate, but also goes against the best ideals of American society: "life, liberty, and the pursuit of happiness" as well as "justice for all." American society must coalesce around those lofty ideals and put an end to using egregious Native American stereotyping in mascots and sports names.

We are hopeful audience coalescence can move American society toward social justice, and their advocacy and activism have produced some promising results. Through our activities in the AAA and SLA's LSJ Task Group we were able to put forward an initiative for the AAA to issue a public statement condemning the use of sports mascots and racist monikers. The AAA Executive Committee approved the statement on March 20, 2015 and can be found on the Association website (americananthro.org). We have presented at conferences as coauthors, as well as independently, to diverse audiences and venues. Each presentation was a new opportunity to expose the hypocrisy behind the use of Native American mascots and names, as well as to build a coalition that would distribute the work across disciplines, audiences, and communities. In each case, audience members realized that their own lack of awareness of the harm the stereotypes and racist monikers caused for Native American youth was an aspect of naturalized racism. This realization prompted understanding and alignment toward redressing the harmful practices and public displays.

One of the critical components for audience coalescence is the dual intention of identifying the problem as well as providing a means to remedy the problem. It was clear to us that promoting knowledge of the injustice behind White racism toward Native Americans is only the first step. We know we have to also continue to empower allies and advocates to take their own advocacy to their audiences and communities. That is why we continue to address this issue in our classes, in our writing, and in our professional public presentations. The key message for potential allies is to go from "making a difference" to "being the difference." We believe that "to combat centuries of colonialism and racism, it is essential to turn audiences into networks of social justice ... [becoming] active participants in envisioning a socially just present and future" (Avineri and Perley 2019: 154–5).

There are hopeful signs that those coalitions are taking root and that change is happening. Such changes include retiring mascots and changing mascot names as tangible remediation efforts, but also include changes in intangible properties such as ideational awareness as genuine respect and honor for America's first peoples. The summer of 2020 highlights the significance of audience coalescence through the current social justice movement Black Lives Matter. The call to address police violence against Black men was expanded to include systemic racism against all minoritized populations. This widening of focus brought new coalitions of activists together condemning the use of the racist moniker of the Washington professional football team. Resultant public and economic pressure on Dan Snyder, owner of the Washington professional football team, compelled him to retire the racist moniker despite his earlier "NEVER" stance. While this is a significant accomplishment for social justice there is still much to do. During this past Super Bowl, fans witnessed ongoing displays of racist behavior on the part of Kansas City Chiefs fans. There was outrage from Native American activists, but also from other Kansas City Chiefs fans. One account comes from a chef in a Kansas City restaurant who witnessed the "tomahawk chop" in his restaurant and commented "It doesn't show Kansas City pride ... it makes us look stupid."[17] The challenge before us is to address the stupidity that naturalized racism continues to succor and reveal the pathology of bullying that is perpetuated by these racist activities. Our contribution to this chapter is our latest example of coalition-building and healing for both Native Americans, as well as all Americans. It is our hope the readers of this chapter become aware of the harm mascots and monikers inflict on Native American youth and join our coalition to remediate the injustice these displays of naturalized racism perpetuate.

(Mis)Understanding the "30 million word gap"

Eric J. Johnson

In a promotional video for his Early Learning Initiative, former president Barack Obama makes the following claim: "We know that right now, during the first three years of life, a child born into a low-income family hears 30 million fewer words than a child born into a well-off family" (Obama 2014). The fact that a president of the United States highlighted this statistic about language and socioeconomic status as taken-for-granted knowledge (i.e., "We know that . . .") is significant and merits interrogation. Although few would argue against the president's use of research to back his vision for enhancing educational opportunities for underprivileged families, his use of the "30 million words" statistic reflects an underlying ethnocentric and classist view of language that: 1) is not grounded in the science of linguistics; and 2) continues to perpetuate, rather than mitigate, social inequities. This topic resonates deeply with my previous experiences as a high school teacher in a low-income school district, my current role as a faculty member in a teacher preparation program, and my commitment to language and social justice-oriented research.

What is the "language gap"?

The notion of the 30 million "word gap" stems from Hart and Risley's (1995) research on communication patterns in families from different socioeconomic levels, and claims that by age 3, children from more affluent households are exposed to approximately 30 million more words than children from low-income backgrounds. They concluded that this "word gap" is responsible for inferior cognitive development and eventual lower academic achievement (Hart and Risley 1995). I argue that the "language gap" is a misleading, and dangerous, concept because it is founded on a deficit perspective of low-income and linguistically diverse communities and prioritizes language patterns in school settings as inherently superior. Their conclusions consider the quantity of words to which children are exposed as the principal factor in cognitive development, which eventually manifests in their (in)capacity for learning in school settings. This view of language does not take into consideration the sociocultural influences involved in language development and communicative competence, nor is it based on describing features of language from a linguistic perspective. Scrutinizing the "language gap" through an anthropological lens brings these types of issues to the foreground and counters them with an asset-based narrative of language use and communication.

Despite serious theoretical and methodological weaknesses in Hart and Risley's study, the "word gap" concept has been widely embraced by policymakers and educators across the US. Moreover, current research premised on the "word gap" has extended across multiple linguistic dimensions, including quality of communication (Hoff 2003), language processing (Fernald et al. 2013), and health-related issues stemming from language use (Crow and O'Leary 2015). This expanded genealogy of the "word gap" is commonly described as "language gap" research. Unfortunately, the "language gap" literature generally omits research in fields such as linguistic anthropology, applied linguistics, sociolinguistics, and educational linguistics that have demonstrated how to view language based on communicative competence within, and across, different sociocultural contexts. In response to these areas of "language gap" research, there has been a growing body of literature that explicitly calls out this concept in terms of its sociolinguistic inaccuracies (Sperry et al. 2019), underlying deficit orientations (Avineri et al. 2015), theoretical and methodological deficiencies (Johnson 2017, Paugh and Riley 2019), influence on educators' perspectives of their students (Adair et al. 2017), and its prevalence across broader social discourses in the media, academia, and policy spheres (Johnson et al. 2017).

The swell of "language gap" scholarship over the past twenty years has incited a spike in programs and policies aimed at mitigating linguistic "deficiencies" of families from low-income backgrounds. Large-scale initiatives like *Providence Talks*, the *Thirty Million Words Initiative*, and *Too Small to Fail* are examples of programs designed to "help" children by changing how their parents talk. Moreover, the increase of "language gap" programs and research has received widespread publicity in the public media (Pondiscio 2019), further reinforcing deficit orientations toward culturally and linguistically diverse communities while also promoting dominant group norms of language use (Johnson et al. 2017). Even though a few media articles that problematize the "language gap" do exist (Rothschild 2016), the vast majority are based on the misguided assumption that language patterns found in school contexts are inherently superior to those of low-income communities.

Counternarratives to the "language gap"

Highlighting educational disparities across different socioeconomic, linguistic, and cultural groups is also a major concern in anthropological research; though, in fields like linguistic anthropology, it is common for researchers to look at a variety of sociocultural factors (e.g., educator demographics, teacher preparation, policy development, standardized testing, etc.) as contributing to academic challenges. It is important to acknowledge and applaud "language gap" researchers' efforts to point out socioeconomic inequities and to draw attention to the importance of language in academic development. That said, I am critical of the way the "language gap" assumes the linguistic superiority of a certain variety of language—school-based English in this case—without recognizing the ideological influences that feed into that perspective. During the 2014 meeting of the SLA's LSJ Task Group, this topic was brought up as a significant point of concern. Since then, I have engaged in collaborations with others to promote dialogue surrounding the "language gap," including:

1. university teaching and guest lecturing;
2. formal academic publishing and conference presentations;
3. media exposure;
4. professional development workshops; and
5. community outreach presentations.

As an instructor in a teacher preparation program, my lessons involving the "language gap" focus on how to equip students with the strategies to build on their culturally and linguistically diverse students' language abilities within academic contexts—instead of eschewing them as deficits. I have found Arnold and Faudree's (2019) cogent examples of how to critically teach this topic in university settings especially useful. Additionally, to support instructors who are interested in integrating the "language gap" topic into their courses, the SLA provides a repository of teaching materials and resources on their website, linguisticanthrology.org (Society for Linguistic Anthropology 2017). Nevertheless, the overall scarcity of scholarship and instructional materials on how to teach counterperspectives of the "language gap" exposes the need for more pedagogical examples and guidance.

As a researcher, I have contributed to a variety of publications focused on critiquing the language gap—most notable are collaborations with colleagues in academic journals (Avineri et al. 2015; Johnson 2017) and association newsletters (Avineri et al. 2016; Blum et al. 2015). I have participated in AAA and AAAL conference panel presentations, with a primary audience of academic researchers. Scholarship is considered to be the standard through which research is validated; however, its scope may be limited in terms of broader social impact. While the "language gap" spans research disciplines in academia, few scholars commit to turning academic advocacy into action. The LSJ Task Group is an example of how academic researchers collaborate to extend research into the public realm through teaching, writing in public outlets, offering trainings, and holding community gatherings. Considering the prevalence of pro "language-gap" research in academic literature and how it has been embraced in the media (Johnson et al. 2017), more academic scholarship that counters the "language gap" is needed.

We have also collaborated to stimulate dialogue in other contexts. One such collaboration was with LSJ colleagues to write an op-ed article in 2014, which we submitted to the *New York Times*, *Washington Post*, *LA Times*, *Chicago Tribune*, and *San Francisco Chronicle*—all of which rejected our critical take on the "language gap." Determining the exact reasons for not being accepted for publication in these media outlets is difficult considering the volume of op-ed submissions and rejection rates for those newspapers. That said, it is disconcerting, and dubious, that none of the newspapers were open to this type of discussion at the time, especially considering the widespread media attention that "language gap" remediation programs have received. However, the *Atlantic* reached out to me and LSJ colleague Netta Avineri about an interview for an article highlighting counterperspectives to the "language gap" (Rothschild 2016). Although the article in the *Atlantic* was not published explicitly as an LSJ effort, it does demonstrate that our effort to advance this issue into the broader public view is being acknowledged. Since then, additional counterperspectives have been voiced in the media and online (Kamenetz 2018).

Finally, I have facilitated multiple workshops for educators in school districts across the state of Washington to illustrate misperceptions surrounding the "language gap" as well as strategies for rethinking classroom instruction and family engagement. For example, I have been able to deliver three professional development trainings based on countering the "language gap" at the Washington Association for Bilingual Education annual conference for educators from around the state. Although it is difficult to know how all of the participants in these workshops ultimately applied the information presented in these trainings, I have had conversations with teachers about rethinking their views toward students' home-language skills and applying this perspective in academic settings. I have taken a similar approach during presentations for community organizations, family engagement workshops with parents, meetings with Washington's department of education, and even at an administrative training event with a local library system. I contend that any social justice effort that engages people to consider positions of advocacy is worthwhile and should be supported, regardless of direct evidence of widespread social impact.

My emphasis has consistently involved challenging individuals to rethink commonsense notions of communication and language so that linguistic diversity is not seen as a deficit. Whereas heightening a broader awareness of linguistic strengths can propel our understanding of language diversity forward, truly moving beyond a "language gap" orientation involves reframing the conversation about the academic achievement disparities that emerge across different socioeconomic status groups. Addressing the root causes of the persistent educational inequities confronting individuals from culturally, linguistically, and economically marginalized communities merits a deeper examination of how teachers are prepared and professionally mentored to effectively engage students and families from all backgrounds. While anthropological research demonstrates that language gaps do not exist, we must recognize that the ideologically (re)produced "language gap" *concept* does very much exist. Creating safe environments to flesh out this concept's shortcomings and allow people to reconsider their own biases is a positive step toward moving past "gaps" and forging more linguistically supportive platforms for educational reform.

Conclusion

Netta Avineri

Applied linguistic anthropology necessitates a sensitivity to time, scale, audience, positionality, modality, and impact. As these case studies demonstrate, this approach involves long-term, in-depth understanding of issues, contexts, and communities alongside active engagement in collaboration with others. It becomes evident that systemic change takes time and is an ongoing battle, with successes, challenges, and disappointments. The authors highlight how critical it is to have a supportive community of practice, such as the LSJ Task Group, with whom to collaborate when combating problematic ideologies and practices. Through an email list of committed professionals, the LSJ Task Group provides a forum for exploring complex issues and a means to mobilize and raise critical awareness toward collective action in a dynamic and responsive way. Each member of the inclusive group can become exposed to issues, approaches, and initiatives through observation and direct engagement. LSJ discussion members can see how others have engaged similar issues while they may address issues more locally (e.g., through teaching or other professional activities). In this way, the listserv and conference meetings become fertile spaces for peer socialization into a more social justice-oriented community of practice.

This approach involves a recognition that frequently issues related to language and social justice operate at multiple scales. For example, when looking at sports team mascot names at the level of both national sports teams and local sports teams, one can see the iconization and rhematization of the stereotypes associated with the mascot's symbolic practices mapped onto indigeneity in general and vice versa. Or when Obama talks on a national stage about the "language gap" one can feel those reverberations in what happens at individual schools and with individual students. Therefore, an applied linguistic anthropology must recognize how the micro, meso, and macro levels are all connected in terms of media (e.g., I-word), policies (e.g., Census Bureau), and institutions (e.g., national sports teams, schooling).

As each of the authors discuss, their positionalities, both personal and professional, shape their interests in the issues as well as their collaborative approach to addressing them. Academics can offer these positionalities and expertise toward broader activist efforts. Their firsthand experiences provide important lessons in how to recognize one's own positionality and how to build upon that in coalition with others. As Zentella and Johnson highlight, it is essential for academics to model responsible research design and analysis to counteract pervasive, misleading arguments based on faulty assumptions. As Rosa and Perley demonstrate, racist representations of both Indigenous and migrant groups take on a life of their own. These are examples of the many social issues that applied linguistic anthropologists can uniquely address through engagement in multiple venues.

In addition, this approach entails a broadening of audiences, activities, and modalities. The case studies each highlight how the authors, in collaboration with others, engage with diverse publics through presentations and conferences, op-eds and media engagement, teaching, mentorship, and beyond. Applied linguistic anthropologists are uniquely positioned to broaden their range of language practices and genres in the service of mobilizing toward social change.

Lastly, this approach highlights the importance of considering various forms of "success" and "impact." For example, some might consider the re-examination of assumptions or awareness raising as sufficient impact, whereas others may believe that policy change is a better metric of success. Activism and advocacy involve collaboration at multiple levels, and, therefore, an exploration of impact is central to effective social change. Reconceptualizing what impact involves within both academic and institutional structures is key to this endeavor as well (cf., Lawson and Sayers 2017). Overall, the authors have demonstrated how in-depth observation, reflection, and critique; recognition of one's own positionalities; processes of collaboration; and actions for social change are central to an applied linguistic anthropological approach. One must also recognize the inherent tensions involved in both exploring issues in depth while seeking to redress the societal inequities that become evident during that exploration. Through observation, critique, reflection, and collaboration, scholars of language can use these tools and dispositions to move meaningfully toward social change, justice, and liberation.

Notes

1. Here and throughout the chapter we have used the word "minoritized" to encapsulate both the numerical minority situation of many groups as well as the status of being positioned as marginal/subordinate regardless of numbers. For some groups, numerical minority status has particular salience (e.g., Native Americans being only 3% of the US population). "Minoritization" may also be a problematic conceptualization (e.g., Native Americans being "minoritized" rather than seen as sovereign peoples). See this chapter for "audience coalescence" as a strategy to overcome such numerical odds and reframe minoritizing ideologies.
2. "PULSE | English as a Second Language," *The New York Times*, December 7, 1992: B1.
3. Latinu, Zentella's alternative to Latinx, is gender non-binary and respects Spanish phonology. The authors of this chapter vary in their preference for an inclusive term.
4. Limited English proficient children were problematically referred to as "LEP-ers."
5. Drop the I-Word. *RaceForward.org*. Available online: https://www.raceforward.org/practice/tools/drop-i-word
6. Jonathan Rosa, "Contesting Representations of Immigration," *Anthropology News*, October 2013. Available online: http://linguisticanthropology.org/wp-content/uploads/2015/02/Jonathan-Rosa-Contesting-Representations-of-Immigration.pdf
7. Mónica Novoa, "The Associated Press Updates Its Stylebook, Still Clings to I-Word," *Colorlines*, November 10, 2011. Available online: www.colorlines.com/articles/associated-press-updates-its-stylebook-still-clings-i-word
8. Margaret Sullivan, "Readers Won't Benefit if Times Bans the Term 'Illegal Immigrant,'" *The New York Times*, October 2, 2012. Available online: https://publiceditor.blogs.nytimes.com/2012/10/02/readers-wont-benefit-if-times-bans-the-term-illegal-immigrant/?_r=0
9. Cristina Costantini, "Linguistics Tell New York Times that 'Illegal' is Neither 'Neutral' nor 'Accurate,'" *ABC News/Univision*, October 1, 2012. Available online: http://

abcnews.go.com/ABC_Univision/linguists-york-times-illegal-neutral-%20accurate/story?id=17366512
10 Cindy Y. Rodriguez, "Language like 'Illegal Immigrant' Seen as a Challenge During Immigration Debate," *CNN*, April 4, 2013. Available online: http://www.cnn.com/2013/04/04/us/illegal-immigrant-term-still-a-challenge
11 Gene Demby, "In Immigration Debate, 'Undocumented' Vs. 'Illegal' is More than Just Semantics," *NPR*, January 30, 2013. Available online: https://www.npr.org/sections/itsallpolitics/2013/01/30/170677880/in-immigration-debate-undocumented-vs-illegal-is-more-than-just-semantics
12 Lauren Gambino, "'No Human Being is Illegal': Linguists Argue Against Mislabeling of Immigrants," *The Guardian*, December 6, 2015. Available online: https://www.theguardian.com/us-news/2015/dec/06/illegal-immigrant-label-offensive-wrong-activists-say
13 Cristina Costantini, "Associated Press Drops 'Illegal Immigrant' from Stylebook," *ABC News/Univision*, April 2, 2013. Available online: https://abcnews.go.com/ABC_Univision/press-drops-illegal-immigrant-standards-book/story?id=18862824
14 Roque Planas, "USA Today Drops 'Illegal Immigrant,'" *The Huffington Post*, April 11, 2013. Available online: http://www.huffingtonpost.com/2013/04/11/usa-today-illegal-immigrant_n_3062479.html
15 Jamilah King, "Los Angeles Times Drops 'Illegal Immigrant,'" *Colorlines*, May 2, 2013. Available online: https://www.colorlines.com/articles/los-angeles-times-drops-illegal-immigrant.
16 Bert Gambini, "Research shows Native American imagery hurts all ethnic groups, says UB psychologist," The University of Buffalo news website, March 11, 2015. Available online: http://www.buffalo.edu/research/research-services/click-implementation/announcements.host.html/content/shared/university/news/news-center-releases/2015/03/021.detail.html
17 John Eligon, "Celebrating the Kansas City Chiefs, the Chop Divides," *The New York Times*, January 29, 2020. Available online: https://www.nytimes.com/2020/01/29/sports/football/chiefs-tomahawk-chop.html

References

Adair, J. K., K. S. S. Colegrove, and M. E. McManus (2017), "How the Word Gap Argument Negatively Impacts Young Children of Latinx Immigrants' Conceptualizations of Learning," *Harvard Educational Review*, 87(3): 309–34.
American Anthropology Association (2008), "Statement on Language Questions in the US Census," 6 February. Available online: https://www.americananthro.org/ConnectWithAAA/Content.aspx?ItemNumber=2596

American Anthropology Association (2011), "American Anthropological Association Spurs Elimination of 'Linguistically Isolated' as Classification by the U. S. Census Bureau," 2 May. Available online: http://linguisticanthropology.org/wp-content/uploads/2015/02/U-S-Census-Bureau.pdf

American Psychological Association (2018), "Summary of the APA Resolution Recommending Retirement of American Indian Mascots." Available online: https://www.apa.org/pi/oema/resources/indian-mascots

Arnold, L., and P. Faudree (2019), "Language and Social Justice: Teaching about the Word Gap," *Teaching American Speech*, 94(2): 283–301.

Avineri, N., E. Johnson, S. Brice-Heath, T. McCarty, E. Ochs, T. Kremer-Sadlik, S. Blum, A. C. Zentella, J. Rosa, N. Flores, H. S. Alim, and D. Paris (2015), "Invited Forum: Bridging the 'Language Gap,'" *Journal of Linguistic Anthropology*, 25(1): 66–86.

Avineri, N., S. D. Blum, E. J. Johnson, K. C. Riley, and A. C. Zentella (2016), "The Gap that Won't Be Filled: An Anthropolitical Critique of the 'Language Gap,'" *Anthropology News*, 29 August. Available online: http://linguisticanthropology.org/blog/2016/08/29/an-news-the-gap-that-wont-be-filled-an-anthropolitical-critique-of-the-language-gap-by-avineri-et-al/

Avineri, N., and B. C. Perley (2019), "Mascots, Name Calling, and Racial Slurs: Seeking Social Justice through Audience Coalescence," in N. Avineri, L. R. Graham, E. J. Johnson, R. C. Riner, and J. Rosa (eds.), *Language and Social Justice in Practice*, pp. 147–56, New York: Routledge.

Bogage, J. (2019), "'Redskins?? More Like White Skins": Graffiti Opposing High School's Mascot Opens Old Wounds," *The Washington Post*, 5 September. Available online: https://www.washingtonpost.com/sports/2019/09/05/redskins-more-like-white-skins-graffiti-opposing-high-schools-mascot-opens-old-wounds/

Blum, S. D., N. Avineri, and E. J. Johnson (2015), "White + Word Gap = Wrong!," *American Anthropological Association* blog, 22 June. Available online: http://blog.aaanet.org/2015/06/22/white-word-gap-wrong

Census Bureau (2010), "*2010 English Language and Ability Terminology in the American Community Survey*," 14 May. Available online: https://www.census.gov/topics/population/language-use/about.html

Costantini, C. (2011), "Anti-Latino Hate Crimes Rise as Immigration Debate Intensifies," *Huffington Post*, 17 October. Available online: www.huffingtonpost.com/2011/10/17/anti-latino-hate-crimes-rise-immigration_n_1015668.html

Costantini, C. (2012), "Linguistics Tell New York Times that 'Illegal' is Neither 'Neutral' nor 'Accurate,'" *ABC News/Univision*, 1 October. Available online: http://abcnews.go.com/ABC_Univision/linguists-york-times-illegal-neutral-%20accurate/story?id=17366512

Costantini, C. (2013), "Associated Press Drops 'Illegal Immigrant' from Stylebook," *ABC News/Univision*, 2 April. Available online: https://abcnews.go.com/ABC_Univision/press-drops-illegal-immigrant-standards-book/story?id=18862824

Crow, S., and A. O'Leary (2015), "Word Health: Addressing the Word Gap as a Public Health Crisis," *Next Generation*, May. Available online: http://thenextgeneration.org/files/Word_Health_v3.pdf

De Genova, N. (2004), "The Legal Production of Mexican/Migrant 'Illegality,'" *Latino Studies*, 2 (2): 160–85.

Demby, G. (2013), "In Immigration Debate, 'Undocumented' Vs. 'Illegal; is More than Just Semantics," *NPR*, 30 January. Available online: https://www.npr.org/sections/itsallpolitics/2013/01/30/170677880/in-immigration-debate-undocumented-vs-illegal-is-more-than-just-semantics

Dockerman, D. (2009), "Statistical Portrait of Hispanics in the United States," *Pew Research Center*, 17 February. Available online: https://www.pewresearch.org/hispanic/2011/02/17/2009-statistical-information-on-hispanics-in-united-states/

"Drop the I-Word," *RaceForward.org*. Available online: https://www.raceforward.org/practice/tools/drop-i-word

Eligon, J. (2020), "Celebrating the Kansas City Chiefs, the Chop Divides," *The New York Times*, 28 January. Available online: www.nytimes.com/2020/01/29/sports/football/chiefs-tomahawk-chop.html

Fernald, A., V. A. Marchman, and A. Weisleder (2013), "SES Differences in Language Processing Skill and Vocabulary Are Evident at 18 Months," *Developmental Science*, 16(2): 234–48.

Gambini, B. (2015), "Research Shows Native American Imagery Hurts All Ethnic Groups, says UB Psychologist," *University of Buffalo*, 11 March. Available online: http://www.buffalo.edu/research/research-services/click-implementation/announcements.host.html/content/shared/university/news/news-center-releases/2015/03/021.detail.html

Gambino, L. (2015), "'No Human Being is Illegal': Linguists Argue Against Mislabeling of Immigrants," *The Guardian*, 6 December. Available online: https://www.theguardian.com/us-news/2015/dec/06/illegal-immigrant-label-offensive-wrong-activists-say

Grabmeier, J. (2019), "A 'Million Word Gap' for Children Who Aren't Read to at Home: That's How Many Fewer Words Some May Hear by Kindergarten," *Science Daily*, 4 April. Available online: https://www.sciencedaily.com/releases/2019/04/190404074947.htm

Hart, B., and T. R. Risley (1995), *Meaningful Differences in the Everyday Experience of Young American Children*, Baltimore: Brookes Publishing.

Hoff, E. (2003), "The Specificity of Environmental Influence: Socioeconomic Status Affects Early Vocabulary Development via Maternal Speech," *Child Development*, 74: 1368–78.

Johnson, E. J. (2017), "Special Journal Issue on the 'Language Gap,'" *International Multilingual Research Journal*, 11(1).

Johnson, E. J., N. Avineri, and D. C. Johnson (2017), "Exposing Gaps in/between Discourses of Linguistic Deficits," *International Multilingual Research Journal*, 11(1): 5–22.

Kamenetz, A. (2018), "Let's Stop Talking about the '30 Million Word Gap,'" *NPR Ed,* 1 June. Available online: https://www.npr.org/sections/ed/2018/06/01/615188051/lets-stop-talking-about-the-30-million-word-gap

King, J. (2013), "Los Angeles Times Drops 'Illegal Immigrant,'" *Colorlines,* 2 May. Available online: https://www.colorlines.com/articles/los-angeles-times-drops-illegal-immigrant

King, R. C. (2016), *Redskins: Insult and Brand,* Lincoln NE: University of Nebraska Press.

Lawson, R., and D. Sayers (2017), *Sociolinguistic Research: Application and Impact,* London and New York: Routledge.

Leeman, J. (2018a), *Questioning the Language Questions: Federal Policy and the Evaluation of the U.S. Census Bureau's Statistics on Language* (Survey Methodology No. 2018–11; Center for Survey Measurement Study Series, p. 20), Research and Methodology Directorate, US Census Bureau.

Leeman, J. (2018b), "It's All About English: The Interplay of Monolingual Ideologies, Language Policies and the U.S. Census Bureau's Statistics on Multilingualism," *International Journal of the Sociology of Language,* 252, 21–43 (13 June). Available online: https://doi.org/10.1515/ijsl-2018-0013

Ngai, M. (2006), "No Human Being Is Illegal," *Women's Studies Quarterly,* 34(3/4): 291–5.

Novoa, M. (2011), "The Associated Press Updates Its Stylebook, Still Clings to I-Word," *Colorlines,* 10 November. Available online: www.colorlines.com/articles/associated-press-updates-its-stylebook-still-clings-i-word

Obama, B. (2014), "President Obama appeals to parents to #closethewordgap," Too Small to Fail speech, 25 June. Available online: https://www.youtube.com/watch?v=gu5P5NbGxEY

Paugh, A. L., and K. C. Riley (2019), "Poverty and Children's Language in Anthropolitical Perspective," *Annual Review of Anthropology,* 48: 297–315.

Pell, S. (2020), "Maine to Become First State to Prohibit Native American Mascots in all Public Schools," *The Washington Post,* 15 February. Available online: https://www.washingtonpost.com/sports/2019/05/17/maine-become-first-state-prohibit-native-american-mascots-all-public-schools/

Planas, R. (2013), "USA Today Drops 'Illegal Immigrant,'" *The Huffington Post,* 11 April. Available online: http://www.huffingtonpost.com/2013/04/11/usa-today-illegal-immigrant_n_3062479.html

Plascencia, L. (2009), "The 'Undocumented' Mexican Migrant Question: Re-Examining the Framing of Law and Illegalization in the United States," *Urban Anthropology,* 38(2–4): 375–434.

Pondiscio, R. (2019), "Don't Dismiss that 30 Million-Word Gap Quite so Fast," *Education Next,* 6 June. Available online: https://www.educationnext.org/dont-dismiss-30-million-word-gap-quite-fast/

"PULSE | English as a Second Language: 'Percentage of children 5 to 17 years old who did not speak English at home' and 'Percentage of children 5 to 17 years old who lived in linguistic isolation.'" (1992), *The New York Times,* 7 December: B1.

Rodriguez, C. Y. (2013), "Language like 'Illegal Immigrant' seen as a Challenge During Immigration Debate," *CNN*, 4 April. Available online: http://www.cnn.com/2013/04/04/us/illegal-immigrant-term-still-a-challenge

Rosa, J. (2013), "Contesting Representations of Immigration," *Anthropology News*, October. Available online: http://linguisticanthropology.org/wp-content/uploads/2015/02/Jonathan-Rosa-Contesting-Representations-of-Immigration.pdf

Rothschild, A. (2016). "Beyond the Word Gap: Are Efforts to Boost Kids' Vocabularies before Kindergarten Missing the Mark?," *The Atlantic*, 22 April. Available online: https://www.theatlantic.com/education/archive/2016/04/beyond-the-word-gap/479448/

Santa Ana, O. (2002), *Brown Tide Rising: Metaphors of Latinos in Contemporary American Public Discourse*, Austin: University of Texas Press.

Santa Ana, O., and C. González de Bustamante (eds.) (2012), *Arizona Firestorm: Global Immigration Realities, National Media, and Provincial Politics*, Lanham: Rowman & Littlefield.

Society for Linguistic Anthropology (2017), "'Language Gap' Teaching Resources." Available online: http://linguisticanthropology.org/socialjustice/initiatives/language-gap-teaching-resources/

Soifer, D. (2009), "Linguistic Isolation Carries a Heavy Cost," *Lexington Institute*, 10 April. Available online: http://lexingtoninstitute.org/linguistic-isolation-carries-a-heavy-cost/

Sperry, D. E., L. L Sperry, and P. J. Miller (2019), "Language Does Matter: But There Is More to Language Than Vocabulary and Directed Speech," *Child Development*, 90(3): 993–7.

Sullivan, M. "Readers Won't Benefit if Times Bans the Term 'Illegal Immigrant,'" *The New York Times*, 2 October. Available online: https://publiceditor.blogs.nytimes.com/2012/10/02/readers-wont-benefit-if-times-bans-the-term-illegal-immigrant/?_r=0

Zentella, A. C. (1995), "The 'Chiquita-fication' of U.S. Latinos and Their Languages, or Why We Need an Anthro-political Linguistics," *SALSA III: The Proceedings of the Symposium about Language and Society at Austin*, 1–18.

Zentella, A. C. (2009), "An Effective Census 2010 / Un Censo Eficaz en el 2010," *El Diario-La Prensa*, 23.

Zentella, A. C. (2011), "Gota a Gota, el Mar se Agota: The Census and Combatting Linguistic Intolerance," *San Diego La Prensa*, 29 April. Available online: http://laprensa-sandiego.org/stories/gota-a-gota-el-mar-se-agota-the-census-and-combatting-linguistic-intolerance/

Afterword: Crossing Borders, Rethinking Expertise, and Becoming *Collaborative* Linguists

Betsy Rymes

It takes a solidity and depth of purpose—courage—to cross borders and then, once on the other side, to work to make yourself understood, to step outside the criteria of judgment you've grown accustomed to. After years of recognition in one stream of life, the current runs strong. It's hard to go against that current, to turn from a lifetime working among one group of people and their shared assumptions and look to broader horizons. Even more difficult: Once you turn upstream and face those new horizons, it could get ugly. You might not like what you see. People there, those you mean to reach, as you struggle against the current, may not understand you or care about what you're saying. You might not understand them. Having spent your entire adulthood in different worlds of value, crossing into new social worlds—and then offering your services to those worlds—can be dicey. But that work across borders and, in the case of this volume, extending applied linguistics into new realms and cross-disciplinary collaborations must be done.

We now live in an era of precarity and doubt, in which such crossing—into other disciplines and other ways of life—has become more critical. In academia, soothing notions like "tenure," "job security," or even "progress" have become questionable. A world of struggles amid the destruction wrought by global capitalism—our damaged planet, endemic racism, sexism and xenophobia, and the attendant violence—has become more visible and impossible to address within the University walls. The trappings of material and intellectual progress associated with more isolated academic work have lost their sheen. The epistemic privilege that attends academia has also become more tenuous. Our contemporary conditions demand new ways of thinking, the wisdom of all the world, and the *public inquiry* of the kind this book has brought together.

But what can applied linguists do, specifically? How does linguistic expertise manage to have relevant social impact? In *The Mushroom at the End of the World: On the Possibility of Life in Capitalist Ruins* (2015), Anna Tsing points to the need to rethink notions of "progress" precisely by honing our own abilities to notice the details of the world, and to develop an appreciation for the connections between those details, the collaborations that build new ways of living—and thinking—together. Her book is an ethnography of the forms of life that surround one mushroom, the Matsutaki, a mushroom that cannot be cultivated, whose means of production cannot be standardized, and that crops up in the crevices of previous failures, or those spots of ruin left abandoned in the wake of capitalism's "progress." Her study of the mushroom reveals the kinds of unlikely and often happenstance collaborations that build new forms of life within the spoils of a world devastated by capitalism. Applied linguists, by taking a longer look at language and communication, might also draw attention to similar happenstance and hopeful forms of life.

Each of the chapters in this volume point to this possibility for new kinds of knowledge, emerging from collaborative forms of inquiry and partnership with new publics. Each describes working across disciplines and communities, with the hope that these collaborations will bring new ways of noticing, working together to make a world that is inhabitable by everyone. To make this radical shift in noticing and collaboration across borders, however, necessitates that those of us in academia abandon our sense of what counts as progress, and perhaps even what counts as social change. We need to look beyond intellectual challenges faced on our own terms and move on to the rewards of being our best selves among others we don't know or understand—even when that means forgoing assured approval of those from whom we've been trained to expect it. These authors have all taken that brave step.

By bringing together these examples of collaborative research, this volume gives us a rare opportunity to compare, in detail, the promise and pitfalls of *public inquiry*. The candid and open descriptions convey the integrity with which each of the coauthors pursued collaborations. In what follows, I'll focus on how these courageous authors wrestled in various ways with crossing institutional borders, reckoning with new forms of expertise, and finally, the importance of moving from "applied" to "collaborative" positionality as scholars in our increasingly precarious world.

Crossing institutional borders

As researchers and professors in the University, the career of most applied linguists or linguistic anthropologists is spent honing a professional voice and position. All of us probably have a friend whose communicative repertoire is limited to this realm, who feels uncomfortable interacting in other contexts, or with non-academic types. Maybe we even are that friend! Professionally, this can serve us well, as we learn to "talk the talk and walk the walk" of academia. But no one ever teaches us, explicitly, how to cross from academia into public inquiry, the very subject of this volume, and arguably, a necessity for applied work in the service of social impact. How do these authors variably manage that border crossing?

Christina Higgins introduces her work on advocating for Pidgin speakers in Hawai'i with a discussion of her own childhood growing up on military bases, reflecting on how that childhood gave her a certain ease socializing across social boundaries. She contrasts these early years with the relative discomfort she felt once her family joined "civilian life," in which she found herself suddenly cut off from the diversity she had experienced in the first part of her childhood. Through these experiences, she serendipitously developed the ability and desire to be among diverse others rather than to retreat into sameness. Her own "public-facing" scholarship is a natural match for these invisible skills—and the result is highly visible work. Her chapter goes on to describe three different ways she, as a scholar living in Hawai'i, worked within the Pidgin-speaking community to collaboratively develop public-facing projects.

Her role and status as a university professor smoothed her entry into the community and advocacy work, but she didn't lean on that status. Nor did she let it hold her back from genuine collaboration. She made great efforts to hold events or create artifacts that would have an impact to people outside of academia, while sharing with them, her perspective from the scholarly community.

While straddling these two worlds, and upon discovering the vibrance of such border-crossing, it might occur to some to shed their academic identity completely—to become public intellectuals or work outside the University. But for Higgins, rather than making her look back at the ivory tower as irrelevant, these collaborations made her "more enthusiastic about academia than ever" (p. X). Not because she wanted to leave her collaborators behind and return to the dusty halls of academia. Rather, through this project, she was able to see how her decades as a scholar could uplift communities outside academia. Her position provided a platform for the voices and expertise of Pidgin speakers to be heard.

Other authors describe navigating rougher waters as they crossed institutional borders. In her chapter on collaborating with science museums, for example, Leslie Moore describes waiting until post-tenure to begin this work, to be liberated from the pressures of academia. However, even when she was free from the demands of the tenure process, and as she developed the project with partners from the network of museums she was working with, Moore remained bound to her sense of obligation to some institutional role as expert from the University, and to the specific expertise on *repertoires of practice* that she brought to the NSF-funded exploratory study. As Moore brought this line of thinking into the museum world, ideas honed over years as a scholar of multilingualism and early childhood education, it seems her partners also remained bound by the demands of their own institutional roles as museum administrators and teacher educators.

Even as Moore developed a study to explore the repertoires of practice of those multilingual families they were hoping to reach, the institutional "repertoires of practice" of both Moore and her collaborators seemed to function at cross purposes. As ultra-competent professionals in their very different worlds, they enacted an obligation to their institutional roles: Moore, the university professor, took on the expected institutional role of providing theoretical and research expertise, collecting "data," while the museum-based educators took on their expected institutional roles, developing webinars and professional development workshops (and recruiting Moore to this work as well). Institutional roles persisted within a working relationship. Each collaborator sacrificed time for each other's institutional demands. In the end, the team developed a carefully defined division of labor and time, but never seemed to develop a sense of collaborative inquiry. Public inquiry, with each other and with those multilingual families they hoped to serve through this collaboration, seemed to remain out of reach.

Elizabeth Miller's chapter on her role as applied linguist in an interdisciplinary network focused on *social sustainability* also highlights some of the frustrations of border-crossing, even when those borders remain largely within academia. A goal of the NSF-funded research network Miller joined was explicitly to bring researchers together with scholars from other disciplines and with practitioners outside the University, to stimulate new forms of thinking, offering them time to collaborate, away from their entrenched notions of expertise. Miller's role evolved so that she became both a participant in this network and a researcher studying the language of the network. Her findings illuminate both roles: Her careful corpus-assisted discourse analysis points to a form of frustration qualitatively different from Moore's collaboration. The network of scholars that Miller was working with resolutely avoided their own repertoires of practice. Rather than sticking to their disciplinary expertise and expounding on it, Miller's research shows that, when working groups discussed the matter at hand—honing a definition of *social sustainability*—they relied on vagueness and inconclusive talk, even a backing away from expertise. Miller aptly identified this pragmatic move, calling on a useful term from applied linguistics, "strategic ambiguity." The ways the network talked about *social sustainability*—primarily by not being able or even attempting to define it—became the very substance of their ultimately "unfinalizable" finding: The term *social sustainability* need not be pinned down after all—*social sustainability* is necessarily ambiguous, and will remain so, as long as it is necessary.

In spite of ambitious border-crossing plans, Miller's network of collaborators eventually returned to less radical networking as their final conferences resembled more traditional individual presentations and responses. Their return to more business-as-usual styles of conferencing looks like a retreat back to realms where their expertise was tangible and recognized. Within their initial breakout group format of interdisciplinary border-crossing, it seemed interactionally impossible to redistribute expertise and genuinely collaborate—to think together.

While the collaborators in Moore's chapter seemed to hold fast to their expert roles of professor and museum-based educators, the collaborators in Miller's study seemed to relinquish theirs, to the point of never finding a shared task. As Moore's museum group seemed to hold tightly to their own expert roles, Miller's partners retreated from their own expertise when faced with collaboration. Both these moves may be recognizable to those of us in academia: When we come together as a group, individuals can be eager to share their unique expertise, holding fast to their disciplinary knowledge. At the same time, when grouped with peers from other disciplines, with the goal of thinking together about hard questions, individuals can retreat into vagueness or swiftly arrive "off task." Institutional roles can hamper us when we approach hard problems, or the invitation to think in new ways.

Obed Arango and Holly Link, in contrast, by creating and working together at their afterschool program, RevArte, have transcended institutional constraints. While both are accomplished researchers and scholars, they have also become expert border crossers, creating a space in which they work without the institutional role expectations of the University or K-12 public schools. At RevArte, they have intentionally created a space for children to use language creatively, countering the monolingualism and test-centric nature of the traditional K-12 schools these children attend. When Arango and Link discuss their work with immigrant boys at RevArte, there is no note of frustration with their working conditions or their capacity to engage in genuine collaboration within the community. Instead, their work focuses on resistance of oppression, taking a path toward *social justice*, which they define boldly, and with no "strategic ambiguity" as follows:

> more equitable treatment of individuals and groups who have been minoritized based on their socioeconomic, racio-ethnic, linguistic and/or cultural backgrounds, as well as more equitable distribution of opportunities and privileges for them. (p.x).

The collaboration between Link and Arango, and with the children at RevArte, becomes a shared struggle. They call on art, transnational popular culture, multilingualism, multilingual humor, and specifically translanguaging, to engage with their shared frustrations with the anti-immigrant policy, hateful verbiage, and everyday practices of the former US president they refer to as El innombrable. The care and intelligence Link and Arango put into their work with the children, researching, writing, and performing their theater piece remains organic to the needs and concerns of the community within which they are working, and in which they live. The expertise Arango and Link bring to this work isn't flashy, but it's deep and informed. They share a commitment to "Zapatista rage," and an understanding that building Spanish and English awareness in the boys, through translanguaging praxis, will build their sense of dignidad, and the strength of the Latinx community in which they live. Arango and Link's chapter captures moments of creative local artistic production and care that I suspect occur in many other places, but their collaboration within the community and through their afterschool arts center, combined with their commitment to publish and teach about this work, makes these moments visible, ongoing, and more powerful and lasting.

Like Link and Arango, Ellen Skilton explores the potential of theater work to call attention to injustice and provide participants the tools to confront it. She describes work both in and outside of academia, crossing between the practice of improvisational and participatory theater work in the community and in her classroom of student teachers. She specifically focuses on participatory theater works that have pushed people (including herself) to experience hegemonic Whiteness and understand its power, and brings applied linguistics to bear on these experiences through her reading of three analytic stances in linguistics, "markedness, subject-as-seen/subject-as-heard, and indexical inversion." Each of these concepts provides a vocabulary for articulating what the theater performances are accomplishing. The boundary Skilton crosses here is between those technical vocabularies of applied linguistics and the context of applied theater production—with the goal of illuminating how this theater work has the potential to upend hegemonic whiteness. In many respects, rather than orienting to institutional norms, this chapter explicitly focuses on disrupting norms, even when working within institutional boundaries.

In their collaborative work in the healthcare context, Emily Feuerherm and her colleagues struggle to work across institutional borders by building bridges between applied linguistics, community organizations, and the wider medical field. Their focus is on addressing and alleviating the effects of "social determinants of health." Their expertise as applied linguists, in particular, lead them to their projects, as they sought to understand and alleviate the ways that language and communication impede access to information and care. The research of Feuerherm and her colleagues, working with communities in Michigan, Ohio, and Kansas, illustrates how multilingual communities in all these contexts struggle to access and use medical services and practices. In the current state of overwhelming need, and increasingly disparate care across social demographics, collaboration across these communities, across their disparate forms of knowledge and communication has become a humanitarian necessity.

Feuerherm's research team in Flint, Michigan, for example, explicitly attempted to include several community partners to ensure information about lead in the environment reached them all. The immediacy of the problem meant that getting crucial medical information to the community could be a matter of life and death. Connecting the community to healthcare and information through cross-community collaboration is the focus of Feuerherm's work. However, crossing institutional borders in her case, even when the need seems so obvious and the diversity of expertise so critical, eventually proved frustrating. In this case, the slow implementation of university research protocols and conflict of interest documentation slowed the process down. Eventually, after repeated delays from the university, one of the community partners, *La Placita*, the partner who "provided expertise in community organizing, translation and interpreting, and deep local knowledge of the lives and experiences of the target participants" dropped from the collaboration.

As frustrating as it can be, even just reading about the difficulties Feuerherm and her colleagues have faced, it's simultaneously inspiring to learn about the impact applied linguists can potentially have by crossing borders into the world of healthcare. Morelli and Warriner, in their chapter describing the practices of Cultural Health Navigators (CHNs), also zero in on diversity in the healthcare system—emphasizing the importance of finding ways to learn about the specific challenges refuge-background families face in accessing healthcare. And, like the research of Feuerherm and colleagues, Morelli and Warriner uncover the importance of heightened awareness of subtle language and cultural distinctions. They do so by carefully documenting and analyzing the encounters of refugee-based families with doctors and CHNs, by interviewing the CHNs about those encounters, and finally, by using a technique new to most applied linguists, the "critical incident review," in which they circle back to the CHNs after having transcribed interviews, to question them about those points of tension in the interview. This circling back led to the elaboration of some critical problems CHNs have with patients, problems not directly addressed in the interviews.

Much of the knowledge provided by these CHNs, themselves "typically members of the communities they serve," could only have been unearthed through this type of collaborative process. The CHNs could point out certain critical roadblocks to communication that even the CHNs struggled to overcome. For example, CHNs were assigned to patients, it seems, on the basis of named language categories like "Arabic" or "Burmese." However, these broad language categories hide the linguistic diversity of speakers of those languages. One Burmese-speaking CHN, for example, described how one patient from a different ethnic group within the Burmese language community did not share the same understanding of the word "stone" in "kidney stone" that the CHN had translated. An "Arabic" CHN mentioned the challenge of communicating in different varieties of Arabic from multiple Arabic-speaking countries, often struggling to find the exact words to fit what a given patient is feeling. And another CHN described more broadly the limitations of language to convey the complexity and unique characteristics of healthcare to refugees, saying, "we share the same language, but I don't think she gets what we are doing here." These interpreting issues were just one of the many communicative complexities CHNs faced and that were described by Morelli and Warriner's research. The frustrations in institutional crossing here seemed primarily to arise once they learned the immensity of the tasks needing to be accomplished—and looking forward, finding resources to accomplish those.

In the final chapter, Netta Avineri and colleagues describe their efforts as applied linguistic anthropologists. In this case, their border crossings were not into new field sites and research projects, but involved connecting, in the interest of social change, to policymakers and journalists to communicate what they know and care about as linguistic anthropologists. Each of the authors describes their work to change the way specific words and their patterns of use enter public discourse. Each author builds on a foundational premise of linguistic anthropology, that language never simply describes the world, but plays a role in shaping it. Given this premise, certain phrases like "linguistically isolated" in the US Census, or use of the term "illegal" (as in "illegal immigrant"), don't simply describe humans or their contexts, but simultaneously ascribe qualities to them, accentuating one, potentially harmful, perspective. Similarly, cartoonish mascots named "Indians" or "Redskins" paint a caricature of a mythic Native American, invisibilizing the presence of Native Americans in contemporary US society. And, in the educational context, the "30 million word language gap" is a phrase taken up by the media that has shaped the way many Americans view the home lives of low-income and minoritized students, predisposing teachers to negatively prejudge some students, disproportionately children of color, the very first day they step into their classrooms.

These applied linguistic anthropologists want to cross borders to push the public to recognize the power these words and phrases hold and the potential damage they can do. All the authors emphasize as well that even when words change the world may not immediately follow. Using the term "undocumented" rather than "illegal" to describe immigrants will not change entrenched social structures that will no doubt continue even after the press stops using the "I-word." So, Jonathan Rosa emphasizes, a genuinely "applied" linguistic anthropologist will also seek out collaborations that facilitate structural, institutional, or organizational change as well.

Nevertheless, all these examples, and the authors' combined mission to change public discourse, also illustrate the potential power of simply *talking about* language in new ways, and with other people.

Bernard Perley, for example, in his discussion of sports mascots with Native American names, introduces the concept of "audience coalescence" to describe the process of repeatedly talking about the problems surrounding the unthinking use of Native American sports mascots, honing ways to reach different audiences. He describes his own mission as an applied linguistic anthropologist to foster more of those conversations, to build linguistic and ideological awareness among a broader coalition of people. Ana Celia Zentella's work with the Census Board and Jonathan Rosa's work with journalists might also be seen as examples of audience coalescence—building new understandings by talking about words with those who might not usually talk together about those words, even though they may use them frequently in their more isolated social enclaves. And Eric

Johnson emphasizes, in his discussion of the "language gap," that "while anthropological research demonstrates that language gaps do not exist, we must recognize that the ideologically (re)produced 'language gap' *concept* does" (emphasis in the original, p. X). To raise awareness of words and the concepts they spread, we have to talk about the language people are using—and not just among ourselves as academics. We need to talk about language with new people by forming collaborations in new contexts.

Netta Avineri, in the conclusion, points out the importance of another type of collaboration—*within* the more fine-grained borders of one's discipline. The Language and Social Justice Task Group that each of the authors of this chapter comprises exemplifies the importance of regrouping within our discipline even as we go out to collaborate with others. Counteracting long-entrenched understandings of the contributions possible for linguistics and linguistic anthropology, assumptions that exist both among those troubled worlds in which we apply our research and those equally troubled worlds within which we have become scholars, requires the support of peers who work with a shared sense of purpose. Changing how the word and world build one another takes time and commitment, and as Avineri points out, in the case of the Language and Social Justice Task Group, functions best when we have peers with whom we can think together.

Radical redistribution of expertise

The border crossings described in this volume, at their very best moments, give voice to those who might go unheard in more institutionally isolated conversations. Through their border crossings, each of these authors begins to show how expertise varies across contexts. As such, each critiques the inherent value of stand-alone expertise developed as university scholars. They point to the necessity to cross borders, not simply to find a new audience for their own expertise, but to build knowledge together with those residing in new contexts. Each description of collaboration toggles, to different degrees, between an explication of the author's own expertise, and their ongoing work to access, illuminate, and connect with the expertise of individuals residing in different contexts. As these authors engage across communities, they also begin to change what counts as expertise, and as such, what value it has in building new knowledge, communicating in new ways, and solving social problems.

Emily Fuerherm and her colleagues, for example, have focused their knowledge of multilingualism and communication on getting medical expertise to communities who otherwise might not receive it. Without community partners that have deep knowledge of the language and norms of the community, access to healthcare remains out of reach for many. Medical professionals need applied linguists, who need those health advocates who talk with patients and families, puzzling through their communication, working through how words mean differently for other people. If we didn't hear those voices, it would be hard to meaningfully and sensitively convey to those same patients that, for example, the "toasted seeds, herbs, or grasshopper snacks called *chapulines*" that their friends and families send from Mexico might be poisoning their children with lead. Accessing this expertise, and then being able to communicate to families, with sensitivity and respect, why these emotionally laden snacks may be a health threat, requires what Feuerhelm et al. call a "community strengths-based approach." This approach requires not simply medical expertise, but knowledge of language and sociocultural practices that only the community can provide—and that would only be known through border-crossing collaboration.

Similarly, to combat stigma that circulates about Pidgin in Hawai'i, Higgins's expertise as a linguist was important, but she needed to go beyond the bully pulpit of academia, to work specifically with teachers, community members, and museum staff, to find ways for the expertise of Pidgin speakers themselves to have a public platform. She astutely insisted that the collaborative work on Pidgin be aired in new media, away from the University, in spaces where new people will encounter these different voices and views about language.

In another convergence of multiple invaluable forms of expertise, the Cultural Health Navigators role, as described by Morelli and Warriner, illuminates the importance of the nuanced local expertise regarding the provision of linguistic and cultural translators to inform any changes to the healthcare system. When the Burmese CHNs explained the complexity of working with Burmese refugees from various ethnic groups, using different varieties of "Burmese," the onus of the CHN's job of interpretation became clear. Negotiating meaning, even among speakers of the "same" language requires time, patience, commitment—and more resources. Outside knowledge from applied linguists is relevant here: It's commonly understood by applied linguists these days, for example, that "named languages" are artificial constructs, and that relying on those names to understand, interpret, or translate responses to complex social conditions will inevitably backfire. Understanding the relevance of this linguistic knowledge will always rely on expert *local* knowledge, like that provided in this study by the CHNs, as well as the interdisciplinary methods through which that knowledge was brought to attention.

Still, this recognition of local expertise can be difficult to navigate, and institutional structures can enforce the notion that some knowledge counts more than others. Several chapters here have illustrated how attempts at cross-institutional collaboration and public-facing work can be hamstrung by the opposed metrics of expertise used by different institutions. The University and specifically the discipline of applied linguistics also generate expectations for constructs and forms of talk that may counteract goals for public-facing work. The terms Skilton uses from applied linguistics like "markedness" or "indexical inversion" to discuss radical theater engagements may reinvoke the institutional stance of "academic expert." Moore brought "repertoires of practice" to her collaboration. Miller brought the tools of discourse analysis and the term "strategic ambiguity" to interdisciplinary conversations. Avineri and colleagues brought terms like "audience coalescence," "anthropolitical linguistics," and "naturalized racism" to the discussion of their collaboration.

For an applied linguistics audience, journal editors, and the audience of this book, these words are comforting in their familiarity and assured status (or engaging and fresh if we are first encountering them), but they may seem unnecessarily turgid to others. Are those terms necessary or productive in these forms of public inquiry? Or are they the trappings of an institutional role that may counteract the public-facing nature of this work? As applied linguists, our role is also to be mindful of how and where we use our own language and whether it communicates across boundaries or if it builds those boundaries up. We might even work collaboratively to develop shared terms for these recognizable social dynamics. When Rosa coined "The I-Word" as a format to discuss popular use and abuse of the word "illegal," he seems to have been making a terminological border crossing, recognizing the multiple ways the word "illegal" has been circulating in the US, and turning to the networks and the expertise of the media world in crafting messages that reach a broader audience.

Contemporary attempts at social justice advocacy must include what we see hints of in these chapters: Radical redistribution of expertise. The border crossings and the resulting collaborative inquiry must build on a recognition that the communities within which we work have their own questions, their own knowledge desires, their own sense of what counts as important and how to convey it. As border-crossing academics, these authors have all attempted to give voice to that expertise, which otherwise may go unheeded by the scholarly community. In this way, all these chapters represent the work of *collaborative*, rather than simply *applied*, linguists.

From "applied" to "collaborative" linguistics

There is something unavoidably problematic about being "applied" scholars. The term "applied" suggests these linguists are always the outsiders, ready to apply decontextualized theoretical frameworks, conceptual vocabulary, and research-based findings to some "other" conditions—be it schooling, healthcare, linguistic diversity, or public policy. Shifting into the role of "collaborative" instead of "applied" linguists signals that we are not simply offering up one form of expertise to improve upon what local communities, institutions, or disciplines already have going on. We are offering, instead, to join the community to collaboratively explore the ways language works (and doesn't work) for them.

As collaborative linguists, we are developing, in the words of Tsing (2015), "new tools for noticing" (p. 25). Our old tools of noticing usually don't work as seamlessly when we cross contexts. Nevertheless, that word "linguist" in our designation suggests we have to offer some very technical and specific expertise. Too often, this expert voice can silence others and keep us from noticing new forms of expertise. These chapters have illustrated how fruitful it can be to instead draw attention to the fact that everyone is using language, to notice it in new ways, and appeal to the expertise across communities, age groups, professions, and disciplines, about how we use language, very specifically, to get things done in our everyday lives.

Noticing everyday expertise, and situated understandings of language, can lead to important paths of inquiry and public-facing communication. For Higgins, for example, it led her work with others to create a movie about Pidgin that drew, not on her own expertise on Pidgin, but on her ability to cross borders and hear their stories about how Pidgin operated in the lives of Pidgin speakers. Similarly, for Arango and Link, translanguaging offered a way, not to offer some of their own academically centered expertise, but to invite community members into shared inquiry and artistic production. Arango and Link were facilitators as the students chose their topics and followed their own trains of thought—which took them through weeks of research into, of all things, the world of commercial wrestling and Donald Trump, Jr.'s fanship within that world. With the nudging of Arango, the students themselves brought it back to language, when one of the participants comments on the use of Spanish and English in the play:

> I think it's a nice way to put a story, to mix, and it comes also in itself against Donald Trump's plan that he wants only English. I can't really explain it, but to use both languages in itself makes the case for the story. (p. xx)

And as they began work on their follow-up play, again, the students turned to reflect on language, now interested in the meaning of the words "illegal" (Rosa's "I-word"!) and "citizen," and how these have been used to characterize or defame Mexican immigrants in the US. While Arango and Link's expertise entered into the collaboration, the children's perspectives came through loud and clear, voicing the specifics from their world and affirming their identity in that world—the goals Arango and Link shared in their mission for RevArte.

Emerging from the ruins

The wider social role of the University as an institution is now up for grabs.
  Bill Readings, *The University in Ruins*, 1996 (p. 2)

All this work around words, language ideologies, and advocacy can be framed as a struggle. But it also seems, for all these authors, to be engaging, life-affirming, and important. Nobody can stick with this tough work of border-crossing and collaboration without feeling the joy involved in building new forms of knowledge together.

Often, this knowledge-building collaborative dynamic, this renewed talk about how language means and acts in our worlds, emerges Phoenix-like from the rubble and ruin that have resulted from insular understandings of what progress looks like and how it can be achieved. As mentioned in the beginning of this afterword, progress, today, cannot be embraced whole-heartedly. Too often, we have found that the path to "progress" is simultaneously the path to ruination of something, leaving behind injustices to be brushed under the rug, left unexamined—dispossessed people, land, languages, forms of life, or the degradation of our entire planet.

Academia has not been immune to this damaging march of progress. Those of us who work within it can experience our work as inspiring, but simultaneously complicit with institutional mandates that push for progress, growth, and "excellence" (Readings, 1996). Our positions in academia are often sustained by the very power structures we critique in our work in the name of social justice. As Readings wrote way back in 1996, we need to do something: "the wider social role of the University is now up for grabs" (p. 2). The 2020 pandemic has made the foundation of the University's imbrication with capitalist forms of growth (and destruction) even more painfully palpable. Given this reality, how can we, speaking from the center of academia, put forward a picture of something like "social justice"? As this volume illustrates, we can begin to work toward justice if we insist on a new vision for our work: one that does not brush aside the lives and realities of individuals and communities left in the wake of "progress," either our own professional progress as individuals or that of the institution. We need a new vision of scholarship that instead develops by listening to and lifting up—centering—the voices that usually go unheard. All the authors of this volume have begun this work—and I hope this volume functions as inspiration to keep it all going—shaping and reshaping the words and the world we all make and live in, together.

References

Readings, B. (1996), *The University in Ruins*, Cambridge MA: Harvard University Press.

Tsing, A. (2015), *The Mushroom at the End of the World: On the Possibility of Life in Capitalist Ruins*, Princeton: Princeton University Press.

Index

access to healthcare 6, 7, 125, 151, 153, 155–8, 205
activism 2, 180, 181, 188
advocacy 9, 19, 158, 171, 172, 177, 179, 181, 182, 186, 188, 197, 206, 208
anthro-political linguistics 173, 174, 206
applied theater 5, 6, 103, 105–7, 109–12, 117, 201
arts-based 82, 98, 107
audience coalescence 173, 181, 182, 189, 203, 206

census 7, 9, 82, 129, 171, 173–6, 188, 203
collaboration(s) 1–8, 11, 35, 37–9, 48, 51–3, 59, 62, 64, 66, 76, 89, 90, 97, 99, 131, 132, 134, 137, 142, 166, 167, 172, 173, 185–9, 195–201, 203–6, 208
　community-based 167
collective efficacy 140
corpus analysis 59, 66–9, 73, 76
critical incident interview technique 154, 202
Critical Race Theory 84, 109
cross-disciplinary 3, 5, 6, 9, 60, 62, 63, 66, 150, 154, 195
Cultural Health Navigators 6, 149, 150, 202, 205

discourse analysis 60, 64, 66, 67, 71, 72, 127, 198, 206
dual language learner/DLL 5, 35, 36, 39–44, 46–51, 53

embodied 103, 104, 106, 107, 109–11, 113, 115, 119, 122, 154
　analysis 103
　communication 103, 106, 111
　form(s) 8, 107, 109
　practice 104, 109, 113

filmmaking 19, 20, 21

grant(s) (proposal) 23, 31, 32, 38–40, 43–6, 49, 51, 53, 61, 62, 64, 66, 130–2, 135, 140, 143

Hawai'i 13, 16, 17, 19–22, 25, 27, 28, 30, 32, 197
　creole 13, 16, 17
health
　disparities 125, 128, 138, 141, 143, 149, 167
　equity 125–7, 129, 137, 140–3
humor 29, 82, 86, 87, 89, 92, 94, 95, 97, 98, 200

ideology/-ies 10, 42, 60, 107, 109, 110, 112, 129, 171, 175, 181, 187, 189
　discriminatory 10
　English-only 176
　monolingual 176
　language 1, 31, 47, 49, 50, 129, 172, 208
　raciolinguistic/raciolingüísticas 83, 85
　racist 7, 112
immigration 10, 81, 82, 86–9, 91, 94–6, 98, 177–8
indexical inversion 103, 107, 110, 111, 114, 115, 117, 119, 201, 206
informal science (education) 5, 35–50, 52, 53
interdisciplinary 4, 11, 41, 59, 62, 126, 127, 132, 137, 140–2, 151, 155, 171, 179, 198, 199, 205, 206

Latinx(s) 81–83, 7, 98, 99, 123, 178, 189, 200
LangCrit 103, 107, 109
language
　gap/word gap 10, 172, 183–7, 203–4
　rights 9, 14, 19
　socialization 37, 43

linguistic
    discrimination 14, 19
    diversity 37–9, 41, 43, 46–8, 51, 150, 187, 202, 207
    marginalization 128, 142, 149–51, 166
linguistically isolated 9, 173–6, 203
literacy 4, 6, 7, 17, 40, 43, 47, 86, 92, 95, 97, 130, 138–40, 142, 143, 150–1, 153, 155, 156, 163, 165, 166, 176
    health 126, 127, 130, 131, 138, 140, 141, 153, 162, 167

markedness 103, 107–11, 114, 201, 206
    marked 108–10, 115, 118, 121
    unmarked 105, 108–10, 112, 114, 118, 172
mascot names 172, 179, 182, 188
multimodal 49, 50, 85, 98, 106, 110, 163
museum 5, 6, 9, 14, 22–32, 35, 36, 39–44, 46–53, 87, 198, 199, 205
    exhibits 22–5, 27
museum–university partnership 51, 53

Native American(s) 10, 110, 172, 180–2, 189, 190, 203
networking 60, 64, 66, 69, 75, 199

outreach 15, 38, 41, 43, 44, 47, 50, 132, 138, 185

Paulo Freire 82, 84–6, 89, 90, 97
partnership(s) 3, 5–8, 35, 38, 39, 45, 49, 51, 52, 62, 125–30, 132, 137, 141, 143, 150, 151, 196

Patient Centered Outcomes Research (PCOR) 134, 135
Pidgin 9, 13–14, 16–31, 197, 205, 207
praxis 8, 81–7, 90, 94, 95, 97–9, 200
preschool 5, 35–7, 39–44, 48–51
publicly engaged scholars 171

raciolinguistics 14, 103, 107, 109
repertoire(s) 10, 36, 40, 48, 50, 51, 53, 85, 95, 103, 104, 108, 110, 132, 142, 197, 198, 199, 206
    of practice 35, 38, 48, 53, 198, 199, 206

science center 5, 35, 36, 38, 40, 41, 43, 45, 47, 48, 49, 52
social
    change 11, 54, 84, 107, 171–3, 188, 189, 196, 202
    justice 3, 5, 9, 13–16, 61, 69, 70, 81, 82, 85, 90, 97–9, 107, 112, 143, 171, 172, 174, 176, 181–3, 186, 188, 200, 204, 206, 208, 209
    sustainability 8, 59–63, 65–76, 198, 199
storytelling 85
    counter-stories 84, 96, 99
    re-storying 137, 139, 140
strategic ambiguity 74, 75, 199, 200, 206
subject-as-seen/subject-as-heard 103, 107, 109–12, 114, 117, 121, 201
syndemic sensibility 141

translanguaging 8, 81–7, 92, 94, 95, 97–9, 200, 207
translational research 129, 134, 142

www.ingramcontent.com/pod-product-compliance
Lightning Source LLC
Chambersburg PA
CBHW062222300426
44115CB00012BA/2186